THE COLLECTED

F. A. Hayek

VOLUME II

THE ROAD TO SERFDOM

Text and Documents

The Definitive Edition

PLAN OF THE COLLECTED WORKS
Edited by Bruce Caldwell

The plan is provisional. Minor alterations may occur in titles of individual books, and several additional volumes may be added.

THE COLLECTED WORKS OF
F. A. Hayek

VOLUME II

THE ROAD TO SERFDOM
Text and Documents
The Definitive Edition

EDITED BY
BRUCE CALDWELL

The University of Chicago Press

BRUCE CALDWELL is the Joe Rosenthal Excellence Professor in the Department of Economics at the University of North Carolina, Greensboro, and author of *Beyond Positivism: Economic Methodology in the Twentieth Century* and *Hayek's Challenge: An Intellectual Biography of F. A. Hayek,* the latter also published by the University of Chicago Press. He is a past president of the History of Economics Society.

The University of Chicago Press
Routledge, London

16 15 14 13 12 11 10 09 08 07   1   2   3   4   5

ISBN-13: 978-0-226-32054-0 (cloth)
ISBN-13: 978-0-226-32055-7 (paper)
ISBN-10: 0-226-32054-5 (cloth)
ISBN-10: 0-226-32055-3 (paper)

Library of Congress Cataloging-in-Publication Data

Hayek, Friedrich A. von (Friedrich August), 1899–1992.
    The road to serfdom : text and documents / F. A. Hayek ; edited by
Bruce Caldwell. — Definitive ed.
        p.   cm. — (The collected works of F. A. Hayek ; v. 2)
    Includes bibliographical references and index.
    ISBN-13: 978-0-226-32054-0 (cloth : alk. paper)
    ISBN-13: 978-0-226-32055-7 (pbk. : alk. paper)
    ISBN-10: 0-226-32054-5 (cloth : alk. paper)
    ISBN-10: 0-226-32055-3 (pbk. : alk. paper)
    1. Economic policy. 2. Totalitarianism. I. Caldwell, Bruce. II. Title.
III. Series: Hayek, Friedrich A. von (Friedrich August), 1899–1992.
Works. 1989 ; v. 2.

    HB171 .H426 1989 vol. 2
    [HD82]
    330.1 s—dc22
    [338.9]   2006012835

THE COLLECTED WORKS OF F. A. HAYEK

Founding Editor: W. W. Bartley III
General Editor: Bruce Caldwell

Published with the support of

The Hoover Institution on War, Revolution and Peace
Stanford University

The Earhart Foundation

The Pierre F. and Enid Goodrich Foundation

The Morris Foundation, Little Rock

CONTENTS

EDITORIAL FOREWORD

The first volume in *The Collected Works of F. A. Hayek* was the last book that Hayek wrote, *The Fatal Conceit.* It was the first volume in two respects: it was volume 1 in the series, and it was the first published, in 1988. The founding general editor was the philosopher W. W. Bartley III, and he initially envisioned that the series would contain twenty-two volumes—at least, that was what was noted in the material describing the planned series in *The Fatal Conceit.* Wisely, Bartley added the proviso that "the plan is provisional." It is now anticipated that there will be nineteen volumes in all, but the original proviso still applies.

Much has happened since 1988. A second volume produced under Bartley's editorship was published in 1991, but it was a posthumous contribution, Bartley having succumbed to cancer in February 1990. Soon thereafter Stephen Kresge took over the position of general editor, and under him five more volumes were produced. The volumes in the series did not appear in numerical order: to date, volumes 1, 3, 4, 5, 6, 9, and 10 have been published.

In spring 2002 Stephen Kresge asked me whether I might be interested in becoming the next general editor. I was, and after the Hayek family and representatives from the University of Chicago Press and Routledge all signed off, my work began. The first year or so was taken up with getting editorial material shifted from California to North Carolina, rethinking the ordering of the volumes, establishing relationships with existing and potential volume editors, and seeking funds to support the project.

The Road to Serfdom: Text and Documents—The Definitive Edition is the first volume to appear under the new general editorship. Others are on the way. I anticipate fairly steady progress over the next few years as the project moves toward completion.

In the first volume Bill Bartley briefly stated the editorial policy for the series as follows: "The texts of subsequent volumes will be published in corrected, revised and annotated form" and "essays which exist in slightly variant forms, or in several different languages, will be published always in English or in English translation, and only in their most complete and finished form unless some variation, or the timing thereof, is of theoretical or historical significance." These policies will continue to be followed in the present volume and those to come.

For *The Road to Serfdom* the following editorial decisions were made. The British edition came out in March 1944, and the American in September of that year. The text for the American edition was reset, principally to replace phrases like "this country" with "England." Because the American edition is accordingly clearer (that is, it does not presume that the reader knows that "this country" refers to England), it was chosen for the text. Accordingly, "American English" is used throughout—in this regard this volume differs from others in the series, in which "British English" has mainly been used. Typographical errors were silently corrected, except where Hayek provided an incorrect citation. In those cases the correction is made and noted. At many points in the book Hayek quotes others, and his quotations do not always exactly duplicate the original. However, only when his misquoting might affect the meaning of the passage is this noted; in any event, what Hayek originally wrote stands.

Each volume in *The Collected Works* is intended to be a definitive presentation of Hayek's work. As such, when the University of Chicago Press proposed that we add the subtitle "The Definitive Edition" I initially resisted, thinking it inappropriate to single out this volume from the rest. *The Road to Serfdom* is unique, however, in that it is the only piece of Hayek's work to go through numerous editions: the original one in 1944, another in 1956 to which Hayek added a foreword, a 1976 edition to which he added a new preface, and the 1994 50th anniversary edition which carried an introduction by Milton Friedman. The subtitle was added, and I hope that this will always be considered the definitive edition. History suggests, however, that it may not be the last one.

Many have been involved in helping me get started as the new general editor. I owe a special debt to Mrs. Dorothy Morris of the Morris Foundation, Little Rock, who provided me with the "seed money" needed to initiate a search for additional funding for the project. As has been documented in forewords to preceding volumes in the series, Dorothy's husband Walter Morris was instrumental in the creation of *The Collected Works* project, and the Morris Foundation has been constant in its support throughout the years. I first sought financial support for the project at the Mont Pèlerin meetings in London in October 2002, and John Blundell of the Institute of Economic Affairs provided me both advice on how to proceed and assistance in arranging for a fellowship to help defray the costs of attendance. The meeting ultimately led me to David Kennedy and Ingrid Gregg of the Earhart Foundation, and to Emilio Pacheco of the Liberty Fund and the Pierre F. and Enid Goodrich Foundation. These organizations have provided the lion's share of support for the project. Finally, Stephen Kresge has been an advisor, mentor, sounding board, and friend throughout the very long transition from second to third general editor, and beyond. To all of them my most sincere thanks.

I also would like to thank the following people and organizations for granting their permission to reproduce materials and quote from letters: Mr. Frank B. Knight for permission to reproduce Frank Knight's reader's report on *The Road to Serfdom;* Dr. Thomas Marschak for permission to reproduce Jacob Marschak's reader's report on *The Road to Serfdom;* Mr. David Michaelis for permission to quote from Ordway Tead's letter of September 25, 1943, to Fritz Machlup; and the Hoover Institution on War, Revolution, and Peace for permission to quote from materials contained in the Hoover Institution Archives.

Last but not least, I gratefully acknowledge the assistance of Emily Wilcox and Jason Schenker in preparing the manuscript.

Bruce Caldwell
Greensboro, NC

INTRODUCTION

The Road to Serfdom is F. A. Hayek's most well-known book, but its origins were decidedly inauspicious. It began as a memo to the director of the London School of Economics, Sir William Beveridge, written by Hayek in the early 1930s and disputing the then-popular claim that fascism represented the dying gasp of a failed capitalist system. The memo grew into a magazine article, and parts of it were supposed to be incorporated into a much larger book, but during World War II he decided to bring it out separately. Though Hayek had no problem getting Routledge to publish the book in England, three American publishing houses rejected the manuscript before the University of Chicago Press finally accepted it.

The book was written for a British audience, so the director of the Press, Joseph Brandt, did not expect it to be a big seller in the States. Brandt hoped to get the well-known *New York Herald Tribune* journalist and author Walter Lippmann to write the foreword, noting in an internal memo that if he did, it might sell between two and three thousand copies. Otherwise, he estimated, it might sell nine hundred. Unfortunately, Lippmann was busy with his own work and so turned him down, as did the 1940 Republican presidential candidate Wendell Wilkie, whose 1943 book *One World* had been a best-seller.[1] John Chamberlain, the book review editor for the *New York Times*, was ultimately recruited for the job.

One hopes for his sake that Brandt was not the sort who bet money on his hunches. Since its first publication in 1944, the University of Chicago Press estimates that more than 350,000 copies of *The Road to Serfdom* have been sold. Routledge added many thousands more, but we do not know how many exactly: that press was unable to come up with any reliable numbers. There is also no good count on the number of copies that appeared in translation, not least because a portion were *samizdat* copies produced and distributed behind the Iron Curtain during the cold war.[2]

---

[1] Wendell Wilkie, *One World* (New York: Simon and Schuster, 1943).

[2] In his "Note on Publishing History" prepared for the fiftieth anniversary edition of the book, Milton Friedman noted that by 1994 Chicago had sold approximately 250,000 copies, and that

Not everyone, of course, liked (or likes) the book. The intelligentsia, particularly in the United States, greeted its publication with condescension and, occasionally, vitriol. Then a diplomat in the British Embassy in Washington, Isaiah Berlin wrote to a friend in April 1945 that he was "still reading the awful Dr. Hayek."[3] The economist Gardiner Means did not have Berlin's fortitude; after reading 50 pages he reported to William Benton of the *Encyclopaedia Britannica* that he "couldn't stomach any more."[4] The philosopher Rudolf Carnap, writing to Hayek's friend Karl Popper, apparently could not muster even the stamina of Means: "I was somewhat surprised to see your acknowledgement of von Hayek. I have not read his book myself; it is much read and discussed in this country, but praised mostly by the protagonists of free enterprise and unrestricted capitalism, while all leftists regard him as a reactionary."[5]

Those who, like Carnap, have not read Hayek but think that they already know what he is all about should be prepared for some surprises. Those on the left might preview their reading with a peek at chapter 3, where Hayek expounds on some of the government intervention that he was prepared to accept, at least in 1944.[6] Those on the right might want to have a look at his distinction between a liberal and a conservative in his 1956 foreword to the American paperback edition. Both will be surprised by what they find.

In this introduction I trace the origins of Hayek's little book, summoning up the context in which it was produced and showing how it gradually came to its final form. The reactions, both positive and negative, that ultimately turned it into a cultural icon will then be documented. Because it is a controversial work, I will comment upon some of the most persistent criticisms that have been levied against it. Not all of these, I argue, are warranted: Hayek's book may have been widely, but it was not always carefully, read. In my conclusion I will reflect briefly on its lasting messages.[7]

---

nearly twenty authorized translations had been published. The 350,000 figure is an estimate provided by the Press in 2005. Friedman's introduction and note may be found in the appendix.

[3] Letter, Isaiah Berlin to Elizabeth Morrow, April 4, 1945, reprinted in *Isaiah Berlin: Letters, 1928–46*, ed. Henry Hardy (Cambridge: Cambridge University Press, 2004), p. 540.

[4] Letter, Gardiner Means to William Benton, December 28, 1944, in the University of Chicago Press collection, box 230, folder 2, University of Chicago Library, Chicago, Ill.

[5] Letter, Rudolf Carnap to Karl Popper, February 9, 1946, quoted in Mark Notturno, "Popper's Critique of Scientific Socialism, or Carnap and His Co-Workers," *Philosophy of the Social Sciences*, vol. 29, March 1999, p. 41. Given his comment, Carnap may have read A. R. Sweezy's review in the November 5, 1944, issue of *PM*, a leftist outlet, where Hayek's book was dubbed a "textbook for reactionaries."

[6] Readers of his preface to the 1976 edition, in this volume, will see that he amended some of these views in his later years.

[7] This last task, evidently, is of necessity always specific to a time and place, with each new generation of readers taking away from it different lessons. As such, I will simply alert the reader that this introduction was written by an American historian of economic thought, and was last modified in late 2005.

Prelude: The British, Naziism, and Socialism

Friedrich A. Hayek, a young economist from Vienna, came to the London
School of Economics (LSE) in early 1931 to deliver four lectures on monetary
theory, later published as the book *Prices and Production*.[8] The topic was timely—
Britain's economy, stagnant through the 1920s, had only gotten worse with the
onset of the depression—and the presentation was erudite, if at times hard to
follow, owing to Hayek's accent. On the basis of the lectures Hayek was offered
a visiting professorship that began in the Michaelmas (fall) 1931 term, and
a year later he was appointed to the Tooke Chair of Economic Science and
Statistics. He would remain at the LSE until after the war.

The summer before Hayek arrived to teach was a traumatic one in Britain
and across Europe. In addition to the deepening economic depression, financial crises on the continent led to a gold drain in Britain, and ultimately to the
collapse of the Labour government, the abandoning of the gold standard, and,
in autumn, the imposition of protectionist tariffs. Hayek's entrance onto the
London stage was itself accompanied by no little controversy. In August 1931
he caused a stir with the publication of the first half of a review of John Maynard Keynes's new book, *A Treatise on Money*, which drew a heated reply from
Keynes a few months later. His battle with Keynes and, later, with Keynes's
compatriot Piero Sraffa, would occupy no small amount of Hayek's attention
during the 1931–32 academic year.[9]

By the following year, however, Hayek had secured his chair, and for his inaugural lecture, delivered on March 1, 1933, he turned to a new subject.[10] He
began with the following question: Why were economists, whose advice was
often so useful, increasingly regarded by the general public as out of step with
the times during the perilous years that had followed the last war? To answer
it Hayek drew upon intellectual history. He claimed that public opinion was
unduly influenced by an earlier generation of economists who, by criticizing a
theoretical approach to the social sciences, had undermined the credibility of
economic reasoning in general. Once that had been accomplished, people felt free
to propose all manner of utopian solutions to the problem of the depression,

[8]F. A. Hayek, *Prices and Production* (London: Routledge and Sons, 1931). A *Collected Works* edition
of the book is anticipated.

[9]John Maynard Keynes, *A Treatise on Money*, 2 vols. [1930], reprinted as volumes 5 and 6 (1971)
of *The Collected Writings of John Maynard Keynes*, ed. Austin Robinson and Donald Moggridge, 30
vols. (London: Macmillan [for the Royal Economic Society], 1971–89). Hayek's exchanges with
Keynes and Sraffa, including correspondence, is reproduced in *Contra Keynes and Cambridge: Essays,
Correspondence*, ed. Bruce Caldwell, vol. 9 (1995) of *The Collected Works of F. A. Hayek* (Chicago: University of Chicago Press, and London: Routledge).

[10]F. A. Hayek, "The Trend of Economic Thinking," *Economica*, vol. 13, May 1933, pp. 121–37;
reprinted as chapter 1 of *The Trend of Economic Thinking: Essays on Political Economists and Economic
History*, ed. W. W. Bartley III and Stephen Kresge, vol. 3 (1991) of *The Collected Works of F. A. Hayek*,
op. cit., pp. 17–34.

solutions that any serious study of economics would show were infeasible. Toward the end of his talk Hayek cited the new enthusiasm for socialist planning in Britain as an example of such misguided ideas. The economists who had paved the way for these errors were members of the German Historical School, advisors to Bismarck in the last decades of the nineteenth century.

Hayek's choice of the German Historical School economists was significant on a number of levels. First, the German Historical School had before the war been the chief rival of the Austrian School of Economics, of which Hayek was a member.[11] Next, though the German Historical School economists were conservative imperialists, cheerleaders for a strong German Reich and opponents of German social democracy, they also were the architects of numerous social welfare reforms. Bismarck embraced these reforms while at the same time repressing the socialists; indeed, the reforms were designed at least in part to undermine the socialist position and thereby strengthen the Empire. Hayek probably hoped that his audience would see certain parallels to the present day. Only a month before Adolf Hitler, who detested democracy and favored instead the reconstitution of another (third) Reich, had become Chancellor of the Weimar Republic. Within days he had convinced President Hindenburg to sign a decree prohibiting meetings and publications that could endanger public security, a measure aimed squarely at the communists and socialists. The morning before Hayek's address the world had learned that the Reichstag building had been set on fire and burned; the Nazis were quick to blame the act on the communists and used it to justify further acts of repression. A half century before, Bismarck had used an attempt on the Emperor's life to put his own antisocialist laws in place.

After Hayek's speech the situation in Germany continued to deteriorate. In March there were wholesale arrests of communists and harassment of the social democratic leadership. Opposition newspapers were closed, constitutional protections swept away, and a notorious "enabling law" passed that gave Hitler virtually dictatorial powers. On April 1 a nationwide boycott against German Jews was called, and later in the month action against the trade unions began. In May students on university campuses across Germany held book-burning celebrations, cleansing their libraries of suspect volumes. One such event was staged in the Berlin Opernplatz on May 10, 1933, and the martial songs and speeches of the participants were broadcast live across Germany. It was a horrific spring.

Hayek's criticisms of socialism in his address were not well received. He would later recall that, following the talk, "one of the more intelligent students had the cheek to come to see me for the sole purpose of telling me that, though

---

[11] For more on the history of the two schools, see Bruce Caldwell, *Hayek's Challenge: An Intellectual Biography of F. A. Hayek* (Chicago: University of Chicago Press, 2004), chapters 1–4.

hitherto admired by the students, I had wholly destroyed my reputation by taking, in this lecture, a clearly anti-socialist position."[12] But even more disquieting for Hayek was the interpretation of events in Germany that was emerging among the British intelligentsia. Certain prominent members of the German industrial class had initially supported Hitler's rise, and others had acquiesced in it. This, together with the Nazi party's evident persecution of the left, led many in Britain to see Naziism as either a capitalist-inspired movement or, alternatively (if one were a Marxist, and believed that capitalism was doomed to collapse), as a last-ditch attempt by the bourgeoisie to deny the inexorable triumph of socialism. As Hayek recalled, his director at the LSE was one of the ones propagating such an interpretation:

> A very special situation arose in England, already in 1939, that people were seriously believing that National Socialism was a capitalist reaction against socialism. It's difficult to believe now, but the main exponent whom I came across was Lord Beveridge. He was actually convinced that these National Socialists and capitalists were reacting against socialism. So I wrote a memorandum for Beveridge on this subject, then turned it into a journal article. . . .[13]

In his reminiscence Hayek got the date wrong: given his reference in his memorandum to the Berlin student demonstration, and given that it carries the date "Spring 1933," he probably wrote it in May or early June of that year. The memo, titled "Nazi-Socialism," is reproduced for the first time in the appendix of this volume.[14] In it, Hayek rebuts the standard account with the claim that

[12] This reminiscence is taken from a file card that was among a number that Hayek had written to provide information for Bill Bartley, who was to be Hayek's biographer. (Bartley died in 1990 before getting very far along with the biography.) Transcriptions of the file cards are included in an unpublished document that Bartley playfully titled "Hayek Biography: 'Inductive Basis.'" Bartley was a philosopher trained in the Popperian tradition, and the "inductive basis" is a term in that tradition for the body of facts against which theories are tested. The quotation may be found on p. 78.

[13] F. A. Hayek, *Hayek on Hayek: An Autobiographical Dialogue*, ed. Stephen Kresge and Leif Wenar (Chicago: University of Chicago Press, and London: Routledge, 1994), p. 102.

[14] The original memorandum may be found in the Friedrich A. von Hayek Papers, box 105, folder 10, Hoover Institution Archives, Stanford, Calif.

A historiographical note: there is nothing on the "Nazi-Socialism" manuscript to indicate that it was written for Beveridge. And indeed, though I have long known of the existence of the manuscript in the Hayek archives, I assumed it was *not* the Beveridge memo because it carried a date of 1933, and, as noted, Hayek seemed to imply that he had given it to Beveridge in the late 1930s. In the summer of 2004, however, Susan Howson showed me a copy of the identical memo (though with a newly inscribed title and missing the date) that she had found in Beveridge's papers. This is the basis for the claim that this was indeed the Beveridge memo.

As such, the 1939 date that Hayek mentions in his reminiscence appears simply to be an error. The two articles that grew out of the memo were published in 1938 and 1939, so the memo had

National Socialism is a "genuine socialist movement."[15] In support of this interpretation he notes its antagonism to liberalism, its restrictive economic policy, the socialist background of some of its leaders, and its antirationalism. The success of the Nazis was not, he asserted, due to a reactionary desire on the part of the Germans to return to the prewar order, but rather represented a culmination of antiliberal tendencies that had grown since Bismarck's time. In short, socialism and Naziism both grew out of the antiliberal soil that the German Historical School economists had tended. He added the chilling warning that many other countries were following, though at a distance, the same process of development. Finally, Hayek contended that "the inherent logic of collectivism makes it impossible to confine it to a limited sphere" and hinted at how collective action must lead to coercion, but he did not develop this key idea in any detail.[16]

As Hayek noted in his reminiscence, he ultimately turned his 1933 memo into a magazine article, published in April 1938, titled "Freedom and the Economic System." The following year he came out with an expanded version in the form of a public policy pamphlet.[17] If one compares the two articles one can trace an accretion of ideas that would later appear in *The Road to Serfdom*. In the 1938 version, though he continued to stress the links between fascism and socialism, Hayek began to expand on what he saw as the fatal flaw of socialist planning—namely, that it "presupposes a much more complete agreement on the relative importance of the different ends than actually exists, and that, in consequence, in order to be able to plan, the planning authority must impose upon the people that detailed code of values which is lacking."[18] He followed with a much fuller exposition of why even democratic planning, if it were to be successfully carried out, eventually requires the authorities to use a variety of means, from propaganda to coercion, to implement the plan.

In the 1939 version still more ideas were added. Hayek there drew a contrast between central planning and the planning of a general system of rules that occurs under liberalism; he noted how the price system is a mechanism for coor-

---

to have been written before 1938. Furthermore, Beveridge left the LSE for Oxford in 1937, so presumably the date was even earlier. My best guess is that, in his reminiscence, Hayek simply confused the date of the 1939 publication with the date of the memo. I gratefully acknowledge an anonymous reader for the University of Chicago Press whose careful scrutiny of the evidence helped me to reach this conclusion.

[15] F. A. Hayek, "Nazi-Socialism," appendix.

[16] *Ibid.*

[17] Both the 1938 and the 1939 versions of "Freedom and the Economic System" have been reprinted; they appear as chapters 8 and 9 in F. A. Hayek, *Socialism and War: Essays, Documents and Reviews*, ed. Bruce Caldwell, vol. 10 (1997) of *The Collected Works of F. A. Hayek*, op. cit., pp. 181–88, 189–211 respectively.

[18] F. A. Hayek, "Freedom and the Economic System" [1938], op. cit., p. 182.

dinating knowledge; and he made several observations concerning economic policy under a liberal regime.[19] All of these ideas would be incorporated into *The Road to Serfdom*.

On the one hand, Hayek had developed some of his new arguments in the course of fighting a battle against socialism during the middle years of the decade. On the other hand, some of the arguments were not actually new at all. Another debate on the feasibility of socialism had taken place immediately following the First World War, and Hayek's mentor, Ludwig von Mises, had contributed a key argument. This earlier controversy had taken place in mostly German-language publications. When Hayek came to England and encountered similar arguments in favor of planning being made by his academic colleagues and in the press, he decided to educate them about the earlier discussion. In 1935 he published the edited volume, *Collectivist Economic Planning: Critical Studies on the Possibilities of Socialism*.[20] The book contained translations of articles by others, including von Mises's seminal piece "Economic Calculation in the Socialist Commonwealth," as well as introductory and concluding essays by Hayek.[21] In the former Hayek reviewed the earlier Continental debates on socialism; in his concluding essay, titled "The Present State of the Debate," he identified and assessed a number of more recent proposals, among them the idea of reintroducing competition within a socialist state, dubbed "pseudo-competition" by Hayek, which later came to be called "market socialism."[22] This drew a response from the socialist camp, the most prominent being that of the Polish émigré economist Oskar Lange, whose defense of market socialism in a journal article was later reprinted in a book, *On the Economic Theory of Socialism*.[23] Hayek would respond in turn to Lange and to another proponent of socialism, H. D. Dickinson, in a book review a few years later.[24]

Hayek's three essays constitute the written record of his early economic arguments against socialism. But the battle was also taking place in the class-

[19] *Ibid.*, pp. 193–209.

[20] F. A. Hayek, ed., *Collectivist Economic Planning: Critical Studies on the Possibilities of Socialism* (London: Routledge and Sons, 1935; reprinted, Clifton, NJ: Kelley, 1975).

[21] Ludwig von Mises, "Economic Calculation in the Socialist Commonwealth," translated by S. Adler, in F. A. Hayek, ed., *Collectivist Economic Planning*, op. cit., pp. 87–130.

[22] F. A. Hayek, "The Present State of the Debate," in *Collectivist Economic Planning*, op. cit., pp. 210–43. Hayek's introductory essay, titled "The Nature and History of the Problem," and his concluding essay are reprinted as chapters 1 and 2 of F. A. Hayek, *Socialism and War*, op. cit., pp. 53–79, 89–116, respectively. For more background on the debates, see the editor's introduction to that volume.

[23] Oskar Lange, "On the Economic Theory of Socialism," in *On the Economic Theory of Socialism*, ed. Benjamin E. Lippincott (Minneapolis: University of Minnesota Press, 1938; reprinted, New York: McGraw Hill, 1956), pp. 57–143.

[24] F. A. Hayek, "Socialist Calculation: The Competitive 'Solution'" [1940], reprinted as chapter 3 of F. A. Hayek, *Socialism and War*, op. cit., pp. 117–40.

rooms (and doubtless spilling over into the senior commons room, as well) at the LSE. Beginning in the 1933–34 summer term (which ran from late April through June) Hayek began offering a class entitled "Problems of a Collectivist Economy." The socialist response was immediate: the next year students could also enroll in a class titled "Economic Planning in Theory and Practice," taught first by Hugh Dalton and in later years by Evan Durbin.[25] According to the LSE calendar, during the 1936–37 summer term students could hear Hayek from 5 to 6 PM and Durbin from 6 to 7 PM each Thursday night! This may have proved to be too much: the next year their classes were placed in the same time slot on successive days, Durbin on Wednesdays and Hayek on Thursdays.

By the time that World War II was beginning, then, Hayek had criticized, in a book, a journal, and in the classroom, a variety of socialist proposals put forth by his fellow economists. *The Road to Serfdom* is in many respects a continuation of this work, but it is important to recognize that it also goes beyond the academic debates. By the end of the decade there were many other voices calling for the transformation, sometimes radical, of society. A few held a corporativist view of the good society that bordered on fascism; others sought a middle way; still others were avowedly socialist—but one thing all agreed on, that *scientific planning* was necessary if Britain was to survive.

Thus in their two volume work *Soviet Communism: A New Civilization?* Fabian socialists Sidney and Beatrice Webb praised the "Cult of Science" that they had discovered on their visits to the Soviet Union, and held out the hope that scientific planning on a massive scale was the appropriate medicine to aid Britain in its recovery from the depression.[26] The sociologist Karl Mannheim, who fled Frankfurt in 1933 and ultimately gained a position on the LSE faculty, warned that only by adopting a comprehensive system of economic planning could Britain avoid the fate of central Europe. For Mannheim, planning was inevitable; the only question was whether it was going to be totalitarian or democratic. These economists were joined by other highly respected public intellectuals, from natural scientists to politicians.[27]

If planning was the word on everyone's lips, very few were clear about exactly

---

[25] Both Dalton and Durbin served at various points as Labour members of parliament, and Dalton would hold the position of Chancellor of the Exchequer from 1945–47. We will encounter them again later in the introduction.

[26] Sidney and Beatrice Webb, *Soviet Communism: A New Civilization?* 2 vols (London: Longmans, Green, 1935).

[27] See, for example, Sir Daniel Hall and others, *The Frustration of Science* (London: Allen and Unwin, 1935; reprinted, New York: Arno Press, 1975); Findlay MacKenzie, ed., *Planned Society: Yesterday, Today, Tomorrow. A Symposium by Thirty-Five Economists, Sociologists and Statesmen* (New York: Prentice Hall, 1937); and Harold Macmillan, *The Middle Way: A Study of the Problem of Economic and Social Progress in a Free and Democratic Society* (London: Macmillan, 1938). The climate of opinion among the British intelligentsia in the interwar years is reviewed in Bruce Caldwell, *Hayek's Challenge*, op. cit., pp. 232–37.

what it was to entail. The situation was well captured by Hayek's friend and LSE colleague Lionel Robbins, who in 1937 wrote:

> "Planning" is the grand panacea of our age. But unfortunately its meaning is highly ambiguous. In popular discussion it stands for almost any policy which it is wished to present as desirable. . . . When the average citizen, be he Nazi or Communist or Summer School Liberal, warms to the statement that "What the world needs is planning," what he really feels is that the world needs that which is satisfactory.[28]

As Robbins's passage suggests, planners were to be found all along the political spectrum. Sorting out exactly what planning implied for a complex society was to be yet another major theme in Hayek's coming work.

By 1939, in short, most of the elements for Hayek's book were present. But its form was not yet in place. When he was not fighting against socialist planners, Hayek had spent much of the rest of his time in the 1930s exhausting himself writing and rewriting a major theoretical work in economics, ultimately published in 1941 as *The Pure Theory of Capital*.[29] That project was finally winding down in August 1939. In a letter to his old university friend Fritz Machlup, Hayek spoke of a new project, one that, through a study of the relationship between scientific method and social problems, would provide a systematic investigation of intellectual history and reveal the fundamental principles of social development of the last one hundred years (from Saint-Simon to Hitler).[30] This was to become Hayek's Abuse of Reason project, and from it would emerge *The Road to Serfdom*.

Hayek's War Effort

On September 1, 1939, Germany invaded Poland, and two days later England and France declared war. Within a week, Hayek had sent a letter to the di-

[28] Lionel Robbins, *Economic Planning and Economic Order* (London: Macmillan, 1937), p. 3.

[29] For more on this see the editor's introduction to F. A. Hayek, *The Pure Theory of Capital*, ed. Lawrence A. White, vol. 12 (forthcoming) of *The Collected Works of F. A. Hayek*, op. cit.

[30] Letter, F. A. Hayek to Fritz Machlup, August 27, 1939, Fritz Machlup Papers, box 43, folder 15, Hoover Institution Archives. A classmate of Hayek's at the University of Vienna, Machlup (1902–83) went to the United States on a Rockefeller Fellowship in 1933. As the situation in Europe deteriorated Machlup, a Jew, decided to stay in the States, taking a position in 1935 at the University of Buffalo in New York. When the United States entered the war he went to Washington to work at the Office of Alien Property Custodian. Hayek and Machlup corresponded frequently, and this allows us to follow Hayek's activities during the war years very closely. We will see that Machlup also played an important role in helping to find an American publisher for Hayek.

rector general of the British Ministry of Information offering his services to aid with any propaganda campaign that might be directed at the German-speaking countries. He enclosed a memo with various suggestions about how to proceed. Hayek proposed a campaign with a historical dimension, one that demonstrated that the principles of liberty that England and France stood for were the same as those that had been enunciated by the great German poets and thinkers of the past, but showing that these had been eclipsed by "the distorted view of history, on which they have been brought up during the last sixty years," that is, since Bismarck's time.[31] Hayek's efforts had little effect; in a letter from a staff member dated December 30th his offer to help was politely but firmly turned down.

Once the war began in earnest the next May most of his colleagues from the LSE had been called to duty in various government departments. Though he was naturalized as a British subject in 1938, as an émigré Hayek was not offered a post, so he spent the war teaching his classes and writing. Hayek was clearly frustrated that the British government had no place for him, complaining in a letter to Machlup that he was "getting really annoyed by the refusal to use a person like myself on any useful work. . . ."[32] By this time, however, Hayek's intellectual history was well under way. In his letter to Machlup, Hayek provided an outline of the book, noting that "[t]he second part would of course be an elaboration of the central argument of my pamphlet on Freedom and the Economic System."[33] The first part of the book would be called "Hubris," the second, "Nemesis."

Hayek worked on the Abuse of Reason project for the rest of 1940, completing a number of historical chapters and beginning some others on methodology.[34] Toward the end of the year, though, he began transforming the last part of the book into what would become *The Road to Serfdom*, a book that he initially envisioned as coming out "as a sixpence Penguin volume."[35] Why did Hayek decide to abandon his larger historical endeavor—he never completed the

[31] F. A. Hayek, "Some Notes on Propaganda in Germany," p. 2. The memo, which is nine pages long and bears the notation "2nd draft, 12/9/39," may be found in the Hayek Papers, box 61, folder 4, Hoover Institution Archives. Box 61, folder 5 contains Hayek's letter to the director general, dated September 9, 1939, as well as Major Anthony Gishford's letter of December 30.

[32] Letter, F. A. Hayek to Fritz Machlup, June 21, 1940, Machlup Papers, box 43, folder 15, Hoover Institution Archives.

[33] *Ibid.*

[34] These would be published separately as "The Counter-Revolution of Science," *Economica*, *N.S.*, vol. 8, February 1941, pp. 9–36; May 1941, pp. 119–50; August 1941, pp. 281–320; and "Scientism and the Study of Society," *Economica*, *N.S.*, vol. 9, August 1942, pp. 267–91; vol. 10, February 1943, pp. 34–63; vol. 11, February 1944, pp. 27–39. Revised versions of these essays may be found in F. A. Hayek, *The Counter-Revolution of Science* (Glencoe, IL: The Free Press, 1952; reprinted, Indianapolis, IN: Liberty Press, 1979).

[35] Letter, F. A. Hayek to Fritz Machlup, January 2, 1941, Machlup Papers, box 43, folder 15, Hoover Institution Archives.

Abuse of Reason project—to focus on a shorter, more popular, and admittedly "political" tract? We will probably never have a definitive answer, but certain plausible reasons stand out. Were the Allies to lose the war, western civilization in Europe itself would be the cost. But Hayek was also worried about what would transpire if the Allies *won*.

Mobilization for war requires a massive reallocation of resources away from the production of peacetime consumer goods and capital toward the production of war materials. Factories are commandeered, their machines retooled for wartime production, and decisions about what to produce are made at the center. With fewer consumer goods being produced, the prospect of inflation looms (particularly harmful during wartime, because it hurts debtors, just when the government is trying to convince its citizens to become debtors by buying war bonds). To avoid inflation further intervention is necessary, and the standard policy response is to fix prices and institute a system of rationing. This essentially does away with a freely adjusting price system for basic consumer goods. Bluntly put, during war the market system is more or less abandoned, as many parts of the economy are placed under central control. Hayek's fear was that socialists would want to *continue* such controls in peacetime.

There was precedence for such a fear. Even before the First World War had begun, the philosopher Otto Neurath had been touting the doctrine of "war economy" in Eugen von Böhm-Bawerk's economics seminar in Vienna, much to the chagrin of seminar participant Ludwig von Mises. Neurath claimed that central planning under wartime conditions provided an exemplar for how to run an economy in peacetime. His and others' proposals for the socialization of the postwar economy provoked Mises to formulate his initial critique of socialist planning. Interestingly, Neurath was still on the scene when Hayek was writing: when hostilities started in earnest Neurath had fled Holland and would spend the war in Oxford.[36]

The British were not Continental socialists, but still, the danger signs were there. Clearly, the nearly universal sentiment among the intelligentsia in the 1930s that a planned system represented "the middle way" between a failed capitalism and totalitarianisms of the left and right was worrisome. The writings of what Hayek called the "men (and women!) of science" could not be ignored. Look at this message from the weekly magazine *Nature*, taken from an editorial that carried the title "Science and the National War Effort":

---

[36] For more on Neurath, see the editor's introduction to F. A. Hayek, *Socialism and War*, op. cit. There was a brief but fascinating correspondence between Hayek and Neurath at the end of the Second World War. Neurath initiated it by sending Hayek a review of *The Road to Serfdom*, and in a subsequent letter invited him to debate. Hayek put him off, saying he was busy working on a writing project. This would later become *The Sensory Order: An Inquiry into the Foundations of Theoretical Psychology* (Chicago: University of Chicago Press, 1952). The debate never took place, as Neurath died in December 1945. The correspondence may be found in the Hayek Papers, box 40, folder 7, Hoover Institution Archives.

The contribution of science to the war effort should be a major one, for which the Scientific Advisory Committee may well be largely responsible. Moreover, the work must not cease with the end of the war. It does not follow that an organization which is satisfactory under the stress of modern warfare will serve equally well in time of peace; but the principle of the immediate concern of science in formulating policy and in other ways exerting a direct and sufficient influence on the course of government is one to which we must hold fast. Science must seize the opportunity to show that it can lead mankind onward to a better form of society.[37]

The very next week readers of *Nature* would find similar sentiments echoed in Barbara Wootton's review of a book on Marxism: "The whole approach to social and political questions is still pre-scientific. Until we have renounced tribal magic in favour of the detached and relentless accuracy characteristic of science the unconquered social environment will continue to make useless and dangerous our astonishing conquest of the material environment."[38] Progressive opinion was united behind the idea that science was to be enlisted to reconstruct society along more rational lines.

There were also more overtly political forces to be reckoned with, forces whose hopes for the postwar world became increasingly clear as the conflict began to turn in favor of the allies. In early 1942 the Labour Party issued a pamphlet, *The Old World and the New Society*, that laid out the principles for reconstruction after the war. Here are some of its key claims:

> There must be no return to the unplanned competitive world of the inter-War years, in which a privileged few were maintained at the expense of the common good . . .

> A planned society must replace the old competitive system . . .

> The basis for our democracy must be planned production for community use . . .

> As a necessary prerequisite to the reorganization of society, the main Wartime controls in industry and agriculture should be maintained to avoid the scramble for profits which followed the last war.[39]

[37] Editorial, "Science and the National War Effort," *Nature*, vol. 146, October 12, 1940, p. 470.
[38] Barbara Wootton, "Book Review: *Marxism: A Post-Mortem*," *Nature*, vol. 146, October 19, 1940, p. 508.
[39] National Executive Committee of the Labour Party, *The Old World and the New Society: A Report on the Problems of War and Peace Reconstruction* (London: Transport House, n.d.), pp. 3–4. The pamphlet was issued by the Committee "for the consideration of its various Affiliated Organizations

These ideas were incorporated into a resolution proposed by Harold Laski and passed at the Party Conference on May 26, 1942. In his speech defending the resolution, Laski noted that "Nationalization of the essential instruments of production before the war ends, the maintenance of control over production and distribution after the war—this is the spearhead of this resolution."[40]

Party boilerplate is one thing, concrete plans as how to carry it out are quite another. A start at the latter was made in the famous Beveridge Report.[41]

The story of how Hayek's former director at the LSE came to chair the Interdepartmental Committee on Social Insurance and Allied Services is not without interest. The committee was originally set up in early 1941 to respond to trade union complaints about the mishmash of government programs then in existence to provide for unemployment benefits, sick pay, pensions, and the like. The Treasury, busy trying to finance the war, did not want a comprehensive review, fearing it would only lead to recommendations for further expenditures. They pushed for the appointment of a "safe" chairman who would do a patch-up job, and made sure that the committee was staffed principally with equally safe middle-level civil servants. But then the Minister of Labour Ernest Bevin intervened, and ultimately prevailed in having Beveridge appointed to chair the committee, his motivation being, according to one account, to get "the pushy Beveridge at last out of his Ministry"![42]

By December 1941 Beveridge had received only one of the 127 pieces of evidence that his committee would ultimately collect, but this did not deter him from circulating a paper that contained most of the main points that would be contained in the final report. Beveridge turned out to be anything but safe. His proposals provided the foundations for the postwar British welfare state, including the provision of family allowances, comprehensive social insurance, universal health care coverage, and a government obligation to maintain full employment.

Though the Treasury was horrified at the projected cost of the plan, over the course of 1942 Beveridge, through public appearances, radio talks, and the like,

---

prior to discussions at a series of Regional Conferences throughout the country, and at the Annual Conference of the Party, to be held in London at Whitsuntide (May 25–28, 1942)."

[40] Professor H. J. Laski, "A Planned Economic Democracy," *The Labour Party Report of the 41st Annual Conference* (London: Transport House, 1942), p. 111.

[41] Though as William Beveridge's biographer notes, "Already by June 1941 . . . there was a large body of reforming opinion interested in, and with well-formed views upon, the range of problems that Beveridge and his committee were to examine in detail over the next eighteen months." See Jose Harris, *William Beveridge: A Biography*, revised paperback edition (Oxford: Clarendon Press, 1997), pp. 367–68.

[42] Brian Abel-Smith, "The Beveridge Report: Its Origins and Outcomes," in *Beveridge and Social Security: An International Perspective*, ed. John Hill, John Ditch, and Howard Glennerster (Oxford: Clarendon Press, 1994), p. 14.

managed to leak to the press the broad outlines of the report, thereby building up popular support and undermining the ability of the government to either ignore or dismiss it. He was successful as impresario: when the 299-page government document was finally released on December 2, 1942, the line for it at the government bookshop was said to have been over a mile long.[43] It ultimately sold about a half a million copies, influencing policy not just in Britain, but worldwide. (In America, an edition that was "reproduced photographically from the English edition" to ensure a speedy delivery was quickly made available and sold about fifty thousand copies.)[44]

The Beveridge Report was an immediate success. The British economy had been stagnant throughout the interwar period, and no one wanted a return to such deprivation. The common sacrifices that the war necessitated bred a feeling that all should similarly share more equally in the reconstruction to come. Universal medical provision was itself virtually a fact of life during the first few years of the war, certainly for anyone injured by aerial bombing or whose work was tied to the war effort—and whose work was not, in one way or another? The war, then, was transforming the climate, and Beveridge's hope—and he was not alone—was to build on this transformation in the future.[45] Indeed, the first of the "Three Guiding Principles of Recommendations" with which he began his report made the link explicit: "Now, when the war is abolishing landmarks of every kind, is the opportunity for using experience in a clear field. A revolutionary moment in the world's history is a time for revolutions, not for patching."[46]

Having come to his majority in interwar Vienna, Hayek doubtless experienced an intense and disquieting sense of déjà vu on reading such words. In his book he sought to reverse the trends that were everywhere evident in Britain. Making the economic case against socialist planning was not enough. He

[43]Janet Beveridge, *Beveridge and His Plan* (London: Hodder and Stoughton, 1954), p. 114. It should probably be pointed out that it was Beveridge's wife who reported on the length of the line, and she was apparently recounting an anecdote that she had received second hand.

[44]Brian Abel-Smith, "The Beveridge Report," op. cit., p. 18.

[45]According to Beveridge's biographer, "the Social Insurance plan formed merely an iceberg tip—and in Beveridge's view perhaps the least important tip—of the very much more ambitious and far-reaching program of social reconstruction that he had in his mind at the time . . . [which] included such possible objectives as the nationalization of land and housing, national minimum wage legislation, public ownership of up to 75 per cent of industrial production, a public enterprise board to direct both public and private investment, and permanent state control of income, prices, and manpower planning." See Jose Harris, "Beveridge's Social and Political Thought," in *Beveridge and Social Security*, op. cit., p. 29. The changes instituted by the postwar Labour government would be far less dramatic than what Beveridge privately hoped for, and the levels of assistance once implemented were less than what he outlined in his report. But the welfare state was established, and with it the presumption that the state would be responsible for, and capable of, maintaining "full employment."

[46]Sir William Beveridge, *Social Insurance and Allied Services* (New York: Macmillan, 1942), p. 6.

needed to remind the British of their liberal democratic heritage, to contrast it with the collectivist or corporativist authoritarian modes of social organization promoted by its enemies, and finally, to make clear (notwithstanding the rhetoric of "planning for freedom") that the actual implementation of a centrally planned society would be inimical to liberty.

Finding an American Publisher

In a letter dated August 8, 1942, Hayek asked Fritz Machlup, who was by then in Washington at the Office of Alien Property Custodian, for his help in securing an American publisher. Machlup's wartime letters to Hayek may have helped him to realize that his message might be needed as an antidote in the States as well as in Britain: "If you talk here with people over 40 years of age—except Hansen—they sound sane and relatively conservative. It is the generation brought up by Keynes and Hansen, which is blind to the political implications of their economic views."[47] By summer's end Hayek sent Machlup a typescript that included all but the final three substantive chapters, two of which would deal with his recommendations for the postwar period. He would mail these to his friend over the course of the next year.[48]

Machlup's first stop was Macmillan, but they turned him down.[49] Machlup later reported to Hayek what they said in their letter: "Frankly, we are doubtful of the sale which we could secure for it, and I personally cannot but feel that Professor Hayek is a little outside the stream of much present-day thought, both here and in England."[50] Machlup's next move was, at Hayek's request, to send the (by now completed) typescript to Walter Lippmann, who would promote it to Little, Brown. This was done, but they also declined, on the grounds that

[47] Letter, Fritz Machlup to F. A. Hayek, October 23, 1942, Hayek Papers, box 36, folder 17, Hoover Institution Archives, copyright Stanford University.

[48] In a letter dated June 13, 1943, Hayek reported that he had sent Machlup copies of chapters 13 and 14 "about two months ago" and was now sending him the final chapter (chapter 15) as well as a new preface and table of contents. Machlup confirmed their arrival in his letter of August 9, 1943. Both letters may be found in the Machlup Papers, box 43, folder 15, Hoover Institution Archives. It should perhaps be noted that there are sixteen, not fifteen, chapters in the final published version, but the last chapter is only a two-page conclusion that was added later.

[49] Machlup was an editorial consultant for the academic publishing house Blakiston Company, and they told him that they would be happy to publish the book should Hayek want to, but lacking a trade department they would not be able to provide any real marketing for the book. So Machlup decided to see if he could drum up interest elsewhere.

[50] Letter, Fritz Machlup to F. A. Hayek, January 21, 1943, Machlup Papers, box 43, folder 15, Hoover Institution Archives, copyright Stanford University. It is difficult to resist adding the sentence with which Machlup's correspondent, Mr. Putnam, ended his paragraph: "If, however, the book is published by someone else and becomes a best-seller in the non-fiction field, just put it down to one of those mistakes in judgment which we all make." Indeed.

"the exposition was too difficult for the general reader."[51] Machlup then turned to Henry Gideonse, by now the President of Brooklyn College, but who previously had served as the editor of the series of public policy pamphlets in which "Freedom and the Economic System" had appeared. Gideonse took the manuscript with his strong endorsement to Ordway Tead, the economics editor at Harper and Brothers. This initiative also failed. In a sentence that in some ways exemplifies his own complaint, Tead explained why Harper would not publish it: "I do feel that the volume is labored, is over-written and that he can say all that he has to say in about half the space."[52]

Nearly a year had gone by and Machlup's search for an American publisher had yielded nothing. It was at this point that Aaron Director came to the rescue.[53] Director worked alongside Machlup in Washington, and had read the typescript in the summer of 1943. In October, Director wrote to fellow Chicago economists Frank Knight and Henry Simons to see if the University of Chicago Press might want to consider publishing it. Though he never received an answer, apparently Knight did recommend that the Press have a look. Toward the end of the next month Director sent the galley proofs from the English edition (which had arrived in the interim) to Chicago, asking for an immediate decision.[54]

The Press complied, asking Knight to evaluate the manuscript. In his reader's report, dated December 10, 1943, the irascible Chicago professor provided a decidedly lukewarm endorsement. He began the report by calling the book "a masterly performance of the job it undertakes" and admitted that he was

[51]Letter, Fritz Machlup to Harry Gideonse, September 9, 1943, Machlup Papers, box 43, folder 15, Hoover Institution Archives, copyright Stanford University.
[52]Letter, Ordway Tead to Fritz Machlup, September 25, 1943, Machlup Papers, box 43, folder 15, Hoover Institution Archives. Tead added that "Also, it is so completely in the negative vein as to leave the reader without any clue as to what line to take in thought or policy," a complaint others would echo.
[53]Aaron Director (1901–2004) did his graduate work in economics at Chicago, and taught there briefly before leaving for a job at the Treasury Department in 1933. He also spent some time in the 1930s at the LSE, where he met Hayek. In 1946 Director joined the Law School faculty at Chicago, and helped found the law and economics movement during his tenure there. His sister, Rose, married Milton Friedman.
[54]As Press editor John Scoon recounted in a letter dated May 2, 1945, to C. Hartley Grattan, "The idea of the Press's publishing it in this country was suggested by a member of the Department of Economics at the University who had previously known Hayek and his work; almost simultaneously another friend of the author's, once at the University but then in Washington with the government, suggested the book to us and got us the page proofs." Scoon's letter may be found in the University of Chicago Press collection, box 230, folder 3, University of Chicago Library. Scoon and Press director Joseph Brandt both joined the Press in January 1944, so Scoon's account of the process by which the book came to Chicago is second hand. Nonetheless, his letter is filled with interesting information (Milton Friedman also made use of parts of it in his "Note on Publishing History"), and it is published for the first time in the appendix.

sympathetic to its main conclusions. But he followed this with a two-page discussion of the book's weaknesses, concluding that, "'[i]n sum, the book is an able piece of work, but limited in scope and somewhat one-sided in treatment. I doubt whether it would have a very wide market in this country, or would change the position of many readers.'"[55]

Knight's distinctly ambivalent report could easily have resulted in the Press rejecting the manuscript. Instead, Acting Editor John T. McNeill took it to mean that it was worthy of further consideration. On December 14 he asked another Chicago economist, Jacob Marschak, to provide a second reader's report. Marschak, a socialist, was far more complimentary, writing six days later that "Hayek's book may start in this country a more scholarly kind of debate. . . . It is written with the passion and the burning clarity of a great doctrinaire. . . . This book cannot be bypassed."[56] Based on the two reports, the publication committee at the Press decided to undertake an American edition. The acceptance letter to Hayek was dated December 28, 1943.

There were still details to be settled, and Machlup acted in Hayek's behalf concerning most of these, even to the point of accepting Chicago's offer for Hayek in early January—it was nearly a month later when Hayek finally got the news.[57] One major decision was to completely reset the type, this because in the British edition Hayek frequently referred to England as "this country."[58] Two other changes were suggested by the Press, but both were rejected. The first was to change the name to *Socialism: The Road to Serfdom*. Both Machlup and Hayek thought that the proposed title was misleading, because socialism was only one of a subset of doctrines the book criticized. Central planning could be undertaken by parties on the right as well as the left; this was Hayek's point when he dedicated the book to socialists of *all* parties. The other proposal was to eliminate the aphorisms with which Hayek began each chapter. Hayek was sufficiently appalled by the latter suggestion that he followed up his letter of protest with a cable reading "Cannot consent to omission of quotations from Road to Serfdom."[59] The quotations were retained, including one from David

[55] Frank Knight, reader's report, December 10, 1943, University of Chicago Press collection, box 230, folder 1, University of Chicago Library. The report is published for the first time in the appendix.

[56] Jacob Marschak, reader's report, December 20, 1943, University of Chicago Press collection, box 230, folder 1, University of Chicago Library. The report is published for the first time in the appendix.

[57] See Hayek's letter to Machlup, February 2, 1944, Machlup Papers, box 43, folder 15, Hoover Institution Archives.

[58] As noted in the editorial foreword, the text of the American edition serves as the basis for the present edition.

[59] In a letter dated June 26, 1944, Hayek explained to editor Scoon why the quotations were so important: "The whole tone of the chapter is sometimes determined by the fact that the main idea is summarized in the quotation at the head, and I sometimes deliberately omit to state a main con-

Hume on the title page. Inexplicably, a quotation from Tocqueville that appeared on the title page of the British edition *was* dropped from the original American one, and in some of the later reprints the Hume quotation was moved off of the title page to the following one. Both have been restored to their rightful place on the title page in the current edition.[60]

Publication: From Minor Hit to Cultural Icon

The Road to Serfdom appeared on March 10, 1944, in England. The initial print run was 2,000 copies, and due to the strong demand (it sold out in about a month's time) a second printing of 2,500 was immediately ordered. That one quickly sold out as well, but nothing further could be done until a new paper quota was announced in July. Paper shortages would plague British production of the book for the duration and beyond.[61] July also saw the publication of an Australian edition.[62]

The American edition, with a run of 2,000 copies, came out on September 18, 1944, a Monday, though advance copies had been sent to reviewers earlier. Henry Hazlitt's laudatory front page review appeared in the next Sunday's *New York Times Book Review* section, and another graced the pages of the *Herald Tribune*. By September 28 a second and third printing had been ordered, bringing the total to 17,000 copies.[63] The Press had a minor hit on its hands.

At the end of October a letter arrived at the Press that would help turn it into

---

clusion because it is expressed in the quotation. I should it regard as a major calamity to the book if they have really to be omitted. . . ." The letter may be found in the University of Chicago Press collection, box 230, folder 1, University of Chicago Library.

[60] An editorial anecdote: the book is filled with quotations of others, and unfortunately, Hayek often failed to get the quotations exactly right, even those at the head of his chapters. In a letter dated February 26, 1944, Hayek asked Machlup to correct one of his quotes, Acton's famous line, "Power tends to corrupt, and absolute power corrupts absolutely." Unfortunately, even in his correction Hayek got it wrong, telling Machlup it should read, "Power tends to corrupt, and absolute power tends to corrupt absolutely"! Machlup dutifully passed the "correction" on, but presumably the actual quote was sufficiently famous that the Chicago Press copyeditor caught the error, for the correct phrasing appeared in the book. The letter is found in the Machlup Papers, box 43, folder 15, Hoover Institution Archives.

[61] As Jeremy Shearmur, "Hayek, *The Road to Serfdom,* and the British Conservative Party," *Journal of the History of Economic Thought,* forthcoming, reports, an abridged British edition was published by Routledge using paper that had been transferred from the allocation provided to the British Conservative Party. The abridgement was done by a conservative MP, Commander Archibald James, and in the place of the title page quotations from Hume and Tocqueville, the abridged edition carried a quotation from Winston Churchill, the leader of the Conservative Party!

[62] F. A. Hayek, *The Road to Serfdom* (Sydney: Dymock's Book Arcade, Ltd., 1944).

[63] For more details on the early history of its publication in America, see John Scoon's letter of May 2, 1945 to C. Hartley Grattan, which is reprinted in the appendix.

a major hit and a cultural icon. On the recommendation of Henry Gideonse, the Press had sent a copy of the book to Max Eastman, then a "roving editor" for *The Reader's Digest*. Eastman liked it so much that he asked the owner and editor-in-chief, DeWitt Wallace, for permission to do a condensation.[64] This appeared in April 1945, and it carried with it an offer of reprints, available through the Book-of-the-Month Club, for a nickel apiece. (Bulk orders were also possible: if one wanted 1,000 copies, it cost $18.) *The Reader's Digest* had at the time a circulation of about 8,750,000, and over a million of the reprints were eventually printed and distributed.[65]

Hayek arrived in the States in the beginning of April 1945 for a five-week lecture tour to promote his book. He crossed the Atlantic by boat, and while he was in transit the *Reader's Digest* issue appeared. Though the tour was initially envisioned to consist of academic lectures before various university departments of economics, by the time he arrived the tour had been turned over to a professional organization (the National Concerts and Artists Corporation) that had added a number of public appearances. The first event, a lecture sponsored by the Town Hall Club in New York, drew an overflow crowd of more than 3,000 listeners and was broadcast over the radio. Hayek was initially overwhelmed by the idea of speaking to such large, popular audiences, but, as he later recounted, he eventually warmed to the task.[66]

But it is also clear (and quite understandable, given his personality) that Hayek was a bit embarrassed by all the adulation, especially from those who might have gotten their only knowledge of his views from a 20-page condensation (or worse, from the cartoon edition that had appeared in the February 1945 issue of *Look* magazine).[67] He seemed particularly worried about being misinterpreted. Thus in a Chicago newspaper under a banner that read in part

[64] Hayek mentioned Eastman, who was initially sympathetic to the Russian Revolution but subsequently recanted, in chapter 2, p. 79. Cf. the foreword to the 1956 American paperback edition, this volume, p. 41.

[65] *Reader's Digest* provided its circulation figures for 1945. Croswell Bowen, "How Big Business Raised the Battle Cry of 'Serfdom,'" *PM*, Sunday, October 14, 1945, p. 13, estimated the *Reader's Digest* readership at 10 million, and is also the source for the Book-of-the-Month Club reprint figure. (Newsstand sales may account for the discrepancy between the circulation and readership figures for the *Reader's Digest*.) In his "Note on Publishing History" Milton Friedman estimated the reprint figure as 600,000 (rather than "more than one million"), but this was probably based on John Scoon's identical estimate in his letter of May 2, 1945. The number presumably had grown between May and October when Bowen's article appeared.

[66] Hayek recounts the story of his trip in more detail in *Hayek on Hayek*, op. cit., pp. 103–5.

[67] Both the *Reader's Digest* condensation and the cartoon version from *Look* are reprinted in a pamphlet released by the Institute of Economic Affairs: F. A. Hayek, *Reader's Digest Condensed Version of The Road to Serfdom*, Rediscovered Riches no. 5 (London: IEA Health and Welfare Unit, 1999). The Director of the IEA John Blundell reported to me on February 25, 2005, that in the last year there had been over 40,000 downloads from their website of a PDF containing the text of the condensed version of *The Road to Serfdom*.

"Friedrich Hayek Comments on Uses to Which His Book Has Been Put" he stated, "I was at first a bit puzzled and even alarmed when I found that a book written in no party spirit and not meant to support any popular philosophy should have been so exclusively welcomed by one party and so thoroughly excoriated by the other."[68] He repeatedly emphasized in his talks before business groups that he was not against government intervention per se: "I think what is needed is a clear set of principles which enables us to distinguish between the legitimate fields of government activities and the illegitimate fields of government activity. You must cease to argue for and against government activity as such."[69]

He also feared that certain parts of his message would be ignored. For example, businessmen who might be quite eager to get "government off of our backs" might be equally eager to demand that the government protect their industries from foreign competition. Responding to a question about tariffs in a discussion following his speech in Washington, DC, Hayek bluntly asserted: "If you have any comprehension of my philosophy at all, you must know that one thing I stand for above all else is free trade throughout the world." The man offering the anecdote added that, with that, "the temperature of the room went down at least 10 degrees."[70]

The trip to the United States gave Hayek his "15 minutes of fame," but it was also important for more substantive reasons. On the trip he first encountered Mr. Harold Luhnow, a Kansas City businessman who was interested in funding a study of how to foster an effective competitive order in the United States. After subsequent negotiations it was agreed that the study would be undertaken at the University of Chicago, and though it was never completed, the project helped to bring together in one place the various principals who would help create the "Chicago School of Economics"—Aaron Director, Milton Friedman, and, later, George Stigler. These men would all attend, in 1947, the first meeting of the Mont Pèlerin Society, an international society of scholars founded by Hayek whose goal was "to contribute to the preservation and improvement of the free society."[71] A few years later Hayek would himself emigrate from Lon-

[68] F. A. Hayek, "Planning and 'The Road to Serfdom': Friedrich Hayek Comments on Uses to Which His Book Has Been Put," *Chicago Sun Book Week*, May 6, 1945.

[69] F. A. Hayek, "The Road to Serfdom, an Address before the Economic Club of Detroit," April 23, 1945, p. 6. A transcript of the address may be found in the Hayek Papers, box 106, folder 8, Hoover Institution Archives.

[70] Marquis W. Childs, "Apostle Hot Potato: Austrian for Whom Senator Hawkes Gave Party Embarrassed Republicans," *Newark Evening News*, May 6, 1945.

[71] This is from the closing sentence of the Society's "Statement of Aims," adopted April 10, 1947, and reproduced in Fritz Machlup, ed., *Essays on Hayek* (New York: New York University Press, 1976), p. xiii.

don to the University of Chicago, though there he would join the Committee on Social Thought rather than the Economics Department.[72]

If Hayek was surprised by the enthusiastic reception of the book in some quarters, he was likely equally surprised at how it was savaged in others. Hayek had expected criticism, of course, and as an academic was looking forward to it, for it would mean that people were engaging his arguments.[73] He doubtless had in mind the sort of response he received from the English socialist Barbara Wootton, whose "courteous and frank" work Hayek mentioned in his 1956 foreword to the American paperback edition.[74] And indeed, with the exception of some Labour Party politicians, Hayek's challengers in Britain by and large took his views seriously, and responded to them accordingly.[75]

The situation was different in the United States. The worst of the lot, Herman Finer's scabrous *Road to Reaction*, was also picked out for mentioning by Hayek in the 1956 foreword. The overarching message of the book was evident in its very first sentence: "Friedrich A. Hayek's *The Road to Serfdom* constitutes the most sinister offensive against democracy to emerge from a democratic country for many decades."[76] According to Finer, Hayek's call for constitutionalism and advocacy of the rule of law was indicative of his antidemocratic biases, the "very essence" of Hayek's argument being "the idea *that democracy is dangerous and ought to be limited*."[77] Toward the end of the book (published, we remember, in 1945) we find Finer remarking on "the thoroughly Hitlerian contempt for the democratic man so perfectly expressed by Hayek."[78] Other pun-

---

[72] As Hayek later recounted in *Hayek on Hayek*, op. cit., p. 103, "practically all my contacts that led to later visits and finally made my move to Chicago possible were made during this trip."

[73] In a letter to Machlup dated March 20, 1944, Hayek noted with some surprise the initial warm reception the book had received in the British press, then added, "But I hope the attacks will begin soon." The letter may be found in the Machlup Papers, box 43, folder 15, Hoover Institution Archives.

[74] See the foreword to the 1956 American paperback edition, this volume, p. 40.

[75] During the 1945 election both Clement Atlee and Hugh Dalton, soon to be the Labour Prime Minister and Chancellor of the Exchequer, respectively, accused Winston Churchill of getting his ideas from Friedrich August von (with an emphasis on the "von") Hayek. In one speech (later dubbed the "Gestapo" speech), Churchill had predicted that a Labour victory would lead to a severe restriction on individual liberties. For more on all this see F. A. Hayek, *Hayek on Hayek*, op. cit., pp. 106–7; cf. Jeremy Shearmur, "Hayek, *The Road to Serfdom*, and the British Conservative Party," op. cit.

[76] Herman Finer, *Road to Reaction* (Boston: Little, Brown and Company, 1945), p. ix.

[77] *Ibid.*, p. 36. It is true that Hayek believed that constitutional limits were essential for protecting individuals against the "tyranny of the majority." But he was an opponent of planning, not of democracy. And indeed, if his arguments are correct, democracy is much more likely to be preserved under liberal political and economic institutions than under planning, whatever form it might take.

[78] *Ibid.*, p. 210.

dits of the day took different tacks: George Soule, for example, was quick to label him "the darling of the Chamber of Commerce."[79] The left-leaning *PM* newspaper launched an exposé showing how business interests promoted the "selling" of Hayek's message. The author's concluding sentences capture well many people's perception of the reception of the book in America: "Hayek's book—and the *Look* and *Reader's Digest* treatments of it—gave big business a wonderful opportunity to spread distrust and fear of the New Deal. Big business seized the opportunity."[80]

Perhaps recognizing that nothing sells like controversy, the Press sent Hayek a copy of Finer's book when it appeared in December 1945, and asked whether he might want to add a new chapter to the end of the next edition of *The Road to Serfdom*, in which he would reply to his critics. Hayek worked on such a postscript on and off over the next few years. A partially completed draft, dated 1948, exists in his archives, and elements of this would ultimately be incorporated into the 1956 foreword.[81] It is notable, and characteristic, that Hayek's response there was not to lash out at his critics, but rather to try to explain the differences in the receptions he received in England and the United States, again by emphasizing the different experiences that people in the two countries had had with socialism.[82]

It is hard to imagine that Hayek's book would have become so widely known, remembered decades after its original publication, had it not been for the *Reader's Digest* condensation. This allowed Hayek's message to reach many more people, and in at least one instance with dramatic effect: Antony Fisher, the founder of the Institute of Economic Affairs, and after it a prime mover in the foundation of many other conservative think tanks, was inspired to wage the war of ideas after having read the condensation and then speaking with Hayek in his LSE office in the summer of 1945.[83] But the condensation also turned the book into a symbol for both his admirers and his critics. The sad result is that, as John Scoon put it, "People still tend to go off half-cocked about it; why don't they *read* it and find out what Hayek actually says!"[84] In the next

[79] George Soule, "The Gospel according to Hazlitt: A Review of *Economics in One Lesson*," *The New Republic*, vol. 115, August 19, 1946, p. 202.

[80] Croswell Bowen, "How Big Business . . . ," op. cit., p. 16.

[81] F. A. Hayek, "Postscript," Hayek Papers, box 106, folder 8, Hoover Institution Archives.

[82] See the foreword to the 1956 American paperback edition, this volume, pp. 41–42. A perusal of the 1948 "postscript" shows that Hayek's initial response was less measured, and apparently even in 1955 the penultimate draft of the "Foreword" contained some lines about Rexford Tugwell and Wesley Clair Mitchell that prompted concern from an editor at the Press. These lines were dropped from the final version. See Alexander Morin's letter to Hayek of August 18, 1955, University of Chicago Press collection, box 230, folder 4, University of Chicago Library.

[83] See John Blundell, "Introduction: Hayek, Fisher and *The Road to Serfdom*," in F. A. Hayek, *Reader's Digest Condensed Version of The Road to Serfdom*, op. cit., pp. 16–25.

[84] John Scoon to C. Hartley Grattan, May 2, 1945, op. cit., reprinted in the appendix.

section some oft-heard criticisms of the book are briefly reviewed and assessed. We will see that some are less justified than others.

Some Prominent Criticisms

One of the earliest criticisms concerned the historical accuracy of his claims. A good example is the objection raised by Frank Knight, who in his reader's report insisted that German history was far more complicated than Hayek had portrayed it; that, for example, the socialist policies in place since Bismarck's time comprised only one element in explaining the subsequent trajectory of the country. I doubt that Hayek would deny this; if he did, he would certainly be on very shaky ground. Nonetheless, if this part of his thesis seems overstated, it is only fair to recall the original structure of Hayek's argument. *The Road to Serfdom* was intended to be the final section of a much larger project, in which Hayek would trace the gradual decline of liberalism in a number of different countries. Hayek's specific arguments about Germany make much more sense within the context of this larger project. His decision to publish as a separate piece the conclusion of his work is akin to offering a punch line without the joke.

We must also remember the sorts of arguments he was trying to confront with his thesis. As Hayek frequently repeated, many intelligent and informed people of his day had been taken in by the claim that National Socialism was the next logical and historical phase of a collapsing capitalism. His point, one that most would accept today as evident, was that fascism and communism both represent totalitarian systems that have much more in common with each other than either does with the sorts of governments and economic systems that exist under liberal free market democracies. The Nazis demonized and persecuted the communists, to be sure, but it was not because they were themselves capitalists. Hayek simply sought to establish the true commonalities.

Another oft-voiced complaint was that Hayek's book was long on criticism but short on or vague concerning proposed alternatives. After ten years of economic depression, many people felt that capitalism had finally breathed its last and that something new had to replace it. What was Hayek offering? Writing in *The New Republic*, Alvin Hansen noted that Hayek distinguished in his book between "good planning" and "bad planning," then asked Hayek to inform his readers precisely how he would draw the line between the two.[85] John Maynard Keynes read the book on the way to the Bretton Woods conference, and delighted Hayek when he wrote him that it was "a grand book" and that "morally and philosophically I find myself in agreement with virtually the whole of it;

[85]Alvin Hansen, "The New Crusade against Planning," *The New Republic*, vol. 112, January 1, 1945, pp. 9–10.

and not only in agreement with it, but in a deeply moved agreement."[86] Keynes went on to say, though, that "You admit here and there that it is a question of knowing where to draw the line. You agree that the line has to be drawn somewhere, and that the logical extreme is not possible. But you give us no guidance whatever as to where to draw it."[87]

Hayek evidently took these criticisms to heart, for in the coming years he would make two further important contributions to political philosophy that would refine and extend the arguments made in *The Road to Serfdom*. In *The Constitution of Liberty* he laid out the philosophical foundations of liberal constitutionalism, wherein a private sphere of individual activity is defined, the state is granted a monopoly on coercion, and then is constitutionally limited by the rule of law in its use of those coercive powers. In the last third of the book Hayek outlined the specific sorts of government policies that were consistent with such a political setup.[88] In *Law, Legislation, and Liberty*, Hayek lamented how western democracies were increasingly circumventing the spirit of liberal constitutionalism by passing coercive legislation, typically under the guise of achieving social justice, but in reality serving well-organized coalitions of special interests. The book also included a unique proposal for legislative reform aimed at re-establishing the ideal of a constitutionally constrained liberal democratic commonwealth.[89]

A third complaint is that Hayek's argument against socialism in *The Road to Serfdom* is unconvincing because, by failing to address "market socialism," it must be viewed as incomplete. Evan Durbin, Hayek's old sparring partner at the LSE, was one of the first to enunciate the argument, chiding Hayek in his review in the *Economic Journal* for making "only one reference to the work of those of us who are both practicing economists and also Socialists, and that in a footnote," thereby neglecting "all recent writings on the subject."[90] According to Durbin, "democratic socialism" need not imply any "rigid programme of production" but only that "the final responsibility for taking economic decisions is transferred from the private company or group of shareholders to the representatives of the community. . . ."[91] Durbin's "democratic socialism" was a variant of the market socialism (sometimes also referred to by Hayek as "com-

---

[86] Letter, John Maynard Keynes to Hayek, June 28, 1944, reprinted in John Maynard Keynes, *Activities 1940–1946. Shaping the Post-War World: Employment and Commodities*, ed. Donald Moggridge, vol. 27 (1980) of *The Collected Writings of John Maynard Keynes*, op. cit., p. 385.

[87] *Ibid.*, p. 386.

[88] F. A. Hayek, *The Constitution of Liberty* (Chicago: University of Chicago Press, 1960).

[89] F. A. Hayek, *Law, Legislation, and Liberty*, 3 vols. (Chicago: University of Chicago Press, 1973–79).

[90] Evan Durbin, "Professor Hayek on Economic Planning and Political Liberty," *Economic Journal*, vol. 55, December 1945, p. 360. Durbin had his own book on democratic socialism: see Evan Durbin, *The Politics of Democratic Socialism: An Essay on Social Policy* (London: Routledge, 1940; reprinted, New York: Kelley, 1969).

[91] *Ibid.*, p. 361.

petitive socialism") that Oskar Lange had articulated in *On the Economic Theory of Socialism*. As was noted earlier, Hayek had already criticized this doctrine in a review of the Lange volume published in 1940. It was to this review that Hayek referred in his long note on market socialism in *The Road to Serfdom*.[92]

Market socialism may sound like an oxymoron, but it is a position that has seldom failed to intrigue economists seeking "the middle way." Market socialists are critics of capitalism, to be sure, but they accept as a starting premise that perfectly competitive markets have certain desirable efficiency characteristics. Crucially, however, they deny that any real world markets resemble those described under perfect competition. The days of atomistic competition disappeared when cartels and monopolies began emerging in the late nineteenth century. Contemporary capitalism, then, lacks the beneficial aspects of competition, while retaining all of its defects. A planned market socialist economy would restore true competition with all of its benefits while simultaneously correcting the myriad social injustices associated with unfettered capitalism. In Lange's specific blueprint for a market socialist society, there exist free markets for both consumer goods and labor, but (because of public ownership of the means of production) no market for productive resources. A Central Planning Board would provide prices, adjusting them up or down (using a "trial-and-error" method) depending on revealed shortages or surpluses.

Market socialism is attractive because it seems to combine the best parts of rival systems: the efficiency of a market-based system and egalitarian policies aimed at promoting social justice, all combined within a democratic polity. In his review, Hayek raised a number of pertinent questions about the details of Lange's plan, most of which suggested that though market socialism *sounded* good, it would not work. One of his key complaints was that Lange had neglected to say how often prices would need to be adjusted in his proposed system. This was an important issue, for even with relatively quick adjustments (something that Hayek thought would be difficult to sustain) Hayek maintained that an extensive system of price fixing would still always be playing catch-up relative to the adjustments that would take place in a market system, and so would be less efficient. In making his points, Hayek wrote, famously, that "it is difficult to suppress the suspicion that this particular proposal has been born out of an excessive preoccupation with problems of the pure theory of stationary equilibrium."[93] Hayek's later and much fuller development of how markets work to coordinate social and economic activity in a world in which knowledge is dispersed—a world very different from that described by the theory of stationary equilibrium—would become one of his central contributions to economics.

---

[92] F. A. Hayek, "Socialist Calculation: The Competitive 'Solution,'" op. cit. Hayek mentions the review in chapter 3, note 4.

[93] *Ibid.*, p. 123.

Hayek, then, had already articulated a set of arguments against market socialism. Why did he relegate them to a note in *The Road to Serfdom*? One clue is given by a letter that Lange wrote to Hayek on July 31, 1940, in which he responded to Hayek's review and tried to clear up a misunderstanding:

> I do not propose price fixing by a real central planning board, as a practical solution. It was used, in my paper, only as a methodological device to show how equilibrium prices can be determined by trial and error even in the absence of a market in the institutional sense of the word. Practically, I should, of course recommend the determination of the prices by a thorough market process whenever this is feasible. . . .[94]

Hayek might be forgiven if he were to infer from this letter that Lange had basically accepted his criticisms about the *practical feasibility* of market socialism. Though obviously Durbin thought differently, Hayek felt that market socialism was little more than an interesting theoretical exercise, the sort of thing that economists like to play with on the blackboard, but not something to be taken seriously as practical proposal.

But even more to the point, Hayek did not write *The Road to Serfdom* chiefly with theoretical economists like Lange or Durbin in mind. Unlike such economists, most advocates of "planning" had not even begun to think through what it meant to have a planned society. For them, planning itself was, as Robbins had put it, a panacea. It was this vague but widespread sentiment for which *The Road to Serfdom* was meant to be an antidote. Hayek was trying to show his readers that planning, everyone's favorite remedy for the ills of the world, might sound good in theory, but would not work in practice (or, at least, not unless the western democracies were prepared to accept severe constraints on personal liberty of the sort on display in the systems against which they currently were fighting.)

This explains, I think, why Hayek did not bother to lay out the argument against market socialism in his book. He felt that market socialism was only a theoretical dream, and that the details of the argument against it would be out of place in a general book. His economist readers, he doubtless presumed, were already aware of the arguments he had made in 1940, arguments he felt had succeeded. If they weren't, he reminded them with a note.

As such, one could understand that Hayek felt a bit miffed by Durbin's insinuation that he had neglected all the recent work. His irritation is evident in the unpublished version of his 1948 postscript.

---

[94] Letter, Oskar Lange to Hayek, July 31, 1940, reprinted in *Economic Theory and Market Socialism—Selected Essays of Oskar Lange*, ed. Tadeusz Kowalik (Cheltenham: Elgar, 1994), p. 298.

Mr. Durbin . . . is especially pained that I have not taken more seriously and devoted no more than a note to the interesting schemes of a competitive socialism which have been put forward in recent years in a number of learned books and articles. I am quite ready to discuss their theoretical merits and have in fact done so at some length in an article quoted in the footnote just referred to. And I shall be very glad to examine these plans further as soon as there are any signs that they are taken seriously by, and exercise any practical influence on the politics of, the socialist parties. But I have yet to find any socialist party which is willing even to consider using competition as the method for organizing economic activity, and until this is the case I cannot see that anyone but the specialist need be bothered with the objections to those ingenious schemes. But I may perhaps be allowed to add that I should have more confidence in the genuineness of the desire to reconcile freedom and socialism by means of a "competitive socialism" if one of the main advocates of these schemes, Professor Oskar Lange, had not chosen to become one of the main spokesmen of the Russian point of view on the Council of the United Nations and if Mr. Durbin were not now himself a member of the Socialist British Government which is doing most of the things of which he apparently disapproves.[95]

Durbin would die in a drowning accident in 1948, which may explain why this passage was never included in the foreword. Alas, Lange's accommodation to the political realities in his native Poland would only increase through time: he went on to write apologetics for Stalin and, renouncing his earlier views on market socialism, even went so far as to forbid their republication in Polish.[96]

Though Lange and Durbin are gone, the dreams for market socialism among economic theorists never seem to die, the most recent revival occurring after the collapse of the Soviet bloc in the last decade of the last century. Its longevity is easy to explain: for those who seek a middle way, market socialism is the ideal system. In more recent discussions, Hayek's original critique has been substantially bolstered by additional arguments, some from the economics of information that identify incentive problems, others from public choice analysis that identify political obstacles that would confront any such regime.[97] But it is perhaps sufficient to say, as Hayek did in 1948, that until a real-world example of such an "ingenious scheme" is forthcoming, it is best considered a

---

[95] F. A. Hayek, "Postscript," Hayek Papers, box 106, folder 8, Hoover Institution Archives. By this point Durbin was a Labour MP and the Parliamentary Secretary of the Ministry of Works.

[96] Tadeusz Kowalik, "Oskar Lange's Market Socialism: The Story of an Intellectual-Political Career" [1991], reprinted in *Why Market Socialism? Voices from Dissent,* ed. Frank Roosevelt and David Belkin (Armonk, New York: M. E. Sharpe, 1994), pp. 137–54.

[97] See Bruce Caldwell, "Hayek and Socialism," *Journal of Economic Literature,* vol. 35, December 1997, pp. 1856–90, for more on the recent debates.

theoretical construct of interest only to specialists, one that has no particular relevance for the world in which we actually live.

A final criticism has sometimes been called the "inevitability thesis" or the "slippery slope" argument: Hayek is claimed to have said that, once a society engages in a little planning, it is doomed to end up in a totalitarian state. Durbin was among those making this charge, writing that Hayek believed that "any departure from the practice of free enterprise, any hope that reason and science may be applied to the direction of economic activity, any attempt at economic planning, must lead us remorselessly to serfdom. . . ."[98] If Durbin's statement of the inevitability thesis seems unusually stark, he was certainly not alone in thinking that Hayek had said that any expansion of state control over the economy would necessarily lead to a totalitarian outcome. Those who so interpreted him spanned the ideological spectrum from Barbara Wootton to George Stigler.[99] Paul Samuelson even expressed the idea diagrammatically in his principles of economics text, drawing political freedom on one axis, economic freedom on the other, and a movement down the curve (slippery slope indeed!) from high to low levels of both being what Hayek supposedly predicted: "that government modification of laissez faire must lead *inevitably* to political serfdom."[100]

This interpretation occurred despite Hayek's frequent protests to the contrary. Sometimes he objected publicly, as he did in the preface to the 1976 edition: "It has frequently been alleged that I have contended that any movement in the direction of socialism is bound to lead to totalitarianism. Even though this danger exists, this is not what the book says."[101] In private he could be both more forceful and explicit, as may be seen in his letter to Paul Samuelson:

> I am afraid in glancing through the 11th edition of your *Economics* I seem to have discovered the source of the false allegation about my book *The Road to Serfdom* which I constantly encounter, most resent and can only regard as a

---

[98] Durbin, op. cit., p. 360. Durbin repeatedly accused Hayek as being either unscientific or hostile to science in his review, nicely exemplifying the positivist worldview against which Hayek so often fought.

[99] See Barbara Wootton, *Freedom under Planning*, op. cit., pp. 28, 36–37, 50, and George Stigler, *Memoirs of an Unregulated Economist* (New York: Basic Books, 1985), p. 146.

[100] Paul Samuelson, *Economics*, 11th ed. (New York: McGraw-Hill, 1980), p. 827.

[101] F. A. Hayek, preface to the 1976 edition, this volume, p. 55. Note that Hayek says "this is not what *the book* says." He may have been implying here that the condensation and cartoon versions of his argument were at least in part responsible for the widespread misreading of his message. And indeed, in the condensed version Hayek's insistence that he is not describing inevitable tendencies is left out, whereas part of the following sentence, not emphasized in the original, is set in italics: "Few recognize that the rise of fascism and naziism [the IEA version mistakenly replaces naziism with Marxism here] was not a reaction against the socialist trends of the preceding period *but a necessary outcome of those tendencies*." See F. A. Hayek, *Reader's Digest Condensed Version of The Road to Serfdom*, op. cit., pp. 31–32.

malicious distortion which has largely succeeded in discrediting my argument . . . [Y]ou assert that I contend that "each step away from the market system and towards the social reform of the welfare state is *inevitably* a journey that must end in a totalitarian state" and that "government modification of market laissez faire must lead *inevitably* to political serfdom." . . .

How anyone who has read my book can in good faith say this when ever since the first edition I say right at the beginning . . . "Nor am I arguing that these developments are inevitable. If they were, there would be no point in writing this. They can be prevented if people realize in time where their efforts may lead. . . ."[102]

Given the ubiquity of the "inevitability thesis" interpretation among both his friends and his foes, as well as Hayek's own insistence that this was not his argument, it is important to try to figure out exactly what has given rise to the confusion.

Hayek's letter to Samuelson allows us to rule out one way of interpreting the word "inevitability." Hayek was decidedly *not* making the historical claim that, no matter what future moves were made in Britain and America, there was no turning back, that a socialist future that would end in totalitarianism was inevitably coming. This kind of inevitability thesis was, after all, exactly what Hayek was criticizing in his essay "Scientism and the Study of Society," when he attacked historicism, the belief that there were historical laws knowledge of which allowed one to predict a necessary future.

A more plausible way to read Hayek's words is to see him as warning that, unless we change our ways, we are headed down the road to serfdom. It was certainly part of Hayek's intent to issue such a warning. He was in particular afraid that we might embark on such a path without really realizing it, or, as he put it in his speech before the Economic Club of Detroit, "the danger is the greater because we may choose the wrong way, not by deliberation and concerted decision, but because we seem to be blundering into it."[103] As the title of his fourth chapter makes clear, some of Hayek's opponents had made the claim that planning was "inevitable," that unless we embraced "planning for freedom" we were headed toward totalitarianism. Hayek presumably was hoping to stand such an argument on its head, to show that, rather than the only means of counteracting totalitarianism, planning itself constituted a significant step along the way toward the totalitarian state.

[102] Letter, Hayek to Paul Samuelson, December 18, 1980, Hayek Papers, box 48, folder 5, Hoover Institution Archives. Hayek was wrong to imply that Samuelson was the source of the misreading, for it was a common one. The archives also contain Samuelson's reply, in which he apologized and promised to try to represent Hayek's views more accurately in any future work.

[103] F. A. Hayek, "The Road to Serfdom, an Address before the Economic Club of Detroit," op. cit., p. 4.

Yet another way to read Hayek is to see him as offering a *logical* rather than a *historical* argument. Hayek recognized that "liberal socialists" value freedom of choice and the honoring of individual preferences. What he denied was that they could maintain those values *and still carry out their proclaimed program of extensive central planning.* As he succinctly put it, "socialism can be put into practice only by methods which most socialists disapprove."[104] Even if it were to begin as a "liberal socialist" experiment (none of the real-world cases have ever done so, one might add), full-scale planning requires that the planning authorities take over all production decisions; to be able to make any decisions at all, they would need to exercise more and more political control. If one tries to create a *truly* planned society, one will not be able to separate out control of the economy from political control. This was Hayek's logical argument against planning, one that he had succinctly articulated in 1939 in "Freedom and the Economic System."

> In the end agreement that planning is necessary, together with the inability of the democratic assembly to agree on a particular plan, must strengthen the demand that the government, or some single individual, should be given powers to act on their own responsibility. It becomes more and more the accepted belief that, if one wants to get things done, the responsible director of affairs must be freed from the fetters of democratic procedure.[105]

Now evidently, in the years since he wrote, the countries that Hayek was most concerned about (the Western European democracies and the United States), despite the rhetoric of their left-wing politicians, did not go to anything like complete central planning or full nationalization of the means of production. For example, though there was a movement in this direction in Britain directly after the war, it reached its high point by the late 1940s, and even then only about 20 per cent of British industry was nationalized.

Those who see Hayek as issuing a prediction of an inevitable trend would view this history as refuting his claim. Those who see him as providing a warning might consider thanking him for saving them from disaster. If one confronts Hayek's logical argument, however, the subsequent paths of the western European democracies are not really tests of Hayek's thesis. To be sure, many of them did develop substantial welfare states, and Hayek spoke about the separate dangers of these in his later writings. But the existence of such states, and

---

[104] This volume, chapter 10, p. 159.

[105] F. A. Hayek, "Freedom and the Economic System" [1939], op. cit., p. 205. When I have described Hayek's argument in seminars, more than once members of the audience have noted its similarities with Arrow's "Impossibility Theorem" in welfare economics.

whatever successes they may or may not have had, does not undermine Hayek's logical argument from *The Road to Serfdom:* a welfare state is not socialism.

The proper way to evaluate Hayek's logical thesis is to ask, How many actually existing, real-world political systems have fully nationalized their means of production and preserved both some measure of economic efficiency and freedom of choice over goods and occupations? Count them up. Then compare the number with those that nationalized their means of production and turned to extensive planning and control, and with it the curtailment of individual liberties. If one agrees that this is the right test, Hayek's position is fully vindicated: full socialism *can* only be put into practice by using methods of which most socialists would disapprove.

The Continuing Relevance of The Road to Serfdom

Reading (or perhaps rereading) *The Road to Serfdom* will be a pleasurable experience for some, and induce apoplexy in others: it continues to be a lightning rod, as well as a Rorschach test, revealing as much about the reader's prior commitments as it does about Hayek's ideas. For younger readers the book may also be a bit of a mystery, for though it has elements of a general treatise (more on which anon), it was also very much (as he himself once admitted) a "tract for the times."[106] Modern readers who are not familiar with the history of the Third Reich may stumble over names like Julius Streicher or Robert Ley. And who today still recalls Sir Richard Acland's "Forward March" movement, or the Temporary National Economic Committee? As editor, I have tried to provide brief notes that place these individuals, groups, and ideas in context, in an effort to make it easier for readers today to enter the world that Hayek inhabited.

At the same time, the book is also filled with timeless ideas. Hayek's immediate objective was to persuade his British audience that their heritage of liberal democracy under the rule of law should be viewed as a national treasure rather than an object of scorn, as a still-vital roadmap for organizing society rather than an embarrassing relic of times gone by. Though much depends on how one defines one's terms, his was a message that invites more than occasional reexamination.

Another theme, evident perhaps more explicitly in this introduction than in specific passages in Hayek's own text, but nonetheless very much a part of his underlying motivation in writing the book, is Hayek's warning concerning the dangers that times of war pose for established civil societies—for it is during

---

[106] See F. A. Hayek, preface to the 1976 edition, this volume, p. 53.

such times when hard-won civil liberties are most likely to be all-too-easily given up. Even more troubling, politicians instinctively recognize the seductive power of war. Times of national emergency permit the invocation of a common cause and a common purpose. War enables leaders to ask for sacrifices. It presents an enemy against which all segments of society may unite. This is true of real war, but because of its ability to unify disparate groups, savvy politicians from all parties find it effective to invoke war metaphors in a host of contexts. The war on drugs, the war on poverty, and the war on terror are but three examples from recent times.[107] What makes these examples even more worrisome than true wars is that none has a logical endpoint; each may be invoked forever.

Hayek's message was to be wary of such martial invocations. His specific fear was that, for a war to be fought effectively, the power and size of the state must grow. No matter what rhetoric they employ, politicians and the bureaucracies over which they preside love power, and power is never easily surrendered once the danger, if there ever was one, has passed. Though eternal vigilance is sage advice, surely "wartime" (or when politicians would try to convince us that it is such a time) is when those who value the preservation of individual liberty must be most on guard.[108]

Finally, what one finds in this book, and in all of Hayek's work, is a clear recognition of the power of ideas. It was perhaps John Maynard Keynes who said it best, in the closing chapter of *The General Theory:*

> the ideas of economists and political philosophers, both when they are right and when they are wrong, are more powerful than commonly understood. Indeed the world is ruled by little else. Practical men, who believe themselves to be quite exempt from any intellectual influences, are usually the slaves of some defunct economist. Madmen in authority, who hear voices in the air, are distilling their frenzy from some academic scribbler of a few years back. I am sure that the power of vested interests is vastly exaggerated compared with the gradual encroachment of ideas.[109]

Hayek would have offered his immediate assent, adding, perhaps, that Keynes's passage carries with it the implication that those who fail to understand the ori-

---

[107] I thank Steven Horwitz for providing these apposite examples in his contributions to a session commemorating the 60th anniversary of the publication of *The Road to Serfdom* held at the 2004 History of Economics Society meetings in Toronto, Canada.

[108] For many depressing examples of Hayek's thesis, see Robert Higgs, *Crisis and Leviathan: Critical Episodes in the Growth of American Government* (New York: Oxford University Press, 1987). This introduction is being written during George W. Bush's presidency, one that provides plentiful additional evidence.

[109] John Maynard Keynes, *The General Theory of Employment, Interest and Money* [1936], reprinted as vol. 7 (1973) of *The Collected Writings of John Maynard Keynes*, op. cit., p. 383.

gins of the ideas do so at their peril. Given the many years of his life that he spent diligently toiling, the perennial advocate of causes that most of his contemporaries thought of as lost, anachronistic, or a return to reaction, perhaps no person better represents the notion of the power of ideas in the twentieth century than does F. A. Hayek.

Bruce Caldwell

THE ROAD TO SERFDOM

It is seldom that liberty of any kind is lost all at once. —David Hume

I should have loved freedom, I believe, at all times, but in the time in which we live I am ready to worship it. —A. de Tocqueville

To the socialists of all parties

PREFACE TO THE ORIGINAL EDITIONS[1]

When a professional student of social affairs writes a political book, his first duty is plainly to say so. This is a political book. I do not wish to disguise this by describing it, as I might perhaps have done, by the more elegant and ambitious name of an essay in social philosophy. But, whatever the name, the essential point remains that all I shall have to say is derived from certain ultimate values. I hope I have adequately discharged in the book itself a second and no less important duty: to make it clear beyond doubt what these ultimate values are on which the whole argument depends.

There is, however, one thing I want to add to this. Though this is a political book, I am as certain as anyone can be that the beliefs set out in it are not determined by my personal interests. I can discover no reason why the kind of society which seems to me desirable should offer greater advantages to me than to the great majority of the people of my country. In fact, I am always told by my socialist colleagues that as an economist I should occupy a much more important position in the kind of society to which I am opposed—provided, of course, that I could bring myself to accept their views. I feel equally certain that my opposition to these views is not due to their being different from those with which I have grown up, since they are the very views which I held as a young man and which have led me to make the study of economics my profession. For those who, in the current fashion, seek interested motives in every profession of a political opinion, I may, perhaps, be allowed to add that I have every possible reason for *not* writing or publishing this book. It is certain to offend many people with whom I wish to live on friendly terms; it has forced me to put aside work for which I feel better qualified and to which I attach greater importance in the long run; and, above all, it is certain to prejudice the reception of the results of the more strictly academic work to which all my inclinations lead me.

If in spite of this I have come to regard the writing of this book as a duty which I must not evade, this was mainly due to a peculiar and serious feature of the discussions of problems of future economic policy at the present time, of which the public is scarcely sufficiently aware. This is the fact that the majority of

---

[1] [This preface appeared in the British, Australian, and American editions. —Ed.]

37

economists have now for some years been absorbed by the war machine, and silenced by their official positions, and that in consequence public opinion on these problems is to an alarming extent guided by amateurs and cranks, by people who have an ax to grind or a pet panacea to sell. In these circumstances one who still has the leisure for literary work is hardly entitled to keep to himself apprehensions which current tendencies must create in the minds of many who cannot publicly express them—though in different circumstances I should have gladly left the discussion of questions of national policy to those who are both better authorized and better qualified for the task.

The central argument of this book was first sketched in an article entitled "Freedom and the Economic System," which appeared in the *Contemporary Review* for April, 1938, and was later reprinted in an enlarged form as one of the "Public Policy Pamphlets" edited by Professor H. D. Gideonse for the University of Chicago Press (1939).[2] I have to thank the editors and publishers of both these publications for permission to reproduce certain passages from them.

F. A. Hayek

[2][F. A. Hayek, "Freedom and the Economic System," *Contemporary Review*, April 1938, pp. 434–42; reprinted as chapter 8 of F. A. Hayek, *Socialism and War: Essays, Documents, Reviews*, op. cit., pp. 181–88. F. A. Hayek, *Freedom and the Economic System* (Chicago: University of Chicago Press, 1939), Public Policy Pamphlet No. 29 in the series edited by Harry D. Gideonse; reprinted as chapter 9 *ibid.*, pp. 189–211. —Ed.]

FOREWORD TO THE 1956
AMERICAN PAPERBACK EDITION

Although this book might in some respects have been different if I had written it in the first instance with American readers primarily in mind, it has by now made for itself too definite if unexpected a place in this country to make any rewriting advisable. Its republication in a new form, however, more than ten years after its first appearance, is perhaps an appropriate occasion for explaining its original aim and for a few comments on the altogether unforeseen and in many ways curious success it has had in this country.

The book was written in England during the war years and was designed almost exclusively for English readers. Indeed, it was addressed mainly to a very special class of readers in England. It was in no spirit of mockery that I dedicated it "To the Socialists of All Parties." It had its origin in many discussions which, during the preceding ten years, I had with friends and colleagues whose sympathies had been inclined toward the left, and it was in continuation of those arguments that I wrote *The Road to Serfdom.*

When Hitler came into power in Germany, I had already been teaching at the University of London for several years, but I kept in close touch with affairs on the Continent and was able to do so until the outbreak of war.[1] What I had thus seen of the origins and evolution of the various totalitarian movements made me feel that English public opinion, particularly among my friends who held "advanced" views on social matters, completely misconceived the nature of those movements. Even before the war I was led by this to state in a brief essay what became the central argument of this book.[2] But after war broke out I felt that this widespread misunderstanding of the political systems of our en-

---

[1] [Hayek was a visiting professor in the Economics Department at the London School of Economics and Political Science (LSE) during the 1931–32 academic year, at the end of which he was appointed to the Tooke Chair of Economic Science and Statistics. The chair was founded at King's College, London, in 1859, the year after Thomas Tooke died. In 1919 the chair was transferred from King's to the LSE, both of which were then part of the University of London. Though Hayek's appointment was technically with the University of London, his teaching took place at the LSE. —Ed.]

[2] [Hayek refers here to "Freedom and the Economic System," op. cit. See the preface to the original editions, note 2. —Ed.]

emies, and soon also of our new ally, Russia, constituted a serious danger which had to be met by a more systematic effort. Also, it was already fairly obvious that England herself was likely to experiment after the war with the same kind of policies which I was convinced had contributed so much to destroy liberty elsewhere.

Thus this book gradually took shape as a warning to the socialist intelligentsia of England; with the inevitable delays of wartime production, it finally appeared there early in the spring of 1944. This date will, incidentally, also explain why I felt that in order to get a hearing I had somewhat to restrain myself in my comments on the regime of our wartime ally[3] and to choose my illustrations mainly from developments in Germany.

It seems that the book appeared at a propitious moment, and I can feel only gratification at the success it had in England, which, though very different in kind, was quantitatively no smaller than it was to be in the United States. On the whole, the book was taken in the spirit in which it was written, and its argument was seriously examined by those to whom it was mainly addressed. Excepting only certain of the leading politicians of the Labour party—who, as if to provide an illustration for my remarks on the nationalist tendencies of socialism, attacked the book on the ground that it was written by a foreigner[4]— the thoughtful and receptive manner in which it was generally examined by persons who must have found its conclusions running counter to their strongest convictions was deeply impressive.[5] The same applies also to the other European countries where the book eventually appeared; and its particularly cordial reception by the post-Nazi generation of Germany, when copies of a translation published in Switzerland at last reached that country, was one of the unforeseen pleasures I derived from its publication.

Rather different was the reception the book had in the United States when it was published here a few months after its appearance in England. I had given little thought to its possible appeal to American readers when writing it. It was then twenty years since I had last been in America as a research student, and during that time I had somewhat lost touch with the development of American ideas.[6] I could not be sure how far my argument had direct relevance to the American scene, and I was not in the least surprised when the book was in fact

---

[3] [That is, the Soviet Union. —Ed.]

[4] [See my introduction to this volume, note 75, for more on this. —Ed.]

[5] The most representative example of British criticism of the book from a left-wing point of view is probably Mrs. Barbara Wootton's courteous and frank study, *Freedom under Planning*, op. cit. It is often quoted in the United States as an effective refutation of my argument, though I cannot help feeling that more than one reader must have gained the impression that, as one American reviewer expressed it, "it seems substantially to confirm Hayek's thesis." See Chester I. Barnard, "Review of *Freedom under Planning*," *Southern Economic Journal*, vol. 12, January 1946, p. 290.

[6] [Hayek visited the United States as a student from March 1923 until May 1924. —Ed.]

rejected by the first three publishing houses approached.[7] It was certainly most unexpected when, after the book was brought out by its present publishers, it soon began to sell at a rate almost unprecedented for a book of this kind, not intended for popular consumption.[8] And I was even more surprised by the violence of the reaction from both political wings, by the lavish praise the book received from some quarters no less than by the passionate hatred it appeared to arouse in others.

Contrary to my experience in England, in America the kind of people to whom this book was mainly addressed seem to have rejected it out of hand as a malicious and disingenuous attack on their finest ideals; they appear never to have paused to examine its argument. The language used and the emotion shown in some of the more adverse criticism the book received were indeed rather extraordinary.[9] But scarcely less surprising to me was the enthusiastic welcome accorded to the book by many whom I never expected to read a volume of this type—and from many more of whom I still doubt whether in fact they ever read it. And I must add that occasionally the manner in which it was

[7] I did not know then, as has since been admitted by a person advising one of the firms, that this appears to have been due not to any doubts of the success of the book but to political prejudice, which went to the extent of representing the book as "unfit for publication by a reputable house." See on this the statement by William Miller quoted by W. T. Couch in "The Sainted Book Burners," *The Freeman*, vol. 5, April 1955, p. 423, and also William Miller, *The Book Industry: A Report of the Public Library Inquiry of the Social Science Research Council* (New York: Columbia University Press, 1949), p. 12. [The first printing of Miller's book on the book industry contained the following sentence: "That university presses have done this is suggested by the publication and promotion by the University of Chicago Press a few years ago of Friedrich A. von Hayek's *The Road to Serfdom*, a sensational book previously rejected by at least one notable trade house which was quite aware of its sales possibilities." What university presses "had done" was to try to increase their profits by looking for profitable best-sellers, regardless of quality. W. T. Couch, then director of the University of Chicago Press, sent Miller a letter on October 7, 1949, stating that Miller had his facts wrong. Couch provided documentary evidence that the Press did not expect a big market for the book, and demanded a retraction of the sentence from subsequent printings of Miller's book. In his reply to Couch, Miller acquiesced to the removal of the offending lines in subsequent printings, but also called Hayek's book "a despicable performance" and went on to make the statements, reproduced by Couch in his article in *The Freeman*, that Hayek alludes to in his note. —Ed.]

[8] Not a little of this was due to the publication of a condensation of this book in the *Reader's Digest*, and I should like to pay here to the editors of this journal a public testimony to the extremely skillful manner in which this was done without my assistance. It is inevitable that the compression of a complex argument to a fraction of its original length produces some oversimplification, but that it was done without distortion and better than I could have done it myself is a remarkable achievement. [Hayek discusses this episode at more length in *Hayek on Hayek*, op. cit., 104–5; cf. my introduction to this volume, pp. 18–22. —Ed.]

[9] To any reader who would like to see a specimen of abuse and invective which is probably unique in contemporary academic discussion I recommend a reading of Professor Herman Finer's *Road to Reaction*, op. cit. [Hayek briefly considered filing a libel suit, and ultimately sent Finer a letter breaking off relations with him. For more on the Finer episode, see my introduction to this volume, p. 21. —Ed.]

used vividly brought home to me the truth of Lord Acton's observation that "at all times sincere friends of freedom have been rare, and its triumphs have been due to minorities, that have prevailed by associating themselves with auxiliaries whose objects often differed from their own; and this association, which is always dangerous, has sometimes been disastrous."[10]

It seems hardly likely that this extraordinary difference in the reception of the book on the two sides of the Atlantic is due entirely to a difference in national temperament. I have since become increasingly convinced that the explanation must lie in a difference of intellectual situation at the time when it arrived. In England, and in Europe generally, the problems with which I dealt had long ceased to be abstract questions. The ideals which I examined had long before come down to earth, and even their most enthusiastic adherents had already seen concretely some of the difficulties and unlooked-for results which their application produced. I was thus writing about phenomena of which almost all my European readers had some more or less close experience, and I was merely arguing systematically and consistently what many had already intuitively felt. There was already a disillusionment about these ideals under way, which their critical examination merely made more vocal or explicit.

In the United States, on the other hand, these ideals were still fresh and more virulent. It was only ten or fifteen years earlier—not forty or fifty, as in England—that a large part of the intelligentsia had caught the infection. And, in spite of the experimentation of the New Deal, their enthusiasm for the new kind of rationally constructed society was still largely unsoiled by practical experience. What to most Europeans had in some measure become *vieux jeux* was to the American radicals still the glittering hope of a better world which they had embraced and nourished during the recent years of the Great Depression.

Opinion moves fast in the United States, and even now it is difficult to remember how comparatively short a time it was before *The Road to Serfdom* appeared that the most extreme kind of economic planning had been seriously advocated and the model of Russia held up for imitation by men who were soon to play an important role in public affairs. It would be easy enough to give chapter and verse for this, but it would be invidious now to single out individuals. Be it enough to mention that in 1934 the newly established National Plan-

[10][John Emerich Edward Dalberg-Acton, First Baron Acton, "The History of Freedom in Antiquity," reprinted in *The History of Freedom and Other Essays* (London: Macmillan, 1907; reprinted, Freeport, NY: Books for Libraries Press, 1967), p. 1. Lord Acton (1834–1902) was a Liberal MP from 1859 to 1864, leader of the Liberal Roman Catholics in England, and founder-editor of the *Cambridge Modern History*, to which he contributed the first two volumes. Hayek once thought of naming the Mont Pèlerin Society the Acton-Tocqueville Society, but Frank Knight opposed naming a liberal movement after two Catholics. The article cited was originally an address delivered to the members of the Bridgnorth Institution at the Agricultural Hall in Bridgnorth, Shropshire, on February 26, 1877. —Ed.]

ning Board[11] devoted a good deal of attention to the example of planning provided by these four countries: Germany, Italy, Russia, and Japan. Ten years later we had of course learned to refer to these same countries as "totalitarian," had fought a long war with three of them, and were soon to start a "cold war" with the fourth. Yet the contention of this book that the political development in those countries had something to do with their economic policies was then still indignantly rejected by the advocates of planning in this country. It suddenly became the fashion to deny that the inspiration of planning had come from Russia and to contend, as one of my eminent critics put it, that it was "a plain fact that Italy, Russia, Japan, and Germany all reached totalitarianism by very different roads."[12]

The whole intellectual climate in the United States at the time *The Road to Serfdom* appeared was thus one in which it was bound either profoundly to shock or greatly to delight the members of sharply divided groups. In consequence, in spite of its apparent success, the book has not had here the kind of effect I should have wished or which it has had elsewhere. It is true that its main conclusions are today widely accepted. If twelve years ago it seemed to many almost sacrilege to suggest that fascism and communism are merely variants of the same totalitarianism which central control of all economic activity tends to produce, this has become almost a commonplace. It is now even widely recognized that democratic socialism is a very precarious and unstable affair, riven with internal contradictions and everywhere producing results most distasteful to many of its advocates.

For this sobered mood the lessons of events and more popular discussions of the problem[13] are certainly more responsible than this book. Nor was my general thesis as such original when it was published. Although similar but earlier warnings may have been largely forgotten, the dangers inherent in the policies which I criticized had been pointed out again and again. Whatever merits this

---

[11] [The National Planning Board was established within the U.S. Department of the Interior to assist in the preparation of a comprehensive plan for public works under the direction of Frederick Delano, Charles Merriam, and Wesley Clair Mitchell. Its last successor agency, the National Resources Planning Board, was abolished in 1943. —Ed.]

[12] [The "eminent critic" was the economist Alvin W. Hansen (1887–1975), a leading American expositor of Keynesian economics, who as a policy advisor also played a role in the development of the social security system and the creation of the Full Employment Act of 1946. The passage Hayek cites is taken from Hansen's review of *The Road to Serfdom*, "The New Crusade against Planning," op. cit., p. 12. —Ed.]

[13] The most effective of these was undoubtedly George Orwell's *1984: A Novel* (New York: New American Library, 1949). The author had earlier kindly reviewed this book. [George Orwell, pseudonym of Eric Arthur Blair (1903–1950), was an English novelist and essayist; he also wrote *Animal Farm*. Orwell's brief review appeared in the *Observer*, April 9, 1944, together with a review of a book by Konni Zilliacus, *The Mirror of the Past, Lest It Reflect the Future* (London: V. Gollancz, 1944). —Ed.]

book possesses consist not in the reiteration of this thesis but in the patient and detailed examination of the reasons why economic planning will produce such unlooked-for results and of the process by which they come about.

It is for this reason that I rather hope that the time may now be more favorable in America for a serious consideration of the true argument of the book than it was when it first appeared. I believe that what is important in it still has to render its service, although I recognize that the hot socialism against which it was mainly directed—that organized movement toward a deliberate organization of economic life by the state as the chief owner of the means of production—is nearly dead in the Western world. The century of socialism in this sense probably came to an end around 1948. Many of its illusions have been discarded even by its leaders, and elsewhere as well as in the United States the very name has lost much of its attraction. Attempts will no doubt be made to rescue the name for movements which are less dogmatic, less doctrinaire, and less systematic. But an argument applicable solely against those clear-cut conceptions of social reform which characterized the socialist movements of the past might today well appear as tilting against windmills.

Yet though hot socialism is probably a thing of the past, some of its conceptions have penetrated far too deeply into the whole structure of current thought to justify complacency. If few people in the Western world now want to remake society from the bottom according to some ideal blueprint, a great many still believe in measures which, though not designed completely to remodel the economy, in their aggregate effect may well unintentionally produce this result. And, even more than at the time when I wrote this book, the advocacy of policies which in the long run cannot be reconciled with the preservation of a free society is no longer a party matter. That hodgepodge of ill-assembled and often inconsistent ideals which under the name of the Welfare State has largely replaced socialism as the goal of the reformers needs very careful sorting out if its results are not to be very similar to those of full-fledged socialism. This is not to say that some of its aims are not both practicable and laudable. But there are many ways in which we can work toward the same goal, and in the present state of opinion there is some danger that our impatience for quick results may lead us to choose instruments which, though perhaps more efficient for achieving the particular ends, are not compatible with the preservation of a free society. The increasing tendency to rely on administrative coercion and discrimination where a modification of the general rules of law might, perhaps more slowly, achieve the same object, and to resort to direct state controls or to the creation of monopolistic institutions where judicious use of financial inducements might evoke spontaneous efforts, is still a powerful legacy of the socialist period which is likely to influence policy for a long time to come.

Just because in the years ahead of us political ideology is not likely to aim at a clearly defined goal but toward piecemeal change, a full understanding of the process through which certain kinds of measures can destroy the bases of an economy based on the market and gradually smother the creative powers of a free civilization seems now of the greatest importance. Only if we understand why and how certain kinds of economic controls tend to paralyze the driving forces of a free society, and which kinds of measures are particularly dangerous in this respect, can we hope that social experimentation will not lead us into situations none of us want.

It is as a contribution to this task that this book is intended. I hope that at least in the quieter atmosphere of the present it will be received as what it was meant to be, not as an exhortation to resistance against any improvement or experimentation, but as a warning that we should insist that any modification in our arrangements should pass certain tests (described in the central chapter on the Rule of Law) before we commit ourselves to courses from which withdrawal may be difficult.

The fact that this book was originally written with only the British public in mind does not appear to have seriously affected its intelligibility for the American reader. But there is one point of phraseology which I ought to explain here to forestall any misunderstanding. I use throughout the term "liberal" in the original, nineteenth-century sense in which it is still current in Britain. In current American usage it often means very nearly the opposite of this. It has been part of the camouflage of leftish movements in this country, helped by the muddleheadedness of many who really believe in liberty, that "liberal" has come to mean the advocacy of almost every kind of government control. I am still puzzled why those in the United States who truly believe in liberty should not only have allowed the left to appropriate this almost indispensable term but should even have assisted by beginning to use it themselves as a term of opprobrium. This seems to be particularly regrettable because of the consequent tendency of many true liberals to describe themselves as conservatives.

It is true, of course, that in the struggle against the believers in the all-powerful state the true liberal must sometimes make common cause with the conservative, and in some circumstances, as in contemporary Britain, he has hardly any other way of actively working for his ideals. But true liberalism is still distinct from conservatism, and there is danger in the two being confused.[14] Conservatism, though a necessary element in any stable society, is not a social program; in its paternalistic, nationalistic, and power-adoring tendencies it is often closer to socialism than true liberalism; and with its traditionalistic, anti-intellectual, and often mystical propensities it will never, except in short periods of disillusionment, appeal to the young and all those others who believe that

---

[14][For more on the distinction between conservatism and liberalism, see F. A. Hayek, "Why I Am Not a Conservative," postscript to *The Constitution of Liberty*, op. cit., pp. 397–411. —Ed.]

some changes are desirable if this world is to become a better place. A conservative movement, by its very nature, is bound to be a defender of established privilege and to lean on the power of government for the protection of privilege. The essence of the liberal position, however, is the denial of all privilege, if privilege is understood in its proper and original meaning of the state granting and protecting rights to some which are not available on equal terms to others.

Perhaps a further word of apology is required for my allowing this book to reappear in entirely unchanged form after the lapse of almost twelve years. I have many times tried to revise it, and there are numerous points I should like to explain at greater length or to state more cautiously or to fortify by more illustration and proof. But all attempts at rewriting only proved that I could never again produce as short a book covering as much of the field; and it seems to me that, whatever other merits it may have, its relative brevity is its greatest. I have thus been forced to the conclusion that whatever I want to add to the argument I must attempt in separate studies. I have begun to do so in various essays, some of which provide a more searching discussion of certain philosophical and economic issues on which the present book only touches.[15] On the special question of the roots of the ideas here criticized and of their connection with some of the most powerful and impressive intellectual movements of this age, I have commented in another volume.[16] And before long I hope to supplement the all-too-brief central chapter of this book by a more extensive treatment of the relation between equality and justice.[17]

There is one particular topic, however, on which the reader will with justice expect me to comment on this occasion, yet which I could even less treat adequately without writing a new book. Little more than a year after *The Road to Serfdom* first appeared, Great Britain had a socialist government which remained in power for six years. And the question of how far this experience has confirmed or refuted my apprehensions is one which I must try to answer at least briefly. If anything, this experience has strengthened my concern and, I believe I may add, has taught the reality of the difficulties I pointed out to many for whom an abstract argument would never have carried conviction. Indeed, it was not long after the Labour government came into power that some of the

[15] F. A. Hayek, *Individualism and Economic Order* (Chicago: University of Chicago Press, 1948). [Among the articles reprinted in this collection are "Individualism: True and False," "Economics and Knowledge," "The Use of Knowledge in Society," "The Meaning of Competition," and three essays on socialist calculation. —Ed.]

[16] F. A. Hayek, *The Counter-Revolution of Science*, op. cit. [The volume contains the essays "Scientism and the Study of Society," "The Counter-Revolution of Science," and "Comte and Hegel." —Ed.]

[17] An advance sketch of my treatment of this subject has been published by the National Bank of Egypt in the form of four lectures on *The Political Ideal of the Rule of Law* (Cairo: The National Bank of Egypt, 1955). [The substance of these lectures was incorporated into chapters 11 and 13–16 of *The Constitution of Liberty*, op. cit. —Ed.]

issues which my critics in America dismissed as bogeys became in Great Britain main topics of political discussion. Soon even official documents were gravely discussing the danger of totalitarianism raised by the policy of economic planning. There is no better illustration of the manner in which the inherent logic of their policies drove an unwilling socialist government into the kind of coercion it disliked than the following passage in the *Economic Survey for 1947* (which the Prime Minister presented to Parliament in February of that year) and its sequel:

> There is an essential difference between totalitarian and democratic planning. The former subordinates all individual desires and preferences to the demand of the State. For this purpose, it uses various methods of compulsion upon the individual which deprive him of his freedom of choice. Such methods may be necessary even in a democratic country during the extreme emergency of a great war. Thus the British people gave their war time Government the power to direct labour. But in normal times the people of a democratic country will not give up their freedom of choice to their Government. A democratic Government must therefore conduct its economic planning in a manner which preserves the maximum possible freedom of choice to the individual citizen.[18]

The interesting point about this profession of laudable intentions is that six months later the same government found itself in peacetime forced to put the conscription of labor back on the statute book.[19] It hardly diminishes the significance of this when it is pointed out that the power was in fact never used because, if it is known that the authorities have power to coerce, few will wait for actual coercion. But it is rather difficult to see how the government could have persisted in its illusions when in the same document it claims that it was now for "the Government to say what is the best use for the resources in the national interest" and to "lay down the economic task for the nation: it must say which things are the most important and what the objectives of policy ought to be."[20]

---

[18][*Economic Survey for 1947*, Cmd. 7046 (London: HMSO, 1947), p. 5. —Ed.]

[19][Hayek refers to the Control of Engagement Order of 1947, issued by the Minister of Labour and, as delegated legislation, not subject to amendment by Parliament. Ivor Thomas, in *The Socialist Tragedy* (London: Latimer House Ltd., 1949), pp. 104–5, offered this succinct description: "Under this Order men between the ages of 18 and 50 and women between the ages of 18 and 40 may not be engaged except through an employment exchange of the Ministry of Labour, apart from certain exempted occupations. Workers in coal mining and agriculture are not permitted to leave those occupations. Other applicants at an employment exchange are offered jobs that in the Government's view have the highest priority. If an applicant refuses to accept a job he can in the last resort be directed, and failure to obey the direction can be punished by fine or imprisonment." —Ed.]

[20][*Economic Survey for 1947*, op. cit., p. 9. —Ed.]

Of course, six years of socialist government in England have not produced anything resembling a totalitarian state. But those who argue that this has disproved the thesis of *The Road to Serfdom* have really missed one of its main points: that the most important change which extensive government control produces is a psychological change, an alteration in the character of the people. This is necessarily a slow affair, a process which extends not over a few years but perhaps over one or two generations. The important point is that the political ideals of a people and its attitude toward authority are as much the effect as the cause of the political institutions under which it lives. This means, among other things, that even a strong tradition of political liberty is no safeguard if the danger is precisely that new institutions and policies will gradually undermine and destroy that spirit. The consequences can of course be averted if that spirit reasserts itself in time and the people not only throw out the party which has been leading them further and further in the dangerous direction but also recognize the nature of the danger and resolutely change their course. There is not yet much ground to believe that the latter has happened in England.

Yet the change undergone by the character of the British people, not merely under its Labour government but in the course of the much longer period during which it has been enjoying the blessings of a paternalistic welfare state, can hardly be mistaken. These changes are not easily demonstrated but are clearly felt if one lives in the country. In illustration, I will cite a few significant passages from a sociological survey dealing with the impact of the surfeit of regulation on the mental attitudes of the young. It is concerned with the situation before the Labour government came into power, in fact, about the time this book was first published, and deals mainly with the effects of those wartime regulations which the Labour government made permanent:

> It is above all in the city that the province of the optional is felt as dwindling away to nothing. At school, in the place of work, on the journey to and fro, even in the very equipment and provisioning of the home, many of the activities normally possible to human beings are either forbidden or enjoined. Special agencies, called Citizen's Advice Bureaus, are set up to steer the bewildered through the forest of rules, and to indicate to the persistent the rare clearings where a private person may still make a choice. . . . [The town lad] is conditioned not to lift a finger without referring mentally to the book of words first. A time-budget of an ordinary city youth for an ordinary working day would show that he spends great stretches of his waking hours going through motions that have been predetermined for him by directives in whose framing he has had no part, whose precise intention he seldom understands, and of whose appropriateness he cannot judge. . . . The inference that what the city lad needs is more discipline and tighter control is too hasty. It would be nearer the mark to say that he is suffering from an overdose of control already. . . . Surveying his parents and his older brothers or sisters he finds them

as regulation bound as himself. He sees them so acclimatised to that state that they seldom plan and carry out under their own steam any new social excursion or enterprise. He thus looks forward to no future period at which a sinewy faculty of responsibility is likely to be of service to himself or others. . . . [The young people] are obliged to stomach so much external and, as it seems to them, meaningless control that they seek escape and recuperation in an absence of discipline as complete as they can make it.[21]

Is it too pessimistic to fear that a generation grown up under these conditions is unlikely to throw off the fetters to which it has grown used? Or does this description not rather fully bear out Tocqueville's prediction of the "new kind of servitude" when

after having thus successively taken each member of the community in its powerful grasp, and fashioned him at will, the supreme power then extends its arm over the whole community. It covers the surface of society with a network of small complicated rules, minute and uniform, through which the most original minds and the most energetic characters cannot penetrate to rise above the crowd. The will of man is not shattered but softened, bent and guided; men are seldom forced by it to act, but they are constantly restrained from acting. Such a power does not destroy, but it prevents existence; it does not tyrannize, but it compresses, enervates, extinguishes, and stupefies a people, till each nation is reduced to be nothing better than a flock of timid and industrial animals, of which government is the shepherd.—I have always thought that servitude of the regular, quiet, and gentle kind which I have just described might be combined more easily than is commonly believed with some of the outward forms of freedom and that it might even establish itself under the wing of the sovereignty of the people.[22]

What Tocqueville did not consider was how long such a government would remain in the hands of benevolent despots when it would be so much more easy

[21]L. J. Barnes, *Youth Service in an English County: A Report Prepared for King George's Jubilee Trust* (London, 1945), pp. 18–21. [The first quoted passage appears on pages 18 and 20 of the report; page 19 contains a chart. The second through fourth appear on page 20, and the last on page 21. —Ed.]

[22]Alexis de Tocqueville, *Democracy in America*, the Henry Reeve text as revised by Francis Bowen, now further corrected and edited with introduction, editorial notes, and bibliographies by Philips Bradley (New York: Alfred A. Knopf, 1945), Vol. 2, Book 4, chapter 6, p. 319. The whole chapter should be read in order to realize with what acute insight Tocqueville was able to foresee the psychological effects of the modern welfare state. It was, incidentally, Tocqueville's frequent reference to the "new servitude" which suggested the title of the present book. [In his penetrating account of democracy in America, French historian Alexis de Tocqueville (1805–1859) observed that the search for greater equality typically is accompanied by greater centralization of government and a corresponding reduction in liberty. The chapter cited is titled, "What Sort of Despotism Democratic Nations Have to Fear." —Ed.]

for any group of ruffians to keep itself indefinitely in power by disregarding all the traditional decencies of political life.

Perhaps I should also remind the reader that I have never accused the socialist parties of deliberately aiming at a totalitarian regime or even suspected that the leaders of the old socialist movements might ever show such inclinations. What I have argued in this book, and what the British experience convinces me even more to be true, is that the unforeseen but inevitable consequences of socialist planning create a state of affairs in which, if the policy is to be pursued, totalitarian forces will get the upper hand. I explicitly stress that "socialism can be put into practice only by methods of which most socialists disapprove" and even add that in this "the old socialist parties were inhibited by their democratic ideals" and that "they did not possess the ruthlessness required for the performance of their chosen task."[23] I am afraid the impression one gained under the Labour government was that these inhibitions were if anything weaker among the British socialists than they had been among their German fellow-socialists twenty-five years earlier. Certainly the German Social Democrats, in the comparable period of the 1920s, under equally or more difficult economic conditions, never approached as closely to totalitarian planning as the British Labour government has done.

Since I cannot here examine the effect of these policies in detail, I will rather quote the summary judgments of other observers who may be less suspect of preconceived opinions. Some of the most damning, in fact, come from men who not long before had themselves been members of the Labour party. Thus Mr. Ivor Thomas, in a book apparently intended to explain why he left that party, comes to the conclusion that "from the point of view of fundamental human liberties there is little to choose between communism, socialism, and national socialism. They all are examples of the collectivist or totalitarian state . . . in its essentials not only is completed socialism the same as communism but it hardly differs from fascism."[24]

The most serious development is the growth of a measure of arbitrary administrative coercion and the progressive destruction of the cherished foundation of British liberty, the Rule of Law, for exactly the reasons here discussed in chapter 6. This process had of course started long before the last Labour government came into power and had been accentuated by the war. But the attempts at economic planning under the Labour government carried it to a point which makes it doubtful whether it can be said that the Rule of Law still

---

[23][Hayek quotes from *The Road to Serfdom*, chapter 10, p. 159. —Ed.]

[24]Ivor Thomas, *The Socialist Tragedy*, op. cit., pp. 241, 242. [Classical scholar, author, journalist, and Labour MP Ivor Thomas (1905–1993) wrote for *The Times* and *The News Chronicle*, and later was an editor at *The Daily Telegraph*. He resigned from the Labour party in 1948 and subsequently joined the Conservative party. Thomas assumed the surname Bulmer-Thomas in 1952. —Ed.]

prevails in Britain. The "New Despotism" of which a Lord Chief Justice had warned Britain as long as twenty-five years ago is, as *The Economist* recently observed, no longer a mere danger but an established fact.[25] It is a despotism exercised by a thoroughly conscientious and honest bureaucracy for what they sincerely believe is the good of the country. But it is nevertheless an arbitrary government, in practice free from effective parliamentary control; and its machinery would be as effective for any other than the beneficent purposes for which it is now used. I doubt whether it was much exaggerated when recently an eminent British jurist, in a careful analysis of these trends, came to the conclusions that "in Britain to-day, we live on the edge of dictatorship. Transition would be easy, swift, and it could be accomplished with complete legality. Already so many steps have been taken in this direction, due to the completeness of power possessed by the Government of the day, and the absence of any real check such as the terms of a written constitution or the existence of an effective second chamber, that those still to be taken are small in comparison."[26]

For a more detailed analysis of the economic policies of the British Labour government and its consequences I cannot do better than refer the reader to Professor John Jewkes's *Ordeal by Planning* (London: Macmillan & Co., 1948). It is the best discussion known to me of a concrete instance of the phenomena discussed in general terms in this book. It supplements it better than anything I could add here and spells out a lesson which is of significance far beyond Great Britain.

It seems now unlikely that, even when another Labour government should come into power in Great Britain, it would resume the experiments in large-

---

[25] In an article in the issue of June 19, 1954, discussing the *Report on the Public Inquiry Ordered by the Minister of Agriculture into the Disposal of Land at Crichel Down* (Cmd. 9176; London: H. M. Stationery Office, 1954), a document deserving the most careful study by all those interested in the psychology of a planning bureaucracy. [The *Economist* article Hayek refers to is, "What Is the Public Interest?" vol. 171, June 19, 1954, pp. 951–52. The article notes how, in 1937, the Air Ministry bought against the opposition of its owners a tract of land for a bombing range. The land, part of three farms, was located in Crichel Down, Dorset. After the war the land was transferred to other government ministries and ultimately upgraded and sold to a new buyer. During the whole period the original owners tried unsuccessfully to buy or rent their land back. The episode was taken by *The Economist* as providing "evidence to confirm a suspicion that has been growing on the general public for some time past—that the bureaucracy in Britain has grown arrogantly careless of the rights of the subject" (p. 951). The Lord Chief Justice Hayek refers to in the text is Gordon Hewart, First Baron of Bury (1870–1943), who held the position from 1922–1940. In his book *The New Despotism* (London: Ernest Benn, Ltd., 1929; reprinted, Westport, CT: Greenwood Press, 1975), Hewart criticized Acts of Parliament whose provisions give broad discretion to the ministers and departments that are responsible for carrying them out, discretion that enables them to interpret the Acts as they see fit, without review or meaningful appeal, and even to amend the Acts themselves. Hewart believed that this had "the effect of placing a large and increasing field of departmental authority beyond the reach of the ordinary law" (p. 11). —Ed.]

[26] G. W. Keeton, *The Passing of Parliament* (London: Ernest Benn Ltd., 1952), p. 33.

scale nationalization and planning. But in Britain, as elsewhere in the world, the defeat of the onslaught of systematic socialism has merely given those who are anxious to preserve freedom a breathing space in which to re-examine our ambitions and to discard all those parts of the socialist inheritance which are a danger to a free society. Without such a revised conception of our social aims, we are likely to continue to drift in the same direction in which outright socialism would merely have carried us a little faster.

F. A. Hayek

PREFACE TO THE 1976 EDITION

This book, written in my spare time from 1940 to 1943, while my mind was still mainly occupied with problems of pure economic theory, has unexpectedly become for me the starting point of more than thirty years' work in a new field. This first attempt in the new direction was caused by my annoyance with the complete misinterpretation in English "progressive" circles of the character of the Nazi movement, an annoyance which led me from a memorandum to the then director of the London School of Economics, Sir William Beveridge, through an article in the *Contemporary Review* for 1938, which at the request of Professor Harry G. Gideonse of the University of Chicago I enlarged for publication in his Public Policy Pamphlets,[1] and which, finally and reluctantly, when I found that all my more competent British colleagues were preoccupied with more urgent problems of the conduct of the war, I expanded into this tract for the times. In spite of the wholly unexpected success of the book—in the case of the initially not-contemplated American edition even greater than in that of the British one—I felt for a long time not altogether happy about it. Though I had frankly declared at the outset of the book that it was a political one, I was made to feel by most of my fellow social scientists that I had used my abilities on the wrong side, and I was myself uncomfortable about the possibility that in going beyond technical economics I might have exceeded my competence. I will not speak here about the fury which the book caused in certain circles, or of the curious difference between its reception in Great Britain and that in the United States—about that I did say something twenty years ago in the Preface to the first American paperback edition. Just to indicate the character of a widespread reaction, I will mention merely that one well-known philosopher, who shall be nameless, wrote to another to reproach him for having lauded this scandalous book, which "of course [he] had not read"![2]

But though I tried hard to get back to economics proper, I could not free myself of the feeling that the problems on which I had so undesignedly embarked were more challenging and important than those of economic theory, and that

---

[1] [See the preface to the original editions, note 2. —Ed.]

[2] [The nameless philosopher was the positivist Rudolf Carnap; for the full quotation, see my introduction to this volume, p. 2. —Ed.]

much that I had said in my first sketch needed clarification and elaboration. When I wrote the book, I had by no means sufficiently freed myself from all the prejudices and superstitions dominating general opinion, and even less had I learned to avoid all the prevalent confusions of terms and concepts of which I have since become very conscious. And the discussion of the consequences of socialist policies which the book attempts is of course not complete without an adequate account of what an appropriately run market order requires and can achieve. It was to the latter problem that the further work I have since done in the field was mainly devoted. The first result of these efforts of explaining the nature of an order of freedom was a substantial book called *The Constitution of Liberty* (1960) in which I essentially attempted to restate and make more coherent the doctrines of classical nineteenth-century liberalism. The awareness that such a restatement left certain important questions unanswered led me then to a further effort to provide my own answers in a work of three volumes entitled *Law, Legislation, and Liberty*, of which the first volume appeared in 1973.[3]

In the last twenty years, I have, I believe, learned much about the problems discussed in this book, though I don't think I ever reread the book during this time. Having done so now for the purpose of this Preface, I feel no longer apologetic, but for the first time am rather proud of it—and not least of the insight which made me dedicate it "To the Socialists of All Parties." Indeed, though I have in the interval learned much that I did not know when I wrote it, I was now often surprised by how much I did already see at the beginning of my efforts that later work has confirmed; and though my later efforts will, I hope, be more rewarding to the expert, I am now prepared unhesitatingly to recommend this early book to the general reader who wants a simple and nontechnical introduction to what I believe is still one of the most ominous questions which we have to solve.

The reader will probably ask whether this means that I am still prepared to defend all the main conclusions of this book, and the answer to this is on the whole affirmative. The most important qualification I must add is that during the interval of time terminology has changed and for this reason what I say in the book may be misunderstood. At the time I wrote, socialism meant unambiguously the nationalization of the means of production and the central economic planning which this made possible and necessary. In this sense Sweden, for instance, is today very much less socialistically organized than Great Britain or Austria, though Sweden is commonly regarded as much more socialistic. This is due to the fact that socialism has come to mean chiefly the extensive redistribution of incomes through taxation and the institutions of the welfare

---

[3][The second and third volumes appeared in 1976 and 1979 respectively. See F. A. Hayek, *The Mirage of Social Justice*, vol. 2 (1976), and *The Political Order of a Free People*, vol. 3 (1979) of *Law, Legislation, and Liberty*, op. cit. —Ed.]

state. In the latter kind of socialism the effects I discuss in this book are brought about more slowly, indirectly, and imperfectly. I believe that the ultimate outcome tends to be very much the same, although the process by which it is brought about is not quite the same as that described in this book.

It has frequently been alleged that I have contended that any movement in the direction of socialism is bound to lead to totalitarianism. Even though this danger exists, this is not what the book says. What it contains is a warning that unless we mend the principles of our policy, some very unpleasant consequences will follow which most of those who advocate these policies do not want.

Where I now feel I was wrong in this book is chiefly in that I rather understressed the significance of the experience of communism in Russia—a fault which is perhaps pardonable when it is remembered that when I wrote, Russia was our wartime ally—and that I had not wholly freed myself from all the current interventionist superstitions, and in consequence still made various concessions which I now think unwarranted. And I certainly was not yet fully aware how bad things already were in some respects. I still regarded it, for example, as a rhetorical question when I asked, If Hitler had obtained his unlimited powers in a strictly constitutional manner, "who would suggest that the Rule of Law still prevailed in Germany?" only to discover later that professors Hans Kelsen and Harold J. Laski, and probably many other socialist lawyers and political scientists following these influential authors, had maintained precisely this.[4] Quite generally, further study of the contemporary trends of thought and institutions has, if anything, increased my alarm and concern. And both the influence of socialist ideas and the naïve trust in the good intentions of the holders of totalitarian power have markedly increased since I wrote this book.

I have long resented being more widely known by what I regarded as a pamphlet for the time than by my strictly scientific work. After reexamining what I wrote then in the light of some thirty years' further study of the problems then raised, I no longer do so. Though the book may contain much that I could not, when I wrote it, have convincingly demonstrated, it was a genuine effort to find the truth which I believe has produced insights that will help even those who disagree with me to avoid grave dangers.

F. A. Hayek

[4][English political scientist Harold J. Laski (1893–1950) was a colleague of Hayek's at the LSE and, prior to the Molotov-Ribbentrop nonaggression pact, an avid defender of Stalin and his policies. Hayek remarks on Laski's "pathological" proclivity toward prevarication in *Hayek on Hayek*, op. cit., p. 82. Austrian-born legal theorist Hans Kelsen (1881–1973) taught at Vienna, Cologne, and ultimately at the University of California-Berkeley. Kelsen developed the "pure theory of law" and was known for his defense of legal positivism. —Ed.]

INTRODUCTION

> Few discoveries are more irritating than those which expose the pedigree of ideas. —Lord Acton[1]

Contemporary events differ from history in that we do not know the results they will produce. Looking back, we can assess the significance of past occurrences and trace the consequences they have brought in their train. But while history runs its course, it is not history to us. It leads us into an unknown land, and but rarely can we get a glimpse of what lies ahead. It would be different if it were given to us to live a second time through the same events with all the knowledge of what we have seen before. How different would things appear to us; how important and often alarming would changes seem that we now scarcely notice! It is probably fortunate that man can never have this experience and knows of no laws which history must obey.

Yet, although history never quite repeats itself, and just because no development is inevitable, we can in a measure learn from the past to avoid a repetition of the same process. One need not be a prophet to be aware of impending dangers. An accidental combination of experience and interest will often reveal events to one man under aspects which few yet see.

The following pages are the product of an experience as near as possible to twice living through the same period—or at least twice watching a very similar evolution of ideas. While this is an experience one is not likely to gain in one country, it may in certain circumstance be acquired by living in turn for long periods in different countries. Though the influences to which the trend of thought is subject in most civilized nations are to a large extent similar, they do not necessarily operate at the same time or at the same speed. Thus, by moving from one country to another, one may sometimes twice watch similar phases of intellectual development. The senses have then become peculiarly acute. When one hears for a second time opinions expressed or measures advocated which one has first met twenty or twenty-five years ago, they assume a

---

[1] [Lord Acton, "Review of Sir Erskine May's *Democracy in Europe*" [1878], reprinted in *The History of Freedom and Other Essays*, op. cit., p. 62. —Ed.]

new meaning as symptoms of a definite trend.[2] They suggest, if not the necessity, at least the probability, that developments will take a similar course.

It is necessary now to state the unpalatable truth that it is Germany whose fate we are in some danger of repeating. The danger is not immediate, it is true, and conditions in England and the United States are still so remote from those witnessed in recent years in Germany as to make it difficult to believe that we are moving in the same direction. Yet, though the road be long, it is one on which it becomes more difficult to turn back as one advances. If in the long run we are the makers of our own fate, in the short run we are the captives of the ideas we have created. Only if we recognize the danger in time can we hope to avert it.

It is not to the Germany of Hitler, the Germany of the present war, that England and the United States bear yet any resemblance. But students of the currents of ideas can hardly fail to see that there is more than a superficial similarity between the trend of thought in Germany during and after the last war and the present current of ideas in the democracies. There exists now in these countries certainly the same determination that the organization of the nation which has been achieved for purposes of defense shall be retained for the purposes of creation. There is the same contempt for nineteenth-century liberalism, the same spurious "realism" and even cynicism, the same fatalistic acceptance of "inevitable trends." And at least nine out of every ten of the lessons which our most vociferous reformers are so anxious we should learn from this war are precisely the lessons which the Germans did learn from the last war and which have done much to produce the Nazi system. We shall have opportunity in the course of this book to show that there are a large number of other points where at an interval of fifteen to twenty-five years we seem to follow the example of Germany. Although one does not like to be reminded, it is not so many years since the socialist policy of that country was generally held up by progressives as an example to be imitated, just as in more recent years Sweden has been the model country to which progressive eyes were directed. All those whose memory goes further back know how deeply for at least a generation before the last war German thought and German practice influenced ideals and policy in England and, to some extent, in the United States.

The author has spent about half of his adult life in his native Austria, in close touch with German intellectual life, and the other half in the United States and England. In the latter period he has become increasingly convinced that at least some of the forces which have destroyed freedom in Germany are also at work here and that the character and the source of this danger are, if possible, even less understood than they were in Germany. The supreme tragedy is

---

[2][Hayek alludes here to the trends he identified in his inaugural lecture at the LSE, "The Trend of Economic Thinking," op. cit. —Ed.]

still not seen that in Germany it was largely people of good will, men who were admired and held up as models in the democratic countries, who prepared the way for, if they did not actually create, the forces which now stand for everything they detest. Yet our chance of averting a similar fate depends on our facing the danger and on our being prepared to revise even our most cherished hopes and ambitions if they should prove to be the source of the danger. There are few signs yet that we have the intellectual courage to admit to ourselves that we may have been wrong. Few are ready to recognize that the rise of fascism and naziism was not a reaction against the socialist trends of the preceding period but a necessary outcome of those tendencies. This is a truth which most people were unwilling to see even when the similarities of many of the repellent features of the internal regimes in communist Russia and National Socialist Germany were widely recognized. As a result, many who think themselves infinitely superior to the aberrations of naziism, and sincerely hate all its manifestations, work at the same time for ideals whose realization would lead straight to the abhorred tyranny.

All parallels between developments in different countries are, of course, deceptive; but I am not basing my argument mainly on such parallels. Nor am I arguing that these developments are inevitable. If they were, there would be no point in writing this. They can be prevented if people realize in time where their efforts may lead. But until recently there was little hope that any attempt to make them see the danger would be successful. It seems, however, as if the time were now ripe for a fuller discussion of the whole issue. Not only is the problem now more widely recognized; there are also special reasons which at this juncture make it imperative that we should face the issues squarely.

It will, perhaps, be said that this is not the time to raise an issue on which opinions clash sharply. But the socialism of which we speak is not a party matter, and the questions which we are discussing have little to do with the questions at dispute between political parties. It does not affect our problem that some groups may want less socialism than others; that some want socialism mainly in the interest of one group and others in that of another. The important point is that, if we take the people whose views influence developments, they are now in the democracies in some measure all socialists. If it is no longer fashionable to emphasize that "we are all socialists now," this is so merely because the fact is too obvious.[3] Scarcely anybody doubts that we must continue to move toward socialism, and most people are merely trying to deflect this movement in the interest of a particular class or group.

It is because nearly everybody wants it that we are moving in this direction. There are no objective facts which make it inevitable. We shall have to say

---

[3][The nineteenth century Liberal statesman Sir William Vernon Harcourt (1827–1904) originated the phrase, "We are all socialists now." —Ed.]

something about the alleged inevitability of "planning" later. The main question is where this movement will lead us. Is it not possible that if the people whose convictions now give it an irresistible momentum began to see what only a few yet apprehend, they would recoil in horror and abandon the quest which for half a century has engaged so many people of good will? Where these common beliefs of our generation will lead us is a problem not for one party but for every one of us—a problem of the most momentous significance. Is there a greater tragedy imaginable than that, in our endeavor consciously to shape our future in accordance with high ideals, we should in fact unwittingly produce the very opposite of what we have been striving for?

There is an even more pressing reason why at this time we should seriously endeavor to understand the forces which have created National Socialism: that this will enable us to understand our enemy and the issue at stake between us. It cannot be denied that there is yet little recognition of the positive ideals for which we are fighting. We know that we are fighting for freedom to shape our life according to our own ideas. That is a great deal, but not enough. It is not enough to give us the firm beliefs which we need to resist an enemy who uses propaganda as one of his main weapons not only in the most blatant but also in the most subtle forms. It is still more insufficient when we have to counter this propaganda among the people in the countries under his control and elsewhere, where the effect of this propaganda will not disappear with the defeat of the Axis powers. It is not enough if we are to show to others that what we are fighting for is worth their support, and it is not enough to guide us in the building of a new world safe against the dangers to which the old one has succumbed.

It is a lamentable fact that the democracies in their dealings with the dictators before the war, not less than in their attempts at propaganda and in the discussion of their war aims, have shown an inner insecurity and uncertainty of aim which can be explained only by confusion about their own ideals and the nature of the differences which separated them from the enemy. We have been misled as much because we have refused to believe that the enemy was sincere in the profession of some beliefs which we shared as because we believed in the sincerity of some of his other claims. Have not the parties of the Left as well as those of the Right been deceived by believing that the National Socialist party was in the service of the capitalists and opposed to all forms of socialism? How many features of Hitler's system have not been recommended to us for imitation from the most unexpected quarters, unaware that they are an integral part of that system and incompatible with the free society we hope to preserve? The number of dangerous mistakes we have made before and since the outbreak of war because we do not understand the opponent with whom we are faced is appalling. It seems almost as if we did not want to understand the development which has produced totalitarianism because such an understanding might destroy some of the dearest illusions to which we are determined to cling.

We shall never be successful in our dealings with the Germans until we understand the character and the growth of the ideas which now govern them. The theory which is once again put forth, that the Germans as such are inherently vicious, is hardly tenable and not very creditable to those who hold it. It dishonors the long series of Anglo-Saxon thinkers who during the last hundred years have gladly taken over what was best, and not only what was best, in German thought. It overlooks the fact that, when eighty years ago John Stuart Mill was writing his great essay *On Liberty,* he drew his inspiration, more than from any other men, from two Germans—Goethe and Wilhelm von Humboldt—and forgets the fact that two of the most influential intellectual forebears of National Socialism—Thomas Carlyle and Houston Stewart Chamberlain—were a Scot and an Englishman.[1] In its cruder forms this view is a disgrace to those who by maintaining it adopt the worst features of German racial theories.

The problem is not why the Germans as such are vicious, which congenitally they are probably no more than other peoples, but to determine the circumstances which during the last seventy years have made possible the progressive growth and the ultimate victory of a particular set of ideas, and why in the end this victory has brought the most vicious elements among them to the top. Mere hatred of everything German instead of the particular ideas which now dominate the Germans is, moreover, very dangerous, because it blinds those who indulge in it against a real threat. It is to be feared that this attitude is frequently merely a kind of escapism, caused by an unwillingness to recognize tendencies which are not confined to Germany and by a reluctance to re-examine, and if necessary to discard, beliefs which we have taken over from the Germans and by which we are still as much deluded as the Germans were. It is doubly dangerous because the contention that only the peculiar wickedness of the Germans has produced the Nazi system is likely to become the excuse for forcing on us the very institutions which have produced that wickedness.

[1]As some people may think this statement exaggerated, the testimony of Lord Morley may be worth quoting, who in his *Recollections* speaks of the "acknowledged point" that the main argument of the essay *On Liberty* "was not original but came from Germany." [Hayek quotes from John, Viscount Morley, *Recollections*, vol. 1 (New York: Macmillan, 1917), pp. 61–62. John Morley, First Viscount Morley of Blackburn (1838–1923), was an English statesman and man of letters. He wrote numerous biographies, the most famous of them a four volume work on William Gladstone. German poet, playwright, and scientist Johann Wolfgang von Goethe (1749–1832) was the author of *Faust* and *The Sorrows of Young Werther.* Philologist and statesman Karl Wilhelm von Humboldt (1767–1835) was the first Prussian minister of education and founder of the University of Berlin. Essayist and man of letters Thomas Carlyle (1795–1881), who through various publications helped introduce German culture and literature to English readers, is best known among economists for dubbing the classicals "the dreary professors of a dismal science." English-born author and propagandist Houston Stewart Chamberlain (1855–1927) who lived in Germany from 1885 and who wrote principally on music and philosophy, was known for his support for the doctrine of Aryan supremacy. Hayek's note originally was placed after the name "Humboldt." —Ed.]

The interpretation of the developments in Germany and Italy about to be proffered in this book is very different from that given by most foreign observers and by the majority of exiles from those countries. But if this interpretation is correct, it will also explain why it is almost impossible for a person who, like most of the exiles and the foreign correspondents of English and American newspapers, holds the now prevalent socialist views to see those events in the proper perspective. The superficial and misleading view which sees in National Socialism merely a reaction fomented by those whose privileges or interests were threatened by the advance of socialism was naturally supported by all those who, although they were at one time active in the movement of ideas that has led to National Socialism, have stopped at some point of that development and, by the conflict into which this brought them with the Nazis, were forced to leave their country. But the fact that they were numerically the only significant opposition to the Nazis means no more than that in the wider sense practically all Germans had become socialists and that liberalism in the old sense had been driven out by socialism. As we hope to show, the conflict in existence between the National Socialist "Right" and the "Left" in Germany is the kind of conflict that will always arise between rival socialist factions. If this interpretation is correct, it means, however, that many of those socialist refugees, in clinging to their beliefs, are now, though with the best will in the world, helping to lead their adopted country the way which Germany has gone.

I know that many of my Anglo-Saxon friends have sometimes been shocked by the semi-Fascist views they would occasionally hear expressed by German refugees, whose genuinely socialist convictions could not be doubted. But while these observers put this down to the others' being Germans, the true explanation is that they were socialists whose experience had carried them several stages beyond that yet reached by socialists in England and America. It is true, of course, that German socialists have found much support in their country from certain features of the Prussian tradition; and this kinship between Prussianism and socialism, in which in Germany both sides gloried, gives additional support to our main contention.[5] But it would be a mistake to believe that the

[5] That there did exist a certain kinship between socialism and the organization of the Prussian state, consciously organized from the top as in no other country, is undeniable and was freely recognized already by the early French socialists. Long before the ideal of running the whole state on the same principles as a single factory was to inspire nineteenth-century socialism, the Prussian poet Novalis had already deplored that "no other state has ever been administered so much like a factory as Prussia since the death of Frederick William," in Novalis, *Glauben und Liebe, oder der König and die Königin* [1798] [The cited passage may be found in Novalis, *Schriften*, vol. 2 (Stuttgart: Verlag W. Kohlhammer, 1981, p. 494), and reads "Kein Staat ist mehr als Fabrik verwaltet worden, als Preußen, seit Friedrich Wilhelm des Ersten Tode." Novalis was the pen name of the Prussian poet and novelist Friedrich von Hardenberg (1772–1801), known as the "Prophet of Ro-

specific German rather than the socialist element produced totalitarianism. It was the prevalence of socialist views and not Prussianism that Germany had in common with Italy and Russia—and it was from the masses and not from the classes steeped in the Prussian tradition, and favored by it, that National Socialism arose.

---

manticism." The work from which Hayek quotes may be translated as *Faith and Love, or the King and the Queen*. Novalis anticipated there a future in which universal human spirituality would eliminate the need for government. —Ed.]

ONE

THE ABANDONED ROAD

A program whose basic thesis is, not that the system of free enterprise for profit
has failed in this generation, but that it has not yet been tried.

—F. D. Roosevelt[1]

When the course of civilization takes an unexpected turn—when, instead of
the continuous progress which we have come to expect, we find ourselves
threatened by evils associated by us with past ages of barbarism—we naturally
blame anything but ourselves. Have we not all striven according to our best
lights, and have not many of our finest minds incessantly worked to make this a
better world? Have not all our efforts and hopes been directed toward greater
freedom, justice, and prosperity? If the outcome is so different from our aims—
if, instead of freedom and prosperity, bondage and misery stare us in the
face—is it not clear that sinister forces must have foiled our intentions, that we
are the victims of some evil power which must be conquered before we can resume the road to better things? However much we may differ when we name
the culprit—whether it is the wicked capitalist or the vicious spirit of a particular nation, the stupidity of our elders, or a social system not yet, although we
have struggled against it for half a century, fully overthrown—we all are, or at
last were until recently, certain of one thing: that the leading ideas which during the last generation have become common to most people of good will and
have determined the major changes in our social life cannot have been wrong.
We are ready to accept almost any explanation of the present crisis of our civilization except one: that the present state of the world may be the result of gen-

---

[1] [Franklin D. Roosevelt, "Recommendations to the Congress to Curb Monopolies and the
Concentration of Economic Power," *The Continuing Struggle for Liberalism*, vol. 7 of *The Public Papers
and Addresses of Franklin D. Roosevelt* (New York: Macmillan, 1941), p. 320. The address was delivered on April 29, 1938. Roosevelt lamented in the speech the concentration of power, or "collectivism," in corporate America, and called for a reintroduction of a "democratic competitive
order" through additional federal regulation of business. Hayek was more hopeful at this time
for the future path of the United States relative to Britain regarding free enterprise. For more on
this, see his remarks in "Planning, Science, and Freedom," *Nature*, vol. 143, November 15, 1941,
pp. 581–82, reprinted as chapter 10 of F. A. Hayek, *Socialism and War: Essays, Documents, Reviews*,
op. cit., p. 219. —Ed.]

uine error on our own part and that the pursuit of some of our most cherished ideals has apparently produced results utterly different from those which we expected.

While all our energies are directed to bring this war to a victorious conclusion, it is sometimes difficult to remember that even before the war the values for which we are now fighting were threatened here and destroyed elsewhere. Though for the time being the different ideals are represented by hostile nations fighting for their existence, we must not forget that this conflict has grown out of a struggle of ideas within what, not so long ago, was a common European civilization and that the tendencies which have culminated in the creation of the totalitarian systems were not confined to the countries which have succumbed to them. Though the first task must now be to win the war, to win it will only gain us another opportunity to face the basic problems and to find a way of averting the fate which has overtaken kindred civilizations.

Now, it is somewhat difficult to think of Germany and Italy, or of Russia, not as different worlds but as products of a development of thought in which we have shared; it is, at least so far as our enemies are concerned, easier and more comforting to think that they are entirely different from us and that what happened there cannot happen here. Yet the history of these countries in the years before the rise of the totalitarian system showed few features with which we are not familiar. The external conflict is a result of a transformation of European thought in which others have moved so much faster as to bring them into irreconcilable conflict with our ideals, but which has not left us unaffected.

That a change of ideas and the force of human will have made the world what it is now, though men did not foresee the results, and that no spontaneous change in the facts obliged us thus to adapt our thought is perhaps particularly difficult for the Anglo-Saxon nations to see, just because in this development they have, fortunately for them, lagged behind most of the European peoples. We still think of the ideals which guide us, and have guided us for the past generation, as ideals only to be realized in the future and are not aware how far in the last twenty-five years they have already transformed not only the world but also our own countries. We still believe that until quite recently we were governed by what are vaguely called nineteenth-century ideas or the principle of laissez faire. Compared with some other countries, and from the point of view of those impatient to speed up the change, there may be some justification for such belief. But although until 1931 England and America had followed only slowly on the path on which others had led, even by then they had moved so far that only those whose memory goes back to the years before the last war know what a liberal world has been like.[2]

---

[2] Even in that year the Macmillan Report could already speak of "the change of outlook of the government of this country in recent times, its growing preoccupation, irrespective of party, with the management of the life of the people" and add that "Parliament finds itself increasingly en-

The crucial point of which our people are still so little aware is, however, not merely the magnitude of the changes which have taken place during the last generation but the fact that they mean a complete change in the direction of the evolution of our ideas and social order. For at least twenty-five years before the specter of totalitarianism became a real threat, we had progressively been moving away from the basic ideas on which Western civilization has been built. That this movement on which we have entered with such high hopes and ambitions should have brought us face to face with the totalitarian horror has come as a profound shock to this generation, which still refuses to connect the two facts. Yet this development merely confirms the warnings of the fathers of the liberal philosophy which we still profess. We have progressively abandoned that freedom in economic affairs without which personal and political freedom has never existed in the past. Although we had been warned by some of the greatest political thinkers of the nineteenth century, by Tocqueville and Lord Acton, that socialism means slavery, we have steadily moved in the direction of socialism.[3] And now that we have seen a new form of slavery arise before our eyes, we have so completely forgotten the warning that it scarcely occurs to us that the two things may be connected.[4]

How sharp a break not only with the recent past but with the whole evolution of Western civilization the modern trend toward socialism means becomes clear if we consider it not merely against the background of the nineteenth century but in a longer historical perspective. We are rapidly abandoning not the views merely of Cobden and Bright, of Adam Smith and Hume, or even of Locke and Milton,[5] but one of the salient characteristics of Western civilization

---

gaged in legislation which has for its conscious aim the regulation of the day-to-day affairs of the community and now intervenes in matters formerly thought to be entirely outside its scope." This could be said before, later in the same year, England finally took the headlong plunge and, in the short space of the inglorious years 1931–39, transformed its economic system beyond recognition. [Hayek refers to the *Committee on Finance and Industry Report*, Cmd. 3897 (London: HMSO, 1931). The two passages Hayek quotes from are found on pages 4 and 4–5, respectively. The Committee, chaired by the British jurist Hugo Pattison Macmillan (1873–1952), was charged with discovering the causes behind and formulating remedies for England's depressed economy; it also served as a venue in which J. M. Keynes challenged the "Treasury View." —Ed.]

[3] [For more on Acton and Tocqueville, see the foreword to the 1956 American paperback edition, notes 10 and 22, respectively. —Ed.]

[4] Even much more recent warnings which have proved dreadfully true have been almost entirely forgotten. It is not yet thirty years since Hilaire Belloc, in a book which explains more of what has happened since in Germany than most works written after the event, explained that "the effect of Socialist doctrine on Capitalist society is to produce a third thing different from either of its two begetters—to wit, the Servile State." [French-born British writer and poet Hilaire Belloc (1870–1953), friend to G. K. Chesterton and writer of children's verse, was also the author of *The Servile State* (1912; 2nd ed., London and Edinburgh: T. N. Foulis, 1913; reprinted, Indianapolis: Liberty Classics, 1977), from which the quote is drawn (p. 32). —Ed.]

[5] [English politicians Richard Cobden (1804–1865) and John Bright (1811–1889), both prominent members of the Anti-Corn Law League, were persistent advocates for free trade in

as it has grown from the foundations laid by Christianity and the Greeks and Romans. Not merely nineteenth- and eighteenth-century liberalism, but the basic individualism inherited by us from Erasmus and Montaigne, from Cicero and Tacitus, Pericles and Thucydides, is progressively relinquished.[6]

The Nazi leader who described the National Socialist revolution as a counter-Renaissance spoke more truly than he probably knew. It was the decisive step in the destruction of that civilization which modern man had built up from the age of the Renaissance and which was, above all, an individualist civilization. Individualism has a bad name today, and the term has come to be connected with egotism and selfishness.[7] But the individualism of which we speak in contrast to socialism and all other forms of collectivism has no necessary connection with these. Only gradually in the course of this book shall we be able to make clear the contrast between the two opposing principles. But the essential features of that individualism which, from elements provided by Christianity and the philosophy of classical antiquity, was first fully developed during the Renaissance and has since grown and spread into what we know as Western civilization—are the respect for the individual man *qua* man, that is, the recognition of his own views and tastes as supreme in his own sphere, however narrowly that may be circumscribed, and the belief that it is desirable that men should develop their own individual gifts and bents. "Freedom" and "liberty" are now words so worn with use and abuse that one must hesitate to employ them to express the ideals for which they stood during that period. "Tolerance" is, perhaps, the only word which still preserves the full meaning of the principle

---

nineteenth-century England. Scottish political economist Adam Smith (1723–1790) extolled the system of natural liberty and decried mercantilist restrictions on trade in his classic work, *An Inquiry into the Nature and Causes of the Wealth of Nations.* Scottish philosopher and historian (and close friend of Adam Smith) David Hume (1711–1776) was the author of *A Treatise of Human Nature,* a central work in the empiricist tradition in British philosophy, and of the multivolume *History of England.* English philosopher John Locke (1632–1704), another member of the British empiricist tradition, enunciated the theory of the social contract in his *Two Treatises of Government.* English poet John Milton (1608–1674), author of *Paradise Lost* and *Paradise Regained,* also wrote pamphlets in support of the Commonwealth and of freedom of the press. —Ed.]

[6][Renaissance humanist and cosmopolitan scholar Desiderius Erasmus (1466–1536), "Erasmus of Rotterdam," was the author of *In Praise of Folly.* French writer Michel Eyquem de Montaigne (1533–1592) introduced the essay as a literary form. In his essays he embraced a skeptical attitude toward what could be known and criticized those who held views dogmatically. Roman statesman and man of letters Marcus Tullius Cicero (106–43 BC) was famed for his oratorical skills; his *Philippics* against Mark Antony ultimately cost him his life. In his *Annals* and *Histories,* Roman historian Publius Tacitus (ca. 55–ca. 120) chronicled the Roman Empire in the first century. Under the reign of Athenian statesman Pericles (490–429 BC), architecture, sculpture, and theater in Athens flourished. Greek historian Thucydides (ca. 460–ca. 400 BC) was the author of *History of the Peloponnesian War.* —Ed.]

[7][Hayek criticized the view that individualism is necessarily associated with egoism and selfishness in his article, "Individualism: True and False," op. cit. —Ed.]

which during the whole of this period was in the ascendant and which only in recent times has again been in decline, to disappear completely with the rise of the totalitarian state.

The gradual transformation of a rigidly organized hierarchic system into one where men could at least attempt to shape their own life, where man gained the opportunity of knowing and choosing between different forms of life, is closely associated with the growth of commerce. From the commercial cities of northern Italy the new view of life spread with commerce to the west and north, through France and the southwest of Germany to the Low Countries and the British Isles, taking firm root wherever there was no despotic political power to stifle it. In the Low Countries and Britain it for a long time enjoyed its fullest development and for the first time had an opportunity to grow freely and to become the foundation of the social and political life of these countries. And it was from there that in the late seventeenth and eighteenth centuries it again began to spread in a more fully developed form to the West and East, to the New World and to the center of the European continent, where devastating wars and political oppression had largely submerged the earlier beginnings of a similar growth.[8]

During the whole of this modern period of European history the general direction of social development was one of freeing the individual from the ties which had bound him to the customary or prescribed ways in the pursuit of his ordinary activities. The conscious realization that the spontaneous and uncontrolled efforts of individuals were capable of producing a complex order of economic activities could come only after this development had made some progress. The subsequent elaboration of a consistent argument in favor of economic freedom was the outcome of a free growth of economic activity which had been the undesigned and unforeseen by-product of political freedom.

Perhaps the greatest result of the unchaining of individual energies was the marvelous growth of science which followed the march of individual liberty from Italy to England and beyond. That the inventive faculty of man had been no less in earlier periods is shown by the many highly ingenious automatic toys and other mechanical contrivances constructed while industrial technique still remained stationary and by the development in some industries which, like mining or watch-making, were not subject to restrictive controls. But the few attempts toward a more extended industrial use of mechanical inventions,

---

[8]The most fateful of these developments, pregnant with consequences not yet extinct, was the subjection and partial destruction of the German bourgeoisie by the territorial princes in the fifteenth and sixteenth centuries. [Hayek's readers would have seen analogies between his historical references and the destruction of the influence of the bourgeoisie in Germany after World War I, when hyperinflation wiped out the savings of middle-class German bondholders and helped pave the way for Hitler's rise. The extermination of the kulaks as Stalin consolidated his power was another analogue. —Ed.]

some extraordinarily advanced, were promptly suppressed, and the desire for knowledge was stifled, so long as the dominant views were held to be binding for all: the beliefs of the great majority on what was right and proper were allowed to bar the way of the individual innovator. Only since industrial freedom opened the path to the free use of new knowledge, only since everything could be tried—if somebody could be found to back it at his own risk—and, it should be added, as often as not from outside the authorities officially entrusted with the cultivation of learning, has science made the great strides which in the last hundred and fifty years have changed the face of the world.

As is so often true, the nature of our civilization has been seen more clearly by its enemies than by most of its friends: "the perennial Western malady, the revolt of the individual against the species," as that nineteenth-century totalitarian, Auguste Comte, has described it, was indeed the force which built our civilization.[9] What the nineteenth century added to the individualism of the preceding period was merely to make all classes conscious of freedom, to develop systematically and continuously what had grown in a haphazard and patchy manner, and to spread it from England and Holland over most of the European continent.

The result of this growth surpassed all expectations. Wherever the barriers to the free exercise of human ingenuity were removed, man became rapidly able to satisfy ever widening ranges of desire. And while the rising standard soon led to the discovery of very dark spots in society, spots which men were no longer willing to tolerate, there was probably no class that did not substantially benefit from the general advance. We cannot do justice to this astonishing growth if we measure it by our present standards, which themselves result from this growth and now make many defects obvious. To appreciate what it meant to those who took part in it, we must measure it by the hopes and wishes men held when it began: and there can be no doubt that its success surpassed man's wildest dreams, that by the beginning of the twentieth century the workingman in the Western world had reached a degree of material comfort, security, and personal independence which a hundred years before had seemed scarcely possible.

What in the future will probably appear the most significant and far-reaching effect of this success is the new sense of power over their own fate, the belief in the unbounded possibilities of improving their own lot, which the success al-

---

[9][Auguste Comte, *Système de Politique Positive* (1851–1854), vol. 4 (Paris: Librairie Positiviste, 1912), pp. 368–69. French philosopher and social theorist Auguste Comte (1798–1857) claimed that there are three stages of knowledge—the theological, metaphysical, and positive—with positive being the highest. Positive knowledge had been obtained in many natural sciences, and Comte argued that positivism should be introduced in the study of society. Hayek explicated and criticized Comte's views in his essays "The Counter-Revolution of Science" and "Comte and Hegel," op. cit. —Ed.]

ready achieved created among men. With the success grew ambition—and man had every right to be ambitious. What had been an inspiring promise seemed no longer enough, the rate of progress far too slow; and the principles which had made this progress possible in the past came to be regarded more as obstacles to speedier progress, impatiently to be brushed away, than as the conditions for the preservation and development of what had already been achieved.

There is nothing in the basic principles of liberalism to make it a stationary creed; there are no hard-and-fast rules fixed once and for all. The fundamental principle that in the ordering of our affairs we should make as much use as possible of the spontaneous forces of society, and resort as little as possible to coercion, is capable of an infinite variety of applications. There is, in particular, all the difference between deliberately creating a system within which competition will work as beneficially as possible and passively accepting institutions as they are. Probably nothing has done so much harm to the liberal cause as the wooden insistence of some liberals on certain rough rules of thumb, above all the principle of laissez faire. Yet, in a sense, this was necessary and unavoidable. Against the innumerable interests which could show that particular measures would confer immediate and obvious benefits on some, while the harm they caused was much more indirect and difficult to see, nothing short of some hard-and-fast rule would have been effective. And since a strong presumption in favor of industrial liberty had undoubtedly been established, the temptation to present it as a rule which knew no exceptions was too strong always to be resisted.

But, with this attitude taken by many popularizers of the liberal doctrine, it was almost inevitable that, once their position was penetrated at some points, it should soon collapse as a whole. The position was further weakened by the inevitably slow progress of a policy which aimed at a gradual improvement of the institutional framework of a free society. This progress depended on the growth of our understanding of the social forces and the conditions most favorable to their working in a desirable manner. Since the task was to assist, and where necessary to supplement, their operation, the first requisite was to understand them. The attitude of the liberal toward society is like that of the gardener who tends a plant and, in order to create the conditions most favorable to its growth, must know as much as possible about its structure and the way it functions.

No sensible person should have doubted that the crude rules in which the principles of economic policy of the nineteenth century were expressed were only a beginning—that we had yet much to learn and that there were still immense possibilities of advancement on the lines on which we had moved. But this advance could come only as we gained increasing intellectual mastery of the forces of which we had to make use. There were many obvious tasks, such as our handling of the monetary system and the prevention or control of monopoly, and an even greater number of less obvious but hardly less important tasks to be undertaken in other fields, where there could be no doubt that the governments possessed enormous powers for good and evil; and there was every reason to expect that, with a better understanding of the problems, we should some day be able to use these powers successfully.

But while the progress toward what is commonly called "positive" action was necessarily slow, and while for the immediate improvement liberalism had to rely largely on the gradual increase of wealth which freedom brought about, it had constantly to fight proposals which threatened this progress. It came to be regarded as a "negative" creed because it could offer to particular individuals little more than a share in the common progress—a progress which came to be taken more and more for granted and was no longer recognized as the result of the policy of freedom. It might even be said that the very success of liberalism became the cause of its decline. Because of the success already achieved, man became increasingly unwilling to tolerate the evils still with him which now appeared both unbearable and unnecessary.[10]

Because of the growing impatience with the slow advance of liberal policy, the just irritation with those who used liberal phraseology in defense of antisocial privileges, and the boundless ambition seemingly justified by the material improvements already achieved, it came to pass that toward the turn of the century the belief in the basic tenets of liberalism was more and more relinquished. What had been achieved came to be regarded as a secure and imperishable possession, acquired once and for all. The eyes of the people became fixed on the new demands, the rapid satisfaction of which seemed to be barred by the adherence to the old principles. It became more and more widely accepted that further advance could be expected not along the old lines within the general framework which had made past progress possible but only by a complete remodeling of society. It was no longer a question of adding to or improving the existing machinery but of completely scrapping and replacing it. And, as the hope of the new generation came to be centered on something completely new, interest in and understanding of the functioning of the existing society rapidly declined; and, with the decline of the understanding of the way in which the free system worked, our awareness of what depended on its existence also decreased.

This is not the place to discuss how this change in outlook was fostered by the uncritical transfer to the problems of society of habits of thought engendered by the preoccupation with technological problems, the habits of thought

---

[10] [Hayek makes a similar argument in "The Trend of Economic Thinking," op. cit. —Ed.]

of the natural scientist and the engineer, and how these at the same time tended to discredit the results of the past study of society which did not conform to their prejudices and to impose ideals of organization on a sphere to which they are not appropriate.[11] All we are here concerned to show is how completely, though gradually and by almost imperceptible steps, our attitude toward society has changed. What at every stage of this process of change had appeared a difference of degree only has in its cumulative effect already brought about a fundamental difference between the older liberal attitude toward society and the present approach to social problems. The change amounts to a complete reversal of the trend we have sketched, an entire abandonment of the individualist tradition which has created Western civilization.

According to the views now dominant, the question is no longer how we can make the best use of the spontaneous forces found in a free society. We have in effect undertaken to dispense with the forces which produced unforeseen results and to replace the impersonal and anonymous mechanism of the market by collective and "conscious" direction of all social forces to deliberately chosen goals. The difference cannot be better illustrated than by the extreme position taken in a widely acclaimed book on whose program of so-called "planning for freedom" we shall have to comment yet more than once. "We have never had to set up and direct," writes Dr. Karl Mannheim, "the entire system of nature as we are forced to do today with society. . . . Mankind is tending more and more to regulate the whole of its social life, although it has never attempted to create a second nature."[12]

It is significant that this change in the trend of ideas has coincided with a reversal of the direction in which ideas have traveled in space. For over two hundred years English ideas had been spreading eastward. The rule of freedom which had been achieved in England seemed destined to spread throughout the world. By about 1870 the reign of these ideas had probably reached its easternmost expansion. From then onward it began to retreat, and a different set of

---

[11] The author has made an attempt to trace the beginning of this development in two series of articles on "Scientism and the Study of Society" and "The Counter-Revolution of Science," which appeared in *Economica*, 1941–44. [Revisions of these essays appear in *The Counter-Revolution of Science: Studies in the Abuse of Reason*, op. cit., on pp. 17–182 and 183–363, respectively. —Ed.]

[12] Karl Mannheim, *Man and Society in an Age of Reconstruction: Studies in Modern Social Structure* (London: Kegan Paul, 1940), pp. 175–176. [Hungarian-born sociologist Karl Mannheim (1893–1947) taught at Heidelberg and Frankfurt before fleeing to the LSE in 1933. Having been among the first academics dismissed under Hitler's "Restoration of Civil Service Act" in March 1933, he was invited as a visiting professor under the auspices of the Academic Freedom Committee set up by Beveridge and his LSE colleagues. For more on this, see Ralf Darendorf, *LSE: A History of the London School of Economics and Political Science, 1895–1995* (Oxford: Oxford University Press, 1995), pp. 286–87. Mannheim is remembered today chiefly for his contributions to the sociology of knowledge. —Ed.]

ideas, not really new but very old, began to advance from the East. England lost her intellectual leadership in the political and social sphere and became an importer of ideas. For the next sixty years Germany became the center from which the ideas destined to govern the world in the twentieth century spread east and west. Whether it was Hegel or Marx, List or Schmoller, Sombart or Mannheim, whether it was socialism in its more radical form or merely "organization" or "planning" of a less radical kind, German ideas were everywhere readily imported and German institutions imitated.[13]

Although most of the new ideas, and particularly socialism, did not originate in Germany, it was in Germany that they were perfected and during the last quarter of the nineteenth and the first quarter of the twentieth century that they reached their fullest development. It is now often forgotten how very considerable was the lead which Germany had during this period in the development of the theory and practice of socialism; that a generation before socialism became a serious issue in this country, Germany had a large socialist party in her parliament and that until not very long ago the doctrinal development of socialism was almost entirely carried on in Germany and Austria, so that even today Russian discussion largely carries on where the Germans left off. Most English and American socialists are still unaware that the majority of the problems they begin to discover were thoroughly discussed by German socialists long ago.[14]

The intellectual influence which German thinkers were able to exercise during this period on the whole world was supported not merely by the great material progress of Germany but even more by the extraordinary reputation which German thinkers and scientists had earned during the preceding hundred years when Germany had once more become an integral and even leading member of the common European civilization. But it soon served to assist the spreading from Germany of ideas directed against the foundations of that

[13] [German idealist philosopher Georg Wilhelm Friedrich Hegel (1770–1831) articulated the dialectical method in describing the evolution of consciousness and progression of history, which the revolutionary social theorist Karl Marx (1818–1883) placed within a materialist framework to predict the inevitable collapse of capitalism. In his book *National System of Political Economy*, German-born political economist Friedrich List (1789–1846) advocated trade protectionism. Many of his policy recommendations were also endorsed by the German historical school economists, of whom Gustav Schmoller (1838–1917) was a leader. Schmoller engaged in a *Methodenstreit*, or battle over methods, with Austrian School founder Carl Menger. Historian of the development of capitalism Werner Sombart (1863–1941) was perhaps the last of the historical school economists. Hayek would view his move from left-wing socialism toward anticapitalism of the fascist variety as exemplifying a natural tendency. —Ed.]

[14] [For more on the German socialist tradition, see M. C. Howard and J. E. King, *A History of Marxian Economics, Vol. I 1883–1914* (Princeton: Princeton University Press, 1989). One of Hayek's goals in editing the volume, *Collectivist Economic Planning*, op. cit., was to inform his English readers of some key documents critical of the German-language socialist literature. —Ed.]

civilization. The Germans themselves—or at least those among them who spread these ideas—were fully aware of the conflict: what had been the common heritage of European civilization became to them, long before the Nazis, "Western" civilization—where "Western" was no longer used in the old sense of Occident but had come to mean west of the Rhine. "Western" in this sense was liberalism and democracy, capitalism and individualism, free trade and any form of internationalism or love of peace.

But in spite of the ill-concealed contempt of an ever increasing number of Germans for those "shallow" Western ideals, or perhaps because of it, the people of the West continued to import German ideas and were even induced to believe that their own former convictions had merely been rationalizations of selfish interests, that free trade was a doctrine invented to further British interests, and that the political ideals of England and America were hopelessly outmoded and a thing to be ashamed of.

TWO

THE GREAT UTOPIA

What has always made the state a hell on earth has been precisely that man has tried to make it his heaven. —Hölderlin[1]

That socialism has displaced liberalism as the doctrine held by the great majority of progressives does not simply mean that people had forgotten the warnings of the great liberal thinkers of the past about the consequences of collectivism. It has happened because they were persuaded of the very opposite of what these men had predicted. The extraordinary thing is that the same socialism that was not only early recognized as the gravest threat to freedom, but quite openly began as a reaction against the liberalism of the French Revolution, gained general acceptance under the flag of liberty. It is rarely remembered now that socialism in its beginnings was frankly authoritarian. The French writers who laid the foundations of modern socialism had no doubt that their ideas could be put into practice only by a strong dictatorial government. To them socialism meant an attempt to "terminate the revolution" by a deliberate reorganization of society on hierarchical lines and by the imposition of a coercive "spiritual power." Where freedom was concerned, the founders of socialism made no bones about their intentions. Freedom of thought they regarded as the root-evil of nineteenth-century society, and the first of modern planners, Saint-Simon, even predicted that those who did not obey his proposed planning boards would be "treated as cattle."[2]

---

[1] [Johann Christian Friedrich Hölderlin, *Hyperion, oder der Eremit in Griechenland. Sämtliche Werke*, vol. 3 (Stuttgart: W. Kohlhammer Verlag, 1957), Erster Band, Erstes Buch, p. 31. The quotation in German reads, "Immerhin hat das den Staat zur Hölle gemacht, daß ihn der Mensch zu seinem Himmel machen wollte." —Ed.]

[2] [See Henri Saint-Simon, "Letters from an Inhabitant of Geneva to his Contemporaries," in *Henri Saint-Simon (1760–1825): Selected Writings on Science, Industry and Social Organization*, trans. and ed. Keith Taylor (New York: Holmes and Meier, 1975), p. 78, where Saint-Simon says, "Every man who fails to obey this commandment will be regarded and treated by others as an animal." The social reformer Claude Henri de Rouvroy, Comte de Saint-Simon (1760–1825) was a founder of French socialism. In his account of the origins of "scientism" and of "the abuse of reason," Hayek characterized Saint-Simon as "a megalomaniac visionary." See F. A. Hayek, "The

Only under the influence of the strong democratic currents preceding the revolution of 1848 did socialism begin to ally itself with the forces of freedom. But it took the new "democratic socialism" a long time to live down the suspicions aroused by its antecedents. Nobody saw more clearly than Tocqueville that democracy as an essentially individualist institution stood in an irreconcilable conflict with socialism:

"Democracy extends the sphere of individual freedom," he said in 1848; "socialism restricts it. Democracy attaches all possible value to each man; socialism makes each man a mere agent, a mere number. Democracy and socialism have nothing in common but one word: equality. But notice the difference: while democracy seeks equality in liberty, socialism seeks equality in restraint and servitude."[3]

To allay these suspicions and to harness to its cart the strongest of all political motives—the craving for freedom—socialism began increasingly to make use of the promise of a "new freedom." The coming of socialism was to be the leap from the realm of necessity to the realm of freedom. It was to bring "economic freedom," without which the political freedom already gained was "not worth having." Only socialism was capable of effecting the consummation of the age-long struggle for freedom, in which the attainment of political freedom was but a first step.

The subtle change in meaning to which the word "freedom" was subjected in order that this argument should sound plausible is important. To the great apostles of political freedom the word had meant freedom from coercion, freedom from the arbitrary power of other men, release from the ties which left the individual no choice but obedience to the orders of a superior to whom he was attached. The new freedom promised, however, was to be freedom from necessity, release from the compulsion of the circumstances which inevitably limit the range of choice of all of us, although for some very much more than for others. Before man could be truly free, the "despotism of physical want" had to be broken, the "restraints of the economic system" relaxed.

Counter-Revolution of Science," in *The Counter-Revolution of Science: Studies in the Abuse of Reason*, op. cit., p. 222. The sentence containing the passage that Hayek quotes was apparently deleted by Saint-Simon's disciples from some later versions of the tract. —Ed.]

[3]Alexis de Tocqueville, "Discours prononcé à l'assemblée constituante dans la discussion de projet de constitution (12 Septembre 1848) sur la question du droit au travail," *Oeuvres complètes d'Alexis de Tocqueville*, vol. 9 (Paris: Michel Lévy Frères, 1866), p. 546. [The original passage reads, "La démocratie étend la sphère de l'indépendance individuelle, le socialisme la resserre. La démocratie donne toute sa valeur possible à chaque homme, le socialisme fait de chaque homme un agent, un instrument, un chiffre. La démocratie et le socialisme ne se tiennent que par un mot, l'égalité; mais remarquez la différence: la démocratie veut l'égalité dans la liberté, et le socialisme veut l'égalité dans la gêne et dans la servitude." —Ed.]

Freedom in this sense is, of course, merely another name for power[4] or wealth. Yet, although the promises of this new freedom were often coupled with irresponsible promises of a great increase in material wealth in a socialist society, it was not from such an absolute conquest of the niggardliness of nature that economic freedom was expected. What the promise really amounted to was that the great existing disparities in the range of choice of different people were to disappear. The demand for the new freedom was thus only another name for the old demand for an equal distribution of wealth. But the new name gave the socialists another word in common with the liberals, and they exploited it to the full. And, although the word was used in a different sense by the two groups, few people noticed this and still fewer asked themselves whether the two kinds of freedom promised could really be combined.

There can be no doubt that the promise of greater freedom has become one of the most effective weapons of socialist propaganda and that the belief that socialism would bring freedom is genuine and sincere. But this would only heighten the tragedy if it should prove that what was promised to us as the Road to Freedom was in fact the High Road to Servitude. Unquestionably, the promise of more freedom was responsible for luring more and more liberals along the socialist road, for blinding them to the conflict which exists between the basic principles of socialism and liberalism, and for often enabling socialists to usurp the very name of the old party of freedom. Socialism was embraced by the greater part of the intelligentsia as the apparent heir of the liberal tradition: therefore it is not surprising that to them the idea of socialism's leading to the opposite of liberty should appear inconceivable.

In recent years, however, the old apprehensions of the unforeseen consequences of socialism have once more been strongly voiced from the most unexpected quarters. Observer after observer, in spite of the contrary expectation with which he approached his subject, has been impressed with the extraordinary similarity in many respects of the conditions under "fascism" and "communism." While "progressives" in England and elsewhere were still deluding themselves that communism and fascism represented opposite poles, more and more people began to ask themselves whether these new tyrannies were not

---

[4]The characteristic confusion of freedom with power, which we shall meet again and again throughout this discussion, is too big a subject to be thoroughly examined here. As old as socialism itself, it is so closely allied with it that almost seventy years ago a French scholar, discussing its Saint-Simonian origins, was led to say that this theory of liberty "est à elle seule tout le socialisme" (Paul Janet, *Saint-Simon et le Saint-Simonisme* [Paris: G. Baillière et cie., 1878], p. 26 n.). The most explicit defender of this confusion is, significantly, the leading philosopher of American left-wingism, John Dewey, according to whom "liberty is the effective power to do specific things" so that "the demand for liberty is demand for power." See John Dewey, "Liberty and Social Control," *The Social Frontier*, vol. 2, November 1935, p. 41.

the outcome of the same tendencies. Even communists must have been some-what shaken by such testimonies as that of Max Eastman, Lenin's old friend, who found himself compelled to admit that "instead of being better, Stalin-ism is worse than fascism, more ruthless, barbarous, unjust, immoral, anti-democratic, unredeemed by any hope or scruple," and that it is "better de-scribed as superfascist"; and when we find the same author recognizing that "Stalinism *is* socialism, in the sense of being an inevitable although unforeseen political accompaniment of the nationalization and collectivization which he had relied upon as part of his plan for erecting a classless society,"[5] his conclu-sion clearly achieves wider significance.

Mr. Eastman's case is perhaps the most remarkable, yet he is by no means the first or the only sympathetic observer of the Russian experiment to form simi-lar conclusions. Several years earlier W. H. Chamberlin, who in twelve years in Russia as an American correspondent had seen all his ideals shattered, summed up the conclusions of his studies there and in Germany and Italy in the state-ment that "socialism is certain to prove, in the beginning at least, the road NOT to freedom, but to dictatorship and counter-dictatorships, to civil war of the fiercest kind. Socialism achieved and maintained by democratic means seems definitely to belong to the world of utopias."[6] Similarly a British writer, F. A. Voigt, after many years of close observation of developments in Europe as a foreign correspondent, concludes that "Marxism has led to Fascism and Na-tional Socialism, because, in all essentials, it is Fascism and National Social-ism."[7] And Walter Lippmann has arrived at the conviction that "the generation to which we belong is now learning from experience what happens when men

---

[5] Max Eastman, *Stalin's Russia and the Crisis in Socialism* (New York: W. W. Norton, 1940), the quoted passages are found on p. 82, p. 82, and p. 154, respectively. [Hayek originally listed the quotations as all appearing on p. 82. The American Max Eastman (1883–1969) was the editor and publisher of the radical organ *The Masses*. He traveled to the Soviet Union after the Russian Revolution and married a Russian woman. By the 1930s he had become disillusioned with the Soviet experiment, believing that the original purpose of Lenin's revolution had been subverted by Stalin. As noted in my introduction, p. 19, Eastman condensed *The Road to Serfdom* for *Reader's Digest*. —Ed.]

[6] W. H. Chamberlin, *Collectivism: A False Utopia* (New York: Macmillan, 1937), pp. 202–203. [Author and journalist William Henry Chamberlin (1897–1969) went to Moscow in 1922 as a journalist for the *Christian Science Monitor*. Though initially sympathetic to the revolutionary cause, he quickly became disillusioned with Stalinism. —Ed.]

[7] F. A. Voigt, *Unto Caesar* (New York: G. P. Putnam's Sons, 1938), p. 95. [The English journalist and author Frederick Augustus Voigt (1892–1957) was the Berlin correspondent for the *Manches-ter Guardian* during the interwar years. I could not locate the passage cited in Voigt's book, though the following lines, taken from p. 35, express similar sentiments: "Marxism would be a phenom-enon of little more than historical interest, seeing that it has failed even it its principal stronghold, were it not so closely akin to National Socialism. National Socialism would have been inconceiv-able without Marxism." Voigt notes similarities between Marxism and National Socialism as well as between the persons of Lenin and Hitler in his book. —Ed.]

retreat from freedom to a coercive organization of their affairs. Though they promise themselves a more abundant life, they must in practice renounce it; as the organized direction increases, the variety of ends must give way to uniformity. That is the nemesis of the planned society and the authoritarian principle in human affairs."[8]

Many more similar statements from people in a position to judge might be selected from publications of recent years, particularly from those by men who as citizens of the now totalitarian countries have lived through the transformation and have been forced by their experience to revise many cherished beliefs. We shall quote as one more example a German writer who expresses the same conclusion perhaps more justly than those already quoted.

"The complete collapse of the belief in the attainability of freedom and equality through Marxism," writes Peter Drucker, "has forced Russia to travel the same road toward a totalitarian, purely negative, non-economic society of unfreedom and inequality which Germany has been following. Not that communism and fascism are essentially the same. Fascism is the stage reached after communism has proved an illusion, and it has proved as much an illusion in Stalinist Russia as in pre-Hitler Germany."[9]

No less significant is the intellectual history of many of the Nazi and Fascist leaders. Everyone who has watched the growth of these movements in Italy[10] or in Germany has been struck by the number of leading men, from Mussolini downward (and not excluding Laval and Quisling), who began as socialists and ended as Fascists or Nazis.[11] And what is true of the leaders is even more true of the rank and file of the movement. The relative ease with which a young

---

[8]Walter Lippmann, "The Government of Posterity," *The Atlantic*, vol. 158, November 1936, p. 552. [The American journalist, author, and social commentator Walter Lippmann (1889–1974) wrote for the *New York Herald Tribune*. He won the Pulitzer Prize for international reporting in 1962. —Ed.]

[9]Peter Drucker, *The End of Economic Man: A Study of the New Totalitarianism* (New York: The John Day Co., 1939), pp. 245–246. [In the original, Hayek mistakenly listed the page on which the quotation is found as p. 230. Vienna-born American management consultant Peter Drucker (1909–2005) taught at Bennington College and New York University before his appointment as professor of social sciences at the Claremont Graduate School, now Claremont Graduate University, in California. —Ed.]

[10]An illuminating account of the intellectual history of many of the Fascist leaders will be found in Robert Michels (himself a former Marxist Fascist), *Sozialismus und Fascismus als politische Strömungen in Italien: historische Studien*, vol. 2, *Sozialismus und Fascismus in Italien* (Munich: Meyer and Jessen, 1925), 264–66, 311–12.

[11][French politician Pierre Laval (1883–1945) served as Marshall Pétain's deputy and subsequently as prime minister during the Vichy regime. He was executed as a collaborator following the liberation. Norwegian diplomat Vidkun Quisling (1887–1945) formed the Nasjonal Samlung party, modeled on the German National Socialist party, in 1933, and served as the puppet prime minister during the occupation of Norway. His name has become synonymous with collaboration. Quisling was tried and executed at war's end. —Ed.]

communist could be converted into a Nazi or vice versa was generally known in Germany, best of all to the propagandists of the two parties. Many a university teacher during the 1930s has seen English and American students return from the Continent uncertain whether they were communists or Nazis and certain only that they hated Western liberal civilization.

It is true, of course, that in Germany before 1933, and in Italy before 1922, communists and Nazis or Fascists clashed more frequently with each other than with other parties. They competed for the support of the same type of mind and reserved for each other the hatred of the heretic. But their practice showed how closely they are related. To both, the real enemy, the man with whom they had nothing in common and whom they could not hope to convince, is the liberal of the old type. While to the Nazi the communist, and to the communist the Nazi, and to both the socialist, are potential recruits who are made of the right timber, although they have listened to false prophets, they both know that there can be no compromise between them and those who really believe in individual freedom.

Lest this be doubted by people misled by official propaganda from either side, let me quote one more statement from an authority that ought not to be suspect. In an article under the significant title of "The Rediscovery of Liberalism," Professor Eduard Heimann, one of the leaders of German religious socialism, writes: "Hitlerism proclaims itself as both true democracy and true socialism, and the terrible truth is that there is a grain of truth for such claims— an infinitesimal grain, to be sure, but at any rate enough to serve as a basis for such fantastic distortions. Hitlerism even goes so far as to claim the role of protector of Christianity, and the terrible truth is that even this gross misinterpretation is able to make some impression. But one fact stands out with perfect clarity in all the fog: Hitler has never claimed to represent true liberalism. Liberalism then has the distinction of being the doctrine most hated by Hitler."[12] It should be added that this hatred had little occasion to show itself in practice merely because, by the time Hitler came to power, liberalism was to all intents and purposes dead in Germany. And it was socialism that had killed it.

While to many who have watched the transition from socialism to fascism at close quarters the connection between the two systems has become increasingly

---

[12]Eduard Heimann, "The Rediscovery of Liberalism," *Social Research*, vol. 8, November 1941, p. 479. It deserves to be recalled in this connection that, whatever may have been his reasons, Hitler thought it expedient to declare in one of his public speeches as late as February, 1941, that "basically National Socialism and Marxism are the same." Compare the article, "Herr Hitler's Speech of February 24," *Bulletin of International News* (published by the Royal Institute of International Affairs), vol. 18, March 8, 1941, p. 269. [Eduard Heimann (1889–1967) taught at the University of Hamburg from 1925 to 1933, when he fled Germany and took a position at the New School for Social Research in New York. —Ed.]

obvious, in the democracies the majority of people still believe that socialism and freedom can be combined. There can be no doubt that most socialists here still believe profoundly in the liberal ideal of freedom and that they would recoil if they became convinced that the realization of their program would mean the destruction of freedom. So little is the problem yet seen, so easily do the most irreconcilable ideals still live together, that we can still hear such contradictions in terms as "individualist socialism" seriously discussed. If this is the state of mind which makes us drift into a new world, nothing can be more urgent than that we should seriously examine the real significance of the evolution that has taken place elsewhere. Although our conclusions will only confirm the apprehensions which others have already expressed, the reasons why this development cannot be regarded as accidental will not appear without a rather full examination of the main aspects of this transformation of social life. That democratic socialism, the great utopia of the last few generations, is not only unachievable, but that to strive for it produces something so utterly different that few of those who now wish it would be prepared to accept the consequences, many will not believe until the connection has been laid bare in all its aspects.

THREE

INDIVIDUALISM AND COLLECTIVISM

The socialists believe in two things which are absolutely different and perhaps even contradictory: freedom and organization. —Élie Halévy[1]

Before we can progress with our main problem, an obstacle has yet to be sur-mounted. A confusion largely responsible for the way in which we are drifting into things which nobody wants must be cleared up. This confusion concerns nothing less than the concept of socialism itself. It may mean, and is often used to describe, merely the ideals of social justice, greater equality, and security, which are the ultimate aims of socialism. But it means also the particular method by which most socialists hope to attain these ends and which many competent people regard as the only methods by which they can be fully and quickly attained. In this sense socialism means the abolition of private enter-prise, of private ownership of the means of production, and the creation of a system of "planned economy" in which the entrepreneur working for profit is replaced by a central planning body.

There are many people who call themselves socialists, although they care only about the first, who fervently believe in those ultimate aims of socialism but neither care nor understand how they can be achieved, and who are merely certain that they must be achieved, whatever the cost. But to nearly all those to whom socialism is not merely a hope but an object of practical politics, the characteristic methods of modern socialism are as essential as the ends them-selves. Many people, on the other hand, who value the ultimate ends of social-ism no less than the socialists refuse to support socialism because of the dangers to other values they see in the methods proposed by the socialists. The dispute about socialism has thus become largely a dispute about means and not about ends—although the question whether the different ends of socialism can be simultaneously achieved is also involved.

This would be enough to create confusion. And the confusion has been fur-

---

[1] [Élie Halévy, *L'Ère des tyrannies: Études sur le socialisme et la guerre* (Paris: Gallimard, 1938), p. 208. For an English translation of Halévy's book, see Élie Halévy, *The Era of Tyrannies: Essays on Social-ism and War*, translated by R. K. Webb (New York: New York University Press, 1966). —Ed.]

ther increased by the common practice of denying that those who repudiate the means value the ends. But this is not all. The situation is still more complicated by the fact that the same means, the "economic planning" which is the prime instrument of socialist reform, can be used for many other purposes. We must centrally direct economic activity if we want to make the distribution of income conform to current ideas of social justice. "Planning," therefore, is wanted by all those who demand that "production for use" be substituted for production for profit. But such planning is no less indispensable if the distribution of incomes is to be regulated in a way which to us appears to be the opposite of just. Whether we should wish that more of the good things of this world should go to some racial élite, the Nordic men, or the members of a party or an aristocracy, the methods which we shall have to employ are the same as those which could insure an equalitarian distribution.

It may, perhaps, seem unfair to use the term "socialism" to describe its methods rather than its aims, to use for a particular method a term which for many people stands for an ultimate ideal. It is probably preferable to describe the methods which can be used for a great variety of ends as collectivism and to regard socialism as a species of that genus. Yet, although to most socialists only one species of collectivism will represent true socialism, it must always be remembered that socialism is a species of collectivism and that therefore everything which is true of collectivism as such must apply also to socialism. Nearly all the points which are disputed between socialists and liberals concern the methods common to all forms of collectivism and not the particular ends for which socialists want to use them; and all the consequences with which we shall be concerned in this book follow from the methods of collectivism irrespective of the ends for which they are used. It must also not be forgotten that socialism is not only by far the most important species of collectivism or "planning" but that it is socialism which has persuaded liberal-minded people to submit once more to that regimentation of economic life which they had overthrown because, in the words of Adam Smith, it puts governments in a position where "to support themselves they are obliged to be oppressive and tyrannical."[2]

The difficulties caused by the ambiguities of the common political terms are not yet over if we agree to use the term "collectivism" so as to include all types of "planned economy," whatever the end of planning. The meaning of this term becomes somewhat more definite if we make it clear that we mean that sort of planning which is necessary to realize any given distributive ideals. But, as the idea of central economic planning owes its appeal largely to this very

---

[2] Quoted in Dugald Stewart's *Biographical Memoir of Adam Smith* a memorandum written by Smith in 1755. [A reprint of Stewart's 1793 memoir was released by Augustus M. Kelley in 1966, and the quotation from Smith may be found on p. 68. —Ed.]

vagueness of its meaning, it is essential that we should agree on its precise sense before we discuss its consequences.

"Planning" owes its popularity largely to the fact that everybody desires, of course, that we should handle our common problems as rationally as possible and that, in so doing, we should use as much foresight as we can command. In this sense everybody who is not a complete fatalist is a planner, every political act is (or ought to be) an act of planning, and there can be differences only between good and bad, between wise and foresighted and foolish and short-sighted planning. An economist, whose whole task is the study of how men actually do and how they might plan their affairs, is the last person who could object to planning in this general sense. But it is not in this sense that our enthusiasts for a planned society now employ this term, nor merely in this sense that we must plan if we want the distribution of income or wealth to conform to some particular standard. According to the modern planners, and for their purposes, it is not sufficient to design the most rational permanent framework within which the various activities would be conducted by different persons according to their individual plans. This liberal plan, according to them, is no plan—and it is, indeed, not a plan designed to satisfy particular views about who should have what. What our planners demand is a central direction of all economic activity according to a single plan, laying down how the resources of society should be "consciously directed" to serve particular ends in a definite way.

The dispute between the modern planners and their opponents is, therefore, *not* a dispute on whether we ought to choose intelligently between the various possible organizations of society; it is not a dispute on whether we ought to employ foresight and systematic thinking in planning our common affairs. It is a dispute about what is the best way of so doing. The question is whether for this purpose it is better that the holder of coercive power should confine himself in general to creating conditions under which the knowledge and initiative of individuals are given the best scope so that *they* can plan most successfully; or whether a rational utilization of our resources requires *central* direction and organization of all our activities according to some consciously constructed "blueprint." The socialists of all parties have appropriated the term "planning" for planning of the latter type, and it is now generally accepted in this sense. But though this is meant to suggest that this is the only rational way of handling our affairs, it does not, of course, prove this. It remains the point on which the planners and the liberals disagree.

It is important not to confuse opposition against this kind of planning with a dogmatic laissez faire attitude. The liberal argument is in favor of making the best possible use of the forces of competition as a means of coordinating human efforts, not an argument for leaving things just as they are. It is based on the conviction that, where effective competition can be created, it is a better way of guiding individual efforts than any other. It does not deny, but even emphasizes, that, in order that competition should work beneficially, a carefully thought-out legal framework is required and that neither the existing nor the past legal rules are free from grave defects. Nor does it deny that, where it is impossible to create the conditions necessary to make competition effective, we must resort to other methods of guiding economic activity. Economic liberalism is opposed, however, to competition's being supplanted by inferior methods of coordinating individual efforts. And it regards competition as superior not only because it is in most circumstances the most efficient method known but even more because it is the only method by which our activities can be adjusted to each other without coercive or arbitrary intervention of authority. Indeed, one of the main arguments in favor of competition is that it dispenses with the need for "conscious social control" and that it gives the individuals a chance to decide whether the prospects of a particular occupation are sufficient to compensate for the disadvantages and risks connected with it.

The successful use of competition as the principle of social organization precludes certain types of coercive interference with economic life, but it admits of others which sometimes may very considerably assist its work and even requires certain kinds of government action. But there is good reason why the negative requirements, the points where coercion must not be used, have been particularly stressed. It is necessary in the first instance that the parties in the market should be free to sell and buy at any price at which they can find a partner to the transaction and that anybody should be free to produce, sell, and buy anything that may be produced or sold at all. And it is essential that the entry into the different trades should be open to all on equal terms and that the law should not tolerate any attempts by individuals or groups to restrict this entry by open or concealed force. Any attempt to control prices or quantities of particular commodities deprives competition of its power of bringing about an effective coordination of individual efforts, because price changes then cease to register all the relevant changes in circumstances and no longer provide a reliable guide for the individual's actions.

This is not necessarily true, however, of measures merely restricting the allowed methods of production, so long as these restrictions affect all potential producers equally and are not used as an indirect way of controlling prices and quantities. Though all such controls of the methods of production impose extra costs (i.e., make it necessary to use more resources to produce a given output), they may be well worth while. To prohibit the use of certain poisonous substances or to require special precautions in their use, to limit working hours or to require certain sanitary arrangements, is fully compatible with the preservation of competition. The only question here is whether in the particular instance the advantages gained are greater than the social costs which they impose. Nor is the preservation of competition incompatible with an extensive system of social services—so long as the organization of these services is not designed in such a way as to make competition ineffective over wide fields.

It is regrettable, though not difficult to explain, that in the past much less attention has been given to the positive requirements of a successful working of the competitive system than to these negative points. The functioning of a competition not only requires adequate organization of certain institutions like money, markets, and channels of information—some of which can never be adequately provided by private enterprise—but it depends, above all, on the existence of an appropriate legal system, a legal system designed both to preserve competition and to make it operate as beneficially as possible. It is by no means sufficient that the law should recognize the principle of private property and freedom of contract; much depends on the precise definition of the right of property as applied to different things. The systematic study of the forms of legal institutions which will make the competitive system work efficiently has been sadly neglected; and strong arguments can be advanced that serious shortcomings here, particularly with regard to the law of corporations and of patents, not only have made competition work much less effectively than it might have done but have even led to the destruction of competition in many spheres.

There are, finally, undoubted fields where no legal arrangements can create the main condition on which the usefulness of the system of competition and private property depends: namely, that the owner benefits from all the useful services rendered by his property and suffers for all the damages caused to others by its use. Where, for example, it is impracticable to make the enjoyment of certain services dependent on the payment of a price, competition will not produce the services; and the price system becomes similarly ineffective when the damage caused to others by certain uses of property cannot be effectively charged to the owner of that property. In all these instances there is a divergence between the items which enter into private calculation and those which affect social welfare; and, whenever this divergence becomes important, some method other than competition may have to be found to supply the services in question. Thus neither the provision of signposts on the roads nor, in most circumstances, that of the roads themselves can be paid for by every individual user. Nor can certain harmful effects of deforestation, of some methods of farming, or of the smoke and noise of factories be confined to the owner of the property in question or to those who are willing to submit to the damage for an agreed compensation. In such instances we must find some substitute for the regulation by the price mechanism. But the fact that we have to resort to the substitution of direct regulation by authority where the conditions for the proper working of competition cannot be created does not prove that we should suppress competition where it can be made to function.

To create conditions in which competition will be as effective as possible, to supplement it where it cannot be made effective, to provide the services which, in the words of Adam Smith, "though they may be in the highest degree advantageous to a great society, are, however, of such a nature, that the profit could never repay the expense to any individual or small number of individuals"—these tasks provide, indeed, a wide and unquestioned field for state activity.[3] In no system that could be rationally defended would the state just do nothing. An effective competitive system needs an intelligently designed and continuously adjusted legal framework as much as any other. Even the most essential prerequisite of its proper functioning, the prevention of fraud and deception (including exploitation of ignorance), provides a great and by no means yet fully accomplished object of legislative activity.

The task of creating a suitable framework for the beneficial working of competition had, however, not yet been carried very far when states everywhere turned from it to that of supplanting competition by a different and irreconcilable principle. The question was no longer one of making competition work and of supplementing it but of displacing it altogether. It is important to be quite clear about this: the modern movement for planning is a movement against competition as such, a new flag under which all the old enemies of competition have rallied. And although all sorts of interests are now trying to reestablish under this flag privileges which the liberal era swept away, it is socialist propaganda for planning which has restored to respectability among liberal-minded people opposition to competition and which has effectively lulled the healthy suspicion which any attempt to smother competition used to arouse.[4] What in effect unites the socialists of the Left and the Right is this common hostility to

---

[3][The passage Hayek quotes may be found in Adam Smith, *An Inquiry into the Nature and Causes of the Wealth of Nations*, ed. R. H. Campbell and A. S. Skinner, vol. 2 of *The Glasgow Edition of the Works and Correspondence of Adam Smith* (Oxford: Clarendon Press, 1976, 1979; reprinted, Indianapolis: Liberty Press, 1981), book 5, chapter 1, part 3, p. 723. —Ed.]

[4]Of late, it is true, some academic socialists, under the spur of criticism and animated by the same fear of the extinction of freedom in a centrally planned society, have devised a new kind of "competitive socialism" which they hope will avoid the difficulties and dangers of central planning and combine the abolition of private property with the full retention of individual freedom. Although some discussion of this new kind of socialism has taken place in learned journals, it is hardly likely to recommend itself to practical politicians. If it ever did, it would not be difficult to show (as the author has attempted elsewhere—see *Economica* 1940) that these plans rest on a delusion and suffer from an inherent contradiction. It is impossible to assume control over all the productive resources without also deciding for whom and by whom they are to be used. Although under this so-called "competitive socialism" the planning by the central authority would take somewhat more roundabout forms, its effects would not be fundamentally different, and the element of competition would be little more than a sham. [Hayek refers to his paper "Socialist Calculation: The Competitive 'Solution,'" op. cit. In the paper, Hayek reviews and criticizes proposals found in H. D. Dickinson, *Economics of Socialism* (London: Oxford University Press, 1939), and

competition and their common desire to replace it by a directed economy. Though the terms "capitalism" and "socialism" are still generally used to describe the past and the future forms of society, they conceal rather than elucidate the nature of the transition through which we are passing.

Yet, though all the changes we are observing tend in the direction of a comprehensive central direction of economic activity, the universal struggle against competition promises to produce in the first instance something in many respects even worse, a state of affairs which can satisfy neither planners nor liberals: a sort of syndicalist or "corporative" organization of industry, in which competition is more or less suppressed but planning is left in the hands of the independent monopolies of the separate industries. This is the inevitable first result of a situation in which the people are united in their hostility to competition but agree on little else. By destroying competition in industry after industry, this policy puts the consumer at the mercy of the joint monopolist action of capitalists and workers in the best organized industries. Yet, although this is a state of affairs which in wide fields has already existed for some time, and although much of the muddled (and most of the interested) agitation for planning aims at it, it is not a state which is likely to persist or can be rationally justified. Such independent planning by industrial monopolies would, in fact, produce effects opposite to those at which the argument for planning aims. Once this stage is reached, the only alternative to a return to competition is the control of the monopolies by the state—a control which, if it is to be made effective, must become progressively more complete and more detailed. It is this stage we are rapidly approaching. When, shortly before the war, a weekly magazine pointed out that there were many signs that British leaders, at least, were growing accustomed to thinking in terms of national development by controlled monopolies, this was probably a true estimate of the position as it then existed.[5] Since then this process has been greatly accelerated by the war, and its grave defects and dangers will become increasingly obvious as time goes on.

The idea of complete centralization of the direction of economic activity still appalls most people, not only because of the stupendous difficulty of the task, but even more because of the horror inspired by the idea of everything being directed from a single center. If we are, nevertheless, rapidly moving toward such a state, this is largely because most people still believe that it must be possible to find some middle way between "atomistic" competition and central direction. Nothing, indeed, seems at first more plausible, or is more likely to

---

Oskar Lange and Fred M. Taylor, *On the Economic Theory of Socialism*, op. cit. For more on the significance of Hayek's reference to "competitive socialism," see my introduction to this volume, pp. 24–28. —Ed.]

[5][The statement, "There are many signs that British leaders are growing accustomed to think in terms of national development by controlled monopolies . . ." appeared in *The Spectator*, no. 5774, March 3, 1939, p. 337. —Ed.]

appeal to reasonable people, than the idea that our goal must be neither the extreme decentralization of free competition nor the complete centralization of a single plan but some judicious mixture of the two methods. Yet mere common sense proves a treacherous guide in this field. Although competition can bear some admixture of regulation, it cannot be combined with planning to any extent we like without ceasing to operate as an effective guide to production. Nor is "planning" a medicine which, taken in small doses, can produce the effects for which one might hope from its thoroughgoing application. Both competition and central direction become poor and inefficient tools if they are incomplete; they are alternative principles used to solve the same problem, and a mixture of the two means that neither will really work and that the result will be worse than if either system had been consistently relied upon. Or, to express it differently, planning and competition can be combined only by planning for competition but not by planning against competition.

It is of the utmost importance to the argument of this book for the reader to keep in mind that the planning against which all our criticism is directed is solely the planning against competition—the planning which is to be substituted for competition. This is the more important, as we cannot, within the scope of this book, enter into a discussion of the very necessary planning which is required to make competition as effective and beneficial as possible. But as in current usage "planning" has become almost synonymous with the former kind of planning, it will sometimes be inevitable for the sake of brevity to refer to it simply as planning, even though this means leaving to our opponents a very good word meriting a better fate.

FOUR

THE "INEVITABILITY" OF PLANNING

We were the first to assert that the more complicated the forms assumed by
civilization, the more restricted the freedom of the individual must become.
—Benito Mussolini[1]

It is a revealing fact that few planners are content to say that central planning
is desirable. Most of them affirm that we can no longer choose but are compelled by circumstances beyond our control to substitute planning for competition. The myth is deliberately cultivated that we are embarking on the
new course not out of free will but because competition is spontaneously eliminated by technological changes which we neither can reverse nor should
wish to prevent. This argument is rarely developed at any length—it is one of
the assertions taken over by one writer from another until, by mere iteration,
it has come to be accepted as an established fact. It is, nevertheless, devoid of
foundation. The tendency toward monopoly and planning is not the result of
any "objective facts" beyond our control but the product of opinions fostered
and propagated for half a century until they have come to dominate all our
policy.

Of the various arguments employed to demonstrate the inevitability of planning, the one most frequently heard is that technological changes have made
competition impossible in a constantly increasing number of fields and that the
only choice left to us is between control of production by private monopolies
and direction by the government. This belief derives mainly from the Marxist
doctrine of the "concentration of industry," although, like so many Marxist
ideas, it is now found in many circles which have received it at third or fourth
hand and do not know whence it derives.

The historical fact of the progressive growth of monopoly during the last fifty
years and the increasing restriction of the field in which competition rules is, of
course, not disputed—although the extent of the phenomenon is often greatly

[1] [Benito Mussolini, Grand Fascist Council Report, 1929, quoted in E. B. Ashton, *The Fascist:
His State and His Mind* (New York: William Morrow and Co., 1937), p. 63, note 5. —Ed.]

exaggerated.[2] The important question is whether this development is a necessary consequence of the advance of technology or whether it is simply the result of the policies pursued in most countries. We shall presently see that the actual history of this development strongly suggests the latter. But we must first consider in how far modern technological developments are of such a kind as to make the growth of monopolies in wide fields inevitable.

The alleged technological cause of the growth of monopoly is the superiority of the large firm over the small, owing to the greater efficiency of modern methods of mass production. Modern methods, it is asserted, have created conditions in the majority of industries where the production of the large firm can be increased at decreasing costs per unit, with the result that the large firms are everywhere underbidding and driving out the small ones; this process must go on until in each industry only one or at most a few giant firms are left. This argument singles out one effect sometimes accompanying technological progress; it disregards others which work in the opposite direction; and it receives little support from a serious study of the facts. We cannot here investigate this question in detail and must be content to accept the best evidence available. The most comprehensive study of the facts undertaken in recent times is that by the Temporary National Economic Committee on the *Concentration of Economic Power*. The final report of this committee (which certainly cannot be accused of an undue liberal bias) arrives at the conclusion that the view according to which the greater efficiency of large-scale production is the cause of the disappearance of competition "finds scant support in any evidence that is now at hand."[3] And the detailed monograph on the question which was prepared for the committee sums up the answer in this statement:

"The superior efficiency of large establishments has not been demonstrated; the advantages that are supposed to destroy competition have failed to manifest themselves in many fields. Nor do the economies of size, where they exist, invariably necessitate monopoly. . . . The size or the sizes of the optimum efficiency may be reached long before the major part of a supply is subjected to such control. The conclusions that the advantage of large-scale production must lead inevitably to the abolition of competition cannot be accepted. It should be noted, moreover, that monopoly is frequently the product of factors other than the lower costs of greater size. It is attained through collusive agree-

[2] For a fuller discussion of these problems see Professor Lionel Robbins's essay, "The Inevitability of Monopoly," in his book, *The Economic Basis of Class Conflict and Other Essays in Political Economy* (London: Macmillan, 1939), pp. 45–80.

[3] *Final Report and Recommendations of the Temporary National Economic Committee,* United States of America, 77th Congress, 1st Session, Senate Document No. 35, 1941, p. 89. [President Roosevelt's speech, an excerpt from which provides the quotation at the beginning of chapter 1, was the impetus for the formation of the Temporary National Economic Committee. —Ed.]

ment and promoted by public policies. When these agreements are invalidated and when these policies are reversed, competitive conditions can be restored."[4]

An investigation of conditions in England would lead to very similar results. Anyone who has observed how aspiring monopolists regularly seek and frequently obtain the assistance of the power of the state to make their control effective can have little doubt that there is nothing inevitable about this development.

This conclusion is strongly supported by the historical order in which the decline of competition and the growth of monopoly manifested themselves in different countries. If they were the result of technological developments or a necessary product of the evolution of "capitalism," we should expect them to appear first in the countries with the most advanced economic system. In fact, they appeared first during the last third of the nineteenth century in what were then comparatively young industrial countries, the United States and Germany. In the latter country especially, which came to be regarded as the model country typifying the necessary evolution of capitalism, the growth of cartels and syndicates has since 1878 been systematically fostered by deliberate policy. Not only the instrument of protection but direct inducements and ultimately compulsion were used by the governments to further the creation of monopolies for the regulation of prices and sales. It was here that, with the help of the state, the first great experiment in "scientific planning" and "conscious organization of industry" led to the creation of giant monopolies, which were represented as inevitable growths fifty years before the same was done in Great Britain. It is largely due to the influence of German socialist theoreticians, particularly Sombart, generalizing from the experience of their country, that the inevitable development of the competitive system into "monopoly capitalism" became widely accepted.[5] That in the United States a highly protectionist policy made a somewhat similar development possible seemed to confirm this generalization. The development of Germany, however, more than that of the United States, came to be regarded as representative of a universal tendency; and it became a commonplace to speak—to quote a widely read political essay of recent date—of "Germany where all the social and political forces of modern civilization have reached their most advanced form."[6]

How little there was of inevitability in all this, and how much is the result of deliberate policy, becomes clear when we consider the position in England

---

[4] Clair Wilcox, *Competition and Monopoly in American Industry*, Temporary National Economic Committee Monograph, No. 21 (Washington, DC: U.S. Government Printing Office, 1941), p. 314. [In the original Hayek listed the date of publication as 1940, not 1941. —Ed.]

[5] [For more on Sombart, see chapter 1, note 13. —Ed.]

[6] Reinhold Niebuhr, *Moral Man and Immoral Society: A Study in Ethics and Politics* (New York: Charles Scribner's Sons, 1932), p. 182.

until 1931 and the development since that year in which Great Britain also embarked upon a policy of general protection.[7] It is only a dozen years since, except for a few industries which had obtained protection earlier, British industry was on the whole as competitive as, perhaps, at any time in its history. And, although during the 1920s it suffered severely from incompatible policies followed with regard to wages and to money, at least the years up to 1929 compare with regard to employment and general activity not unfavorably with the 1930s. It is only since the transition to protection and the general change in British economic policy accompanying it that the growth of monopolies has proceeded at an amazing rate and has transformed British industry to an extent the public has scarcely yet realized. To argue that this development has anything to do with the technological progress during this period, that technological necessities which in Germany operated in the 1880s and 1890s, made themselves felt here in the 1930s, is not much less absurd than the claim, implied in a statement of Mussolini, that Italy had to abolish individual freedom before other European people because its civilization had marched so far in advance of the rest!

In so far as England is concerned, the thesis that the change in opinion and policy merely follows an inexorable change in the facts can be given a certain appearance of truth, just because the nation has followed at a distance the intellectual developments elsewhere. It could thus be argued that monopolistic organization of industry grew up in spite of the fact that public opinion still favored competition but that outside events frustrated their wishes. The true relation between theory and practice becomes, however, clear as soon as we look to the prototype of this development—Germany. That *there* the suppression of competition was a matter of deliberate policy, that it was undertaken in the service of the ideal which we now call planning, there can be no doubt. In the progressive advance toward a completely planned society the Germans, and all the people who are imitating their example, are merely following the course which nineteenth-century thinkers, particularly Germans, have mapped out for them. The intellectual history of the last sixty or eighty years is indeed a perfect illustration of the truth that in social evolution nothing is inevitable but thinking makes it so.

The assertion that modern technological progress makes planning inevitable can also be interpreted in a different manner. It may mean that the complexity

---

[7][In the summer of 1931 a financial crisis in Britain led to the collapse of the Labour government, the creation of a "National Government" coalition with Ramsey MacDonald at its head, and the abandonment of the gold standard. One of the first moves of the new National Government was the institution of the general protective tariff to which Hayek refers. —Ed.]

of our modern industrial civilization creates new problems with which we cannot hope to deal effectively except by central planning. In a sense this is true—yet not in the wide sense in which it is claimed. It is, for example, a commonplace that many of the problems created by a modern town, like many other problems caused by close contiguity in space, are not adequately solved by competition. But it is not these problems, like those of the "public utilities," etc., which are uppermost in the minds of those who invoke the complexity of modern civilization as an argument for central planning. What they generally suggest is that the increasing difficulty of obtaining a coherent picture of the complete economic process makes it indispensable that things should be coordinated by some central agency if social life is not to dissolve in chaos.

This argument is based on a complete misapprehension of the working of competition. Far from being appropriate only to comparatively simple conditions, it is the very complexity of the division of labor under modern conditions which makes competition the only method by which such coordination can be adequately brought about. There would be no difficulty about efficient control or planning were conditions so simple that a single person or board could effectively survey all the relevant facts. It is only as the factors which have to be taken into account become so numerous that it is impossible to gain a synoptic view of them that decentralization becomes imperative. But, once decentralization is necessary, the problem of coordination arises—a coordination which leaves the separate agencies free to adjust their activities to the facts which only they can know and yet brings about a mutual adjustment of their respective plans. As decentralization has become necessary because nobody can consciously balance all the considerations bearing on the decisions of so many individuals, the coordination can clearly be effected not by "conscious control" but only by arrangements which convey to each agent the information he must possess in order effectively to adjust his decisions to those of others. And because all the details of the changes constantly affecting the conditions of demand and supply of the different commodities can never be fully known, or quickly enough be collected and disseminated, by any one center, what is required is some apparatus of registration which automatically records all the relevant effects of individual actions and whose indications are at the same time the resultant of, and the guide for, all the individual decisions.

This is precisely what the price system does under competition, and which no other system even promises to accomplish. It enables entrepreneurs, by watching the movement of comparatively few prices, as an engineer watches the hands of a few dials, to adjust their activities to those of their fellows. The important point here is that the price system will fulfill this function only if competition prevails, that is, if the individual producer has to adapt himself to price changes and cannot control them. The more complicated the whole, the more dependent we become on that division of knowledge between individuals whose separate efforts are coordinated by the impersonal mechanism for transmitting the relevant information known by us as the price system.

It is no exaggeration to say that if we had had to rely on conscious central planning for the growth of our industrial system, it would never have reached the degree of differentiation, complexity, and flexibility it has attained. Compared with this method of solving the economic problem by means of decentralization plus automatic coordination, the more obvious method of central direction is incredibly clumsy, primitive, and limited in scope. That the division of labor has reached the extent which makes modern civilization possible we owe to the fact that it did not have to be consciously created but that man tumbled on a method by which the division of labor could be extended far beyond the limits within which it could have been planned. Any further growth of its complexity, therefore, far from making central direction more necessary, makes it more important than ever that we should use a technique which does not depend on conscious control.

There is yet another theory which connects the growth of monopolies with technological progress, and which uses arguments almost opposite to those we have just considered; though not often clearly stated, it has also exercised considerable influence. It contends not that modern technique destroys competition but that, on the contrary, it will be impossible to make use of many of the new technological possibilities unless protection against competition is granted, i.e., a monopoly is conferred. This type of argument is not necessarily fraudulent, as the critical reader will perhaps suspect: the obvious answer—that if a new technique for satisfying our wants is really better, it ought to be able to stand up against all competition—does not dispose of all instances to which this argument refers. No doubt in many cases it is used merely as a form of special pleading by interested parties. Even more often it is probably based on a confusion between technical excellence from a narrow engineering point of view and desirability from the point of view of society as a whole.

There remains, however, a group of instances where the argument has some force. It is, for example, at least conceivable that the British automobile industry might be able to supply a car cheaper and better than cars used to be in the United States if everyone in England were made to use the same kind of car or that the use of electricity for all purposes could be made cheaper than coal or gas if everybody could be made to use only electricity. In instances like these it is at least possible that we might all be better off and should prefer the new situation if we had the choice—but that no individual ever gets the choice, because the alternative is either that we should all use the same cheap car (or all should use only electricity) or that we should have the choice between these things with each of them at a much higher price. I do not know whether this is true in either of the instances given. But it must be admitted that it is possible that, by compulsory standardization or the prohibition of variety beyond a certain degree, abundance might be increased in some fields more than sufficiently to compensate for the restriction of the choice of the consumer. It is even conceivable that a new invention may be made some day whose adoption would seem unquestionably beneficial but which could be used only if many or all people were made to avail themselves of it at the same time.

Whether such instances are of any great or lasting importance, they are certainly not instances where it could be legitimately claimed that technical progress makes central direction inevitable. They would merely make it necessary to choose between gaining a particular advantage by compulsion and not obtaining it—or, in most instances, obtaining it a little later, when further technical advance has overcome the particular difficulties. It is true that in such situations we may have to sacrifice a possible immediate gain as the price of our freedom—but we avoid, on the other hand, the necessity of making future developments dependent upon the knowledge which particular people now possess. By sacrificing such possible present advantages, we preserve an important stimulus to further progress. Though in the short run the price we have to pay for variety and freedom of choice may sometimes be high, in the long run even material progress will depend on this very variety, because we can never predict from which of the many forms in which a good or service can be provided something better may develop. It cannot, of course, be asserted that the preservation of freedom at the expense of some addition to our present material comfort will be thus rewarded in all instances. But the argument for freedom is precisely that we ought to leave room for the unforeseeable free growth. It applies, therefore, no less when, on the basis of our present knowledge, compulsion would seem to bring only advantages, and although in a particular instance it may actually do no harm.

In much of the current discussion on the effects of technological progress this progress is presented to us as if it were something outside us which could compel us to use the new knowledge in a particular way. While it is true, of course, that inventions have given us tremendous power, it is absurd to suggest that we must use this power to destroy our most precious inheritance: liberty. It does mean, however, that if we want to preserve it, we must guard it more jealously than ever and that we must be prepared to make sacrifices for it. While there is nothing in modern technological developments which forces us toward comprehensive economic planning, there is a great deal in them which makes infinitely more dangerous the power a planning authority would possess.

While there can thus be little doubt that the movement toward planning is the result of deliberate action and that there are no external necessities which force us to it, it is worth inquiring why so large a proportion of the technical experts

97

should be found in the front rank of the planners. The explanation of this phenomenon is closely connected with an important fact which the critics of the
planners should always keep in mind: that there is little question that almost
every one of the technical ideals of our experts could be realized within a comparatively short time if to achieve them were made the sole aim of humanity.
There is an infinite number of good things, which we all agree are highly desirable as well as possible, but of which we cannot hope to achieve more than a
few within our lifetime, or which we can hope to achieve only very imperfectly.
It is the frustration of his ambitions in his own field which makes the specialist
revolt against the existing order. We all find it difficult to bear to see things left
undone which everybody must admit are both desirable and possible. That
these things cannot all be done at the same time, that any one of them can be
achieved only at the sacrifice of others, can be seen only by taking into account
factors which fall outside any specialism, which can be appreciated only by a
painful intellectual effort—the more painful as it forces us to see against a wider
background the objects to which most of our labors are directed and to balance
them against others which lie outside our immediate interest and for which, for
that reason, we care less.

Every one of the many things which, considered in isolation, it would be possible to achieve in a planned society creates enthusiasts for planning who feel
confident that they will be able to instill into the directors of such a society their
sense of the value of the particular objective; and the hopes of some of them
would undoubtedly be fulfilled, since a planned society would certainly further
some objectives more than is the case at present. It would be foolish to deny
that the instances of planned or semiplanned societies which we know do furnish illustrations in point, good things which the people of these countries owe
entirely to planning. The magnificent motor roads in Germany and Italy are
an instance often quoted—even though they do not represent a kind of planning not equally possible in a liberal society. But it is equally foolish to quote
such instances of technical excellence in particular fields as evidence of the
general superiority of planning. It would be more correct to say that such extreme technical excellence out of line with general conditions is evidence of a
misdirection of resources. Anyone who has driven along the famous German
motor roads and found the amount of traffic on them less than on many a secondary road in England can have little doubt that, so far as peace purposes
are concerned, there was little justification for them. Whether it was not a case
where the planners decided in favor of "guns" instead of "butter" is another
matter.[8] But by our standards there is little ground for enthusiasm.

The illusion of the specialist that in a planned society he would secure more

[8]But as I am correcting this the news comes that maintenance work on the German motor roads
has been suspended!

attention to the objectives for which he cares most is a more general phenomenon than the term "specialist" at first suggests. In our predilections and interests we are all in some measure specialists. And we all think that our personal order of values is not merely personal but that in a free discussion among rational people we would convince the others that ours is the right one. The lover of the countryside who wants above all that its traditional appearance should be preserved and that the blots already made by industry on its fair face should be removed, no less than the health enthusiast who wants all the picturesque but unsanitary old cottages cleared away, or the motorist who wishes the country cut up by big motor roads, the efficiency fanatic who desires the maximum of specialization and mechanization no less than the idealist who for the development of personality wants to preserve as many independent craftsmen as possible, all know that their aim can be fully achieved only by planning—and they all want planning for that reason. But, of course, the adoption of the social planning for which they clamor can only bring out the concealed conflict between their aims.

The movement for planning owes its present strength largely to the fact that, while planning is in the main still an ambition, it unites almost all the single-minded idealists, all the men and women who have devoted their lives to a single task. The hopes they place in planning, however, are the result not of a comprehensive view of society but rather of a very limited view and often the result of a great exaggeration of the importance of the ends they place foremost. This is not to underrate the great pragmatic value of this type of men in a free society like ours, which makes them the subject of just admiration. But it would make the very men who are most anxious to plan society the most dangerous if they were allowed to do so—and the most intolerant of the planning of others. From the saintly and single-minded idealist to the fanatic is often but a step. Though it is the resentment of the frustrated specialist which gives the demand for planning its strongest impetus, there could hardly be a more unbearable—and more irrational—world than one in which the most eminent specialists in each field were allowed to proceed unchecked with the realization of their ideals. Nor can "coordination," as some planners seem to imagine, become a new specialism. The economist is the last to claim that he has the knowledge which the coordinator would need. His plea is for a method which effects such coordination without the need for an omniscient dictator. But that means precisely the retention of some such impersonal, and often unintelligible, checks on individual efforts as those against which all specialists chafe.

FIVE

PLANNING AND DEMOCRACY

> The statesman who should attempt to direct private people in what manner
> they ought to employ their capitals, would not only load himself with a most
> unnecessary attention, but assume an authority which could safely be trusted
> to no council and senate whatever, and which would nowhere be so danger-
> ous as in the hands of a man who had folly and presumption enough to fancy
> himself fit to exercise it. —Adam Smith[1]

The common features of all collectivist systems may be described, in a phrase
ever dear to socialists of all schools, as the deliberate organization of the labors
of society for a definite social goal. That our present society lacks such "conscious" direction toward a single aim, that its activities are guided by the whims
and fancies of irresponsible individuals, has always been one of the main complaints of its socialist critics.

In many ways this puts the basic issue very clearly. And it directs us at once
to the point where the conflict arises between individual freedom and collectivism. The various kinds of collectivism, communism, fascism, etc., differ
among themselves in the nature of the goal toward which they want to direct
the efforts of society. But they all differ from liberalism and individualism in
wanting to organize the whole of society and all its resources for this unitary
end and in refusing to recognize autonomous spheres in which the ends of the
individuals are supreme. In short, they are totalitarian in the true sense of this
new word which we have adopted to describe the unexpected but nevertheless
inseparable manifestations of what in theory we call collectivism.

The "social goal," or "common purpose," for which society is to be organized is usually vaguely described as the "common good," the "general welfare,"
or the "general interest." It does not need much reflection to see that these
terms have no sufficiently definite meaning to determine a particular course

---

[1] [Adam Smith, *An Inquiry into the Nature and Causes of the Wealth of Nations*, ed. R. H. Campbell
and A. S. Skinner, vol. 1 of *The Glasgow Edition of the Works and Correspondence of Adam Smith*, op. cit.,
book 4, chapter 2, p. 456. —Ed.]

of action. The welfare and the happiness of millions cannot be measured on a single scale of less and more. The welfare of a people, like the happiness of a man, depends on a great many things that can be provided in an infinite variety of combinations. It cannot be adequately expressed as a single end, but only as a hierarchy of ends, a comprehensive scale of values in which every need of every person is given its place. To direct all our activities according to a single plan presupposes that every one of our needs is given its rank in an order of values which must be complete enough to make it possible to decide among all the different courses which the planner has to choose. It presupposes, in short, the existence of a complete ethical code in which all the different human values are allotted their due place.

The conception of a complete ethical code is unfamiliar, and it requires some effort of imagination to see what it involves. We are not in the habit of thinking of moral codes as more or less complete. The fact that we are constantly choosing between different values without a social code prescribing how we ought to choose does not surprise us and does not suggest to us that our moral code is incomplete. In our society there is neither occasion nor reason why people should develop common views about what should be done in such situations. But where all the means to be used are the property of society and are to be used in the name of society according to a unitary plan, a "social" view about what ought to be done must guide all decisions. In such a world we should soon find that our moral code is full of gaps.

We are not concerned here with the question whether it would be desirable to have such a complete ethical code. It may merely be pointed out that up to the present the growth of civilization has been accompanied by a steady diminution of the sphere in which individual actions are bound by fixed rules. The rules of which our common moral code consists have progressively become fewer and more general in character. From the primitive man, who was bound by an elaborate ritual in almost every one of his daily activities, who was limited by innumerable taboos, and who could scarcely conceive of doing things in a way different from his fellows, morals have more and more tended to become merely limits circumscribing the sphere within which the individual could behave as he liked. The adoption of a common ethical code comprehensive enough to determine a unitary economic plan would mean a complete reversal of this tendency.

The essential point for us is that no such complete ethical code exists. The attempt to direct all economic activity according to a single plan would raise innumerable questions to which the answer could be provided only by a moral rule, but to which existing morals have no answer and where there exists no agreed view on what ought to be done. People will have either no definite views or conflicting views on such questions, because in the free society in which we have lived there has been no occasion to think about them and still less to form common opinions about them.

Not only do we not possess such an all-inclusive scale of values: it would be impossible for any mind to comprehend the infinite variety of different needs of different people which compete for the available resources and to attach a definite weight to each. For our problem it is of minor importance whether the ends for which any person cares comprehend only his own individual needs, or whether they include the needs of his closer or even those of his more distant fellows—that is, whether he is egoistic or altruistic in the ordinary senses of these words. The point which is so important is the basic fact that it is impossible for any man to survey more than a limited field, to be aware of the urgency of more than a limited number of needs. Whether his interests center round his own physical needs, or whether he takes a warm interest in the welfare of every human being he knows, the ends about which he can be concerned will always be only an infinitesimal fraction of the needs of all men.

This is the fundamental fact on which the whole philosophy of individualism is based. It does not assume, as is often asserted, that man is egoistic or selfish or ought to be. It merely starts from the indisputable fact that the limits of our powers of imagination make it impossible to include in our scale of values more than a sector of the needs of the whole society, and that, since, strictly speaking, scales of value can exist only in individual minds, nothing but partial scales of values exist—scales which are inevitably different and often inconsistent with each other. From this the individualist concludes that the individuals should be allowed, within defined limits, to follow their own values and preferences rather than somebody else's; that within these spheres the individual's system of ends should be supreme and not subject to any dictation by others. It is this recognition of the individual as the ultimate judge of his ends, the belief that as far as possible his own views ought to govern his actions, that forms the essence of the individualist position.

This view does not, of course, exclude the recognition of social ends, or rather of a coincidence of individual ends which makes it advisable for men to combine for their pursuit. But it limits such common action to the instances where individual views coincide; what are called "social ends" are for it merely identical ends of many individuals—or ends to the achievement of which individuals are willing to contribute in return for the assistance they receive in the satisfaction of their own desires. Common action is thus limited to the fields where people agree on common ends. Very frequently these common ends will not be ultimate ends to the individuals but means which different persons can use for different purposes. In fact, people are most likely to agree on common action where the common end is not an ultimate end to them but a means capable of serving a great variety of purposes.

When individuals combine in a joint effort to realize ends they have in common, the organizations, like the state, that they form for this purpose are given their own system of ends and their own means. But any organization thus formed remains one "person" among others, in the case of the state much more powerful than any of the others, it is true, yet still with its separate and limited sphere in which alone its ends are supreme. The limits of this sphere are determined by the extent to which the individuals agree on particular ends; and the probability that they will agree on a particular course of action necessarily decreases as the scope of such action extends. There are certain functions of the state on the exercise of which there will be practical unanimity among its citizens; there will be others on which there will be agreement of a substantial majority; and so on, until we come to fields where, although each individual might wish the state to act in some way, there will be almost as many views about what the government should do as there are different people.

We can rely on voluntary agreement to guide the action of the state only so long as it is confined to spheres where agreement exists. But not only when the state undertakes direct control in fields where there is no such agreement is it bound to suppress individual freedom. We can unfortunately not indefinitely extend the sphere of common action and still leave the individual free in his own sphere. Once the communal sector, in which the state controls all the means, exceeds a certain proportion of the whole, the effects of its actions dominate the whole system. Although the state controls directly the use of only a large part of the available resources, the effects of its decisions on the remaining part of the economic system become so great that indirectly it controls almost everything. Where, as was, for example, true in Germany as early as 1928, the central and local authorities directly control the use of more than half the national income (according to an official German estimate then, 53 per cent),[2] they control indirectly almost the whole economic life of the nation. There is, then, scarcely an individual end which is not dependent for its achievement on the action of the state, and the "social scale of values" which guides the state's action must embrace practically all individual ends.

It is not difficult to see what must be the consequences when democracy embarks upon a course of planning which in its execution requires more agreement than in fact exists. The people may have agreed on adopting a system of directed economy because they have been convinced that it will produce great prosperity. In the discussions leading to the decision, the goal of planning will have been described by some such term as "common welfare," which only con-

---

[2] [In 1927 Hayek became the first director of the newly formed Austrian Institute for Business Cycle Research (*Österreichisches Institut für Konjunkturforschung*); one of his tasks was to collect economic data of the sort he reports on here. —Ed.]

ceals the absence of real agreement on the ends of planning. Agreement will in fact exist only on the mechanism to be used. But it is a mechanism which can be used only for a common end; and the question of the precise goal toward which all activity is to be directed will arise as soon as the executive power has to translate the demand for a single plan into a particular plan. Then it will appear that the agreement on the desirability of planning is not supported by agreement on the ends the plan is to serve. The effect of the people's agreeing that there must be central planning, without agreeing on the ends, will be rather as if a group of people were to commit themselves to take a journey together without agreeing where they want to go: with the result that they may all have to make a journey which most of them do not want at all. That planning creates a situation in which it is necessary for us to agree on a much larger number of topics than we have been used to, and that in a planned system we cannot confine collective action to the tasks on which we can agree but are forced to produce agreement on everything in order that any action can be taken at all, is one of the features which contributes more than most to determining the character of a planned system.

It may be the unanimously expressed will of the people that its parliament should prepare a comprehensive economic plan, yet neither the people nor its representatives need therefore be able to agree on any particular plan. The inability of democratic assemblies to carry out what seems to be a clear mandate of the people will inevitably cause dissatisfaction with democratic institutions. Parliaments come to be regarded as ineffective "talking shops," unable or incompetent to carry out the tasks for which they have been chosen. The conviction grows that if efficient planning is to be done, the direction must be "taken out of politics" and placed in the hands of experts—permanent officials or independent autonomous bodies.

The difficulty is well known to socialists. It will soon be half a century since the Webbs began to complain of "the increased incapacity of the House of Commons to cope with its work."[3] More recently, Professor Laski has elaborated the argument:

"It is common ground that the present parliamentary machine is quite unsuited to pass rapidly a great body of complicated legislation. The National Government, indeed, has in substance admitted this by implementing its economy and tariff measures not by detailed debate in the House of Commons but by a wholesale system of delegated legislation. A Labour Government would,

---

[3] Sidney and Beatrice Webb, *Industrial Democracy* (London, New York, Bombay and Calcutta: Longmans, Green and Co., 1897), p. 800 n. [English social reformers Sidney (1859–1947) and Beatrice (1858–1943) Webb were early members of the Fabian Society and cofounders of the London School of Economics. In the cited passage, the Webbs actually complained of the "increasing incapacity," rather than "increased incapacity," of the House of Commons to cope with its work. —Ed.]

I presume, build upon the amplitude of this precedent. It would confine the House of Commons to the two functions it can properly perform: the ventilation of grievances and the discussion of general principles of its measures. Its Bills would take the form of general formulae conferring wide powers on the appropriate government departments; and those powers would be exercised by Order in Council which could, if desired, be attacked in the House by means of a vote of no confidence. The necessity and value of delegated legislation has recently been strongly reaffirmed by the Donoughmore Committee; and its extension is inevitable if the process of socialisation is not to be wrecked by the normal methods of obstruction which existing parliamentary procedure sanctions."

And to make it quite clear that a socialist government must not allow itself to be too much fettered by democratic procedure, Professor Laski at the end of the same article raised the question "whether in a period of transition to Socialism, a Labour Government can risk the overthrow of its measures as a result of the next general election"—and left it significantly unanswered.[4]

It is important clearly to see the causes of this admitted ineffectiveness of parliaments when it comes to a detailed administration of the economic affairs of a nation. The fault is neither with the individual representatives nor with parliamentary institutions as such but with the contradictions inherent in the task with which they are charged. They are not asked to act where they can agree, but to produce agreement on everything—the whole direction of the resources of the nation. For such a task the system of majority decision is, however, not suited. Majorities will be found where it is a choice between limited alternatives; but it is a superstition to believe that there must be a majority view on everything. There is no reason why there should be a majority in favor of any one of the different possible courses of positive action if their number is legion. Every member of the legislative assembly might prefer some particular plan for

<hr />

[4]H. J. Laski, "Labour and the Constitution," *New Statesman and Nation, N.S.,* no. 81, September 10, 1932, p. 277. In a book *Democracy in Crisis* (Chapel Hill, NC: University of North Carolina Press, 1933), p. 87 in which Professor Laski later elaborated these ideas, his determination that parliamentary democracy must not be allowed to form an obstacle to the realization of socialism is even more plainly expressed: not only would a socialist government "take vast powers and legislate under them by ordinance and decree" and "suspend the classic formulae of normal opposition" but the "continuance of parliamentary government would depend on its [i.e., the Labour government's] possession of guarantees from the Conservative Party that its work of transformation would not be disrupted by repeal in the event of its defeat at the polls"!

As Professor Laski invokes the authority of the Donoughmore Committee, it may be worth recalling that Professor Laski was a member of that committee and presumably one of the authors of its report. [The Donoughmore Committee on Ministers' Powers was set up to investigate the implications of the expansion of delegated legislation; that is, legislation that is enacted by ministers in order to carry out primary legislation that is passed by Parliament. Hayek makes further reference to its findings in the next note. —Ed.]

the direction of economic activity to no plan, yet no one plan may appear preferable to a majority to no plan at all.

Nor can a coherent plan be achieved by breaking it up into parts and voting on particular issues. A democratic assembly voting and amending a comprehensive economic plan clause by clause, as it deliberates on an ordinary bill, makes nonsense. An economic plan, to deserve the name, must have a unitary conception. Even if a parliament could, proceeding step by step, agree on some scheme, it would certainly in the end satisfy nobody. A complex whole in which all the parts must be most carefully adjusted to each other cannot be achieved through a compromise between conflicting views. To draw up an economic plan in this fashion is even less possible than, for example, successfully to plan a military campaign by democratic procedure. As in strategy it would become inevitable to delegate the task to the experts.

Yet the difference is that, while the general who is put in charge of a campaign is given a single end to which, for the duration of the campaign, all the means under his control have to be exclusively devoted, there can be no such single goal given to the economic planner, and no similar limitation of the means imposed upon him. The general has not got to balance different independent aims against each other; there is for him only one supreme goal. But the ends of an economic plan, or of any part of it, cannot be defined apart from the particular plan. It is the essence of the economic problem that the making of an economic plan involves the choice between conflicting or competing ends—different needs of different people. But which ends do so conflict, which will have to be sacrificed if we want to achieve certain others, in short, which are the alternatives between which we must choose, can only be known to those who know all the facts; and only they, the experts, are in a position to decide which of the different ends are to be given preference. It is inevitable that they should impose their scale of preferences on the community for which they plan.

This is not always clearly recognized, and delegation is usually justified by the technical character of the task. But this does not mean that only the technical detail is delegated, or even that the inability of parliaments to understand the technical detail is the root of the difficulty.[5] Alterations in the structure of

[5] It is instructive in this connection briefly to refer to the government document in which in recent years these problems have been discussed. As long as thirteen years ago, that is before England finally abandoned economic liberalism, the process of delegating legislative powers had already been carried to a point where it was felt necessary to appoint a committee to investigate "what safeguards are desirable or necessary to secure the sovereignty of Law." In its report the Donoughmore Committee (*Report of the [Lord Chancellor's] Committee in Ministers' Powers*, Cmd. 4060 [1932]) showed that even at that date Parliament had resorted "to the practice of wholesale and indiscriminate delegation" but regarded this (it was before we had really glanced into the totalitarian abyss!) as an inevitably and relatively innocuous development. And it is probably true that delegation as such need not be a danger to freedom. The interesting point is why delegation had

civil law are no less technical and no more difficult to appreciate in all their implications; yet nobody has yet seriously suggested that legislation there should be delegated to a body of experts. The fact is that in these fields legislation does not go beyond general rules on which true majority agreement can be achieved, while in the direction of economic activity the interests to be reconciled are so divergent that no true agreement is likely to be reached in a democratic assembly.

It should be recognized, however, that it is not the delegation of law-making power as such which is so objectionable. To oppose delegation as such is to oppose a symptom instead of the cause and, as it may be a necessary result of other causes, to weaken the case. So long as the power that is delegated is merely the power to make general rules, there may be very good reasons why such rules should be laid down by local rather than by the central authority. The objectionable feature is that delegation is so often resorted to because the matter in hand cannot be regulated by general rules but only by the exercise of discretion in the decision of particular cases. In these instances delegation means that some authority is given power to make with the force of law what to all intents and purposes are arbitrary decisions (usually described as "judging the case on its merits").

The delegation of particular technical tasks to separate bodies, while a regular feature, is yet only the first step in the process whereby a democracy which embarks on planning progressively relinquishes its powers. The expedient of delegation cannot really remove the causes which make all the advocates of comprehensive planning so impatient with the impotence of democracy. The delegation of particular powers to separate agencies creates a new obstacle to the achievement of a single coordinated plan. Even if, by this expedient, a democracy should succeed in planning every sector of economic activity, it would still have to face the problem of integrating these separate plans into a unitary whole. Many separate plans do not make a planned whole—in fact, as the planners ought to be the first to admit, they may be worse than no plan. But the democratic legislature will long hesitate to relinquish the decisions on really vital issues, and so long as it does so it makes it impossible for anyone

---

become necessary on such a scale. First place among the causes enumerated in the report is given to the fact that "Parliament nowadays passes so many laws every year" and that "much of the detail is so technical as to be unsuitable for Parliamentary discussion." But if this were all there would be no reason why the detail should not be worked out *before* rather than after Parliament passes a law. What is probably in many cases a much more important reason why, "if Parliament were not willing to delegate law-making power, Parliament would be unable to pass the kind and quantity of legislation which public opinion requires" is innocently revealed in the little sentence that "many of the laws affect people's lives so closely that elasticity is essential"! What does this mean if not conferment of arbitrary power—power limited by no fixed principles and which in the opinion of Parliament cannot be limited by definite and unambiguous rules?

else to provide the comprehensive plan. Yet agreement that planning is necessary, together with the inability of democratic assemblies to produce a plan, will evoke stronger and stronger demands that the government or some single individual should be given powers to act on their own responsibility. The belief is becoming more and more widespread that, if things are to get done, the responsible authorities must be freed from the fetters of democratic procedure.

The cry for an economic dictator is a characteristic stage in the movement toward planning. It is now several years since one of the most acute of foreign students of England, the late Élie Halévy, suggested that, "if you take a composite photograph of Lord Eustace Percy, Sir Oswald Mosley, and Sir Stafford Cripps, I think you would find this common feature—you would find them all agreeing to say: 'We are living in economic chaos and we cannot get out of it except under some kind of dictatorial leadership.'"[6] The number of influential public men whose inclusion would not materially alter the features of the "composite photograph" has since grown considerably.

In Germany, even before Hitler came into power, the movement had already progressed much further. It is important to remember that, for some time before 1933, Germany had reached a stage in which it had, in effect, had to be governed dictatorially. Nobody could then doubt that for the time being democracy had broken down and that sincere democrats like Brüning were no more able to govern democratically than Schleicher or von Papen.[7] Hitler did not have to destroy democracy; he merely took advantage of the decay of democracy and at the critical moment obtained the support of many to whom,

[6]Élie Halévy, "Socialism and the Problem of Democratic Parliamentarianism," *International Affairs*, vol. 13, July 1934, p. 501. [The article was an address given on April 24, 1934, at Chatham House, which since 1920 has been the base for the Royal Institute of International Affairs. French historian Élie Halévy (1870–1937) was the author of *The Growth of Philosophical Radicalism*, which traced the emergence of British utilitarianism, and *The Era of Tyrannies*, from which Hayek drew the opening quotation that begins chapter 3. English statesman Lord Eustace Percy (1887–1958) wrote such books as *Democracy on Trial* and *The Heresy of Democracy*. English politician Sir Oswald Mosley (1896–1980) began as a conservative, then switched to the Labour party, becoming an MP and a member of the 1929 Labour government, and finally resigned to become the leader of the British Union of Fascists. Labour politician Sir Stafford Cripps (1889–1952) veered increasingly to the left in the 1930s, and was ultimately ousted from the party in 1939 for his activities with the Popular Front. Percy, Mosley, and Cripps, then, represented different ends of the political spectrum, yet as Hayek and Halévy noted, they had on certain issues expressed very similar views. —Ed.]

[7][German statesman Heinrich Brüning (1885–1970) was the chancellor of Germany from 1930 to 1932, when he was forced to resign by the Nazis. He left Germany two years later. Franz von Papen (1879–1969) took over as chancellor in 1932, and under Hitler served briefly as vice-chancellor, and later as ambassador to Austria and to Turkey. Kurt von Schleicher (1882–1934) succeeded von Papen as chancellor, but Hitler seized power from him in 1933. He and his wife were tried on trumped up charges and executed by the Nazis the next year. —Ed.]

though they detested Hitler, he yet seemed the only man strong enough to get things done.

The argument by which the planners usually try to reconcile us with this development is that, so long as democracy retains ultimate control, the essentials of democracy are not affected. Thus Karl Mannheim writes:

"The only [*sic*] way in which a planned society differs from that of the nineteenth century is that more and more spheres of social life, and ultimately each and all of them, are subjected to state control. But if a few controls can be held in check by parliamentary sovereignty, so can many. . . . In a democratic state sovereignty can be boundlessly strengthened by plenary powers without renouncing democratic control."[8]

This belief overlooks a vital distinction. Parliament can, of course, control the execution of tasks where it can give definite directions, where it has first agreed on the aim and merely delegates the working-out of the detail. The situation is entirely different when the reason for the delegation is that there is no real agreement on the ends, when the body charged with the planning has to choose between ends of whose conflict parliament is not even aware, and when the most that can be done is to present to it a plan which has to be accepted or rejected as a whole. There may and probably will be criticism; but as no majority can agree on an alternative plan, and the parts objected to can almost always be represented as essential parts of the whole, it will remain quite ineffective. Parliamentary discussion may be retained as a useful safety valve and even more as a convenient medium through which the official answers to complaints are disseminated. It may even prevent some flagrant abuses and successfully insist on particular shortcomings being remedied. But it cannot direct. It will at best be reduced to choosing the persons who are to have practically absolute power. The whole system will tend toward that plebiscitarian dictatorship in which the head of the government is from time to time confirmed in his position by popular vote, but where he has all the powers at his command to make certain that the vote will go in the direction he desires.

It is the price of democracy that the possibilities of conscious control are restricted to the fields where true agreement exists and that in some fields things must be left to chance. But in a society which for its functioning depends on central planning this control cannot be made dependent on a majority's being able to agree; it will often be necessary that the will of a small minority be imposed upon the people, because this minority will be the largest group able to agree among themselves on the question at issue. Democratic government has

---

[8]Mannheim, *Man and Society in an Age of Reconstruction*, op. cit., p. 340. [The second half of the quotation appears on page 341. —Ed.]

worked successfully where, and so long as, the functions of government were, by a widely accepted creed, restricted to fields where agreement among a majority could be achieved by free discussion; and it is the great merit of the liberal creed that it reduced the range of subjects on which agreement was necessary to one on which it was likely to exist in a society of free men. It is now often said that democracy will not tolerate "capitalism." If "capitalism" means here a competitive system based on free disposal over private property, it is far more important to realize that only within this system is democracy possible. When it becomes dominated by a collectivist creed, democracy will inevitably destroy itself.

We have no intention, however, of making a fetish of democracy. It may well be true that our generation talks and thinks too much of democracy and too little of the values which it serves. It cannot be said of democracy, as Lord Acton truly said of liberty, that it "is not a means to a higher political end. It is itself the highest political end. It is not for the sake of a good public administration that it is required, but for the security in the pursuit of the highest objects of civil society, and of private life."[9] Democracy is essentially a means, a utilitarian device for safeguarding internal peace and individual freedom. As such it is by no means infallible or certain. Nor must we forget that there has often been much more cultural and spiritual freedom under an autocratic rule than under some democracies—and it is at least conceivable that under the government of a very homogeneous and doctrinaire majority democratic government might be as oppressive as the worst dictatorship. Our point, however, is not that dictatorship must inevitably extirpate freedom but rather that planning leads to dictatorship because dictatorship is the most effective instrument of coercion and the enforcement of ideals and, as such, essential if central planning on a large scale is to be possible. The clash between planning and democracy arises simply from the fact that the latter is an obstacle to the suppression of freedom which the direction of economic activity requires. But in so far as democracy ceases to be a guaranty of individual freedom, it may well persist in some form under a totalitarian regime. A true "dictatorship of the proletariat," even if democratic in form, if it undertook centrally to direct the economic system, would probably destroy personal freedom as completely as any autocracy has ever done.

The fashionable concentration on democracy as the main value threatened is not without danger. It is largely responsible for the misleading and unfounded belief that, so long as the ultimate source of power is the will of the majority, the power cannot be arbitrary. The false assurance which many people derive from this belief is an important cause of the general unawareness of the dangers

---

[9][Lord Acton, "The History of Freedom in Antiquity," op. cit., p. 22. —Ed.]

which we face. There is no justification for the belief that, so long as power is conferred by democratic procedure, it cannot be arbitrary; the contrast suggested by this statement is altogether false: it is not the source but the limitation of power which prevents it from being arbitrary. Democratic control *may* prevent power from becoming arbitrary, but it does not do so by its mere existence. If democracy resolves on a task which necessarily involves the use of power which cannot be guided by fixed rules, it must become arbitrary power.

SIX

PLANNING AND THE RULE OF LAW

> Recent studies in the sociology of law once more confirm that the fundamental principle of formal law by which every case must be judged according to general rational precepts, which have as few exceptions as possible and are based on logical subsumptions, obtains only for the liberal competitive phase of capitalism. —Karl Mannheim[1]

Nothing distinguishes more clearly conditions in a free country from those in a country under arbitrary government than the observance in the former of the great principles known as the Rule of Law. Stripped of all technicalities, this means that government in all its actions is bound by rules fixed and announced beforehand—rules which make it possible to foresee with fair certainty how the authority will use its coercive powers in given circumstances and to plan one's individual affairs on the basis of this knowledge.[2] Though this ideal can never be perfectly achieved, since legislators as well as those to whom the administration of the law is entrusted are fallible men, the essential point, that the discretion left to the executive organs wielding coercive power should be reduced as much as possible, is clear enough. While every law restricts individual freedom to some extent by altering the means which people may use in the pursuit of their aims, under the Rule of Law the government is prevented from stultifying individual efforts by *ad hoc* action. Within the known rules of the game

---

[1] [Karl Mannheim, *Man and Society in an Age of Reconstruction*, op. cit., p. 180. —Ed.]

[2] According to the classical exposition by A. V. Dicey in *Introduction to the Study of the Law of the Constitution*, 8th ed. (London: Macmillan and Co., 1915), p. 198, the Rule of Law "means, in the first place, the absolute supremacy or predominance of regular law as opposed to the influence of arbitrary power, and excludes the existence of arbitrariness, of prerogative, or even of wide discretionary authority on the part of government." Largely as a result of Dicey's work the term has, however, in England acquired a narrower technical meaning which does not concern us here. The wider and older meaning of the concept of the rule or reign of law, which in England had become an established tradition which was more taken for granted than discussed, has been most fully elaborated, just because it raised what were new problems there, in the early nineteenth-century discussion in Germany about the nature of the *Rechtsstaat*. [For more on the latter tradition, see F. A. Hayek, *The Constitution of Liberty*, op. cit., chapter 13. —Ed.]

the individual is free to pursue his personal ends and desires, certain that the powers of government will not be used deliberately to frustrate his efforts.

The distinction we have drawn before between the creation of a permanent framework of laws within which the productive activity is guided by individual decisions and the direction of economic activity by a central authority is thus really a particular case of the more general distinction between the Rule of Law and arbitrary government. Under the first the government confines itself to fixing rules determining the conditions under which the available resources may be used, leaving to the individuals the decision for what ends they are to be used. Under the second the government directs the use of the means of production to particular ends. The first type of rules can be made in advance, in the shape of *formal rules* which do not aim at the wants and needs of particular people. They are intended to be merely instrumental in the pursuit of people's various individual ends. And they are, or ought to be, intended for such long periods that it is impossible to know whether they will assist particular people more than others. They could almost be described as a kind of instrument of production, helping people to predict the behavior of those with whom they must collaborate, rather than as efforts toward the satisfaction of particular needs.

Economic planning of the collectivist kind necessarily involves the very opposite of this. The planning authority cannot confine itself to providing opportunities for unknown people to make whatever use of them they like. It cannot tie itself down in advance to general and formal rules which prevent arbitrariness. It must provide for the actual needs of people as they arise and then choose deliberately between them. It must constantly decide questions which cannot be answered by formal principles only, and, in making these decisions, it must set up distinctions of merit between the needs of different people. When the government has to decide how many pigs are to be raised or how many busses are to be run, which coal mines are to operate, or at what prices shoes are to be sold, these decisions cannot be deduced from formal principles or settled for long periods in advance. They depend inevitably on the circumstances of the moment, and, in making such decisions, it will always be necessary to balance one against the other the interests of various persons and groups. In the end somebody's views will have to decide whose interests are more important; and these views must become part of the law of the land, a new distinction of rank which the coercive apparatus of government imposes upon the people.

The distinction we have just used between formal law or justice and substantive rules is very important and at the same time most difficult to draw precisely in practice. Yet the general principle involved is simple enough. The difference between the two kinds of rules is the same as that between laying down a Rule of the Road, as in the Highway Code, and ordering people where to go; or, better still, between providing signposts and commanding people which road to take. The formal rules tell people in advance what action the state will take in certain types of situation, defined in general terms, without reference to time and place or particular people. They refer to typical situations into which anyone may get and in which the existence of such rules will be useful for a great variety of individual purposes. The knowledge that in such situations the state will act in a definite way, or require people to behave in a certain manner, is provided as a means for people to use in making their own plans. Formal rules are thus merely instrumental in the sense that they are expected to be useful to yet unknown people, for purposes for which these people will decide to use for them, and in circumstances which cannot be foreseen in detail. In fact, that we do *not* know their concrete effect, that we do *not* know what particular ends these rules will further, or which particular people they will assist, that they are merely given the form most likely on the whole to benefit all the people affected by them, is the most important criterion of formal rules in the sense in which we here use this term. They do not involve a choice between particular ends or particular people, because we just cannot know beforehand by whom and in what way they will be used.

In our age, with its passion for conscious control of everything, it may appear paradoxical to claim as a virtue that under one system we shall know less about the particular effect of the measures the state takes than would be true under most other systems and that a method of social control should be deemed superior because of our ignorance of its precise results. Yet this consideration is in fact the rationale of the great liberal principle of the Rule of Law. And the apparent paradox dissolves rapidly when we follow the argument a little further.

This argument is twofold; the first is economic and can here only briefly be stated. The state should confine itself to establishing rules applying to general types of situations and should allow the individuals freedom in everything which depends on the circumstances of time and place, because only the individuals concerned in each instance can fully know these circumstances and adapt their actions to them. If the individuals are to be able to use their knowledge effectively in making plans, they must be able to predict actions of the state which may affect these plans. But if the actions of the state are to be predictable, they must be determined by rules fixed independently of the concrete circumstances which can be neither foreseen nor taken into account beforehand: and the particular effects of such actions will be unpredictable. If, on the other hand, the state were to direct the individual's actions so as to achieve particular ends, its action would have to be decided on the basis of the full circumstances of the moment and would therefore be unpredictable. Hence the familiar fact that the more the state "plans," the more difficult planning becomes for the individual.

The second, moral or political, argument is even more directly relevant to the point under discussion. If the state is precisely to foresee the incidence of its actions, it means that it can leave those affected no choice. Wherever the state can exactly foresee the effects on particular people of alternative courses of action, it is also the state which chooses between the different ends. If we want to create new opportunities open to all, to offer chances of which people can make what use they like, the precise results cannot be foreseen. General rules, genuine laws as distinguished from specific orders, must therefore be intended to operate in circumstances which cannot be foreseen in detail, and, therefore, their effect on particular ends or particular people cannot be known beforehand. It is in this sense alone that it is at all possible for the legislator to be impartial. To be impartial means to have no answer to certain questions—to the kind of questions which, if we have to decide them, we decide by tossing a coin. In a world where everything was precisely foreseen, the state could hardly do anything and remain impartial.

Where the precise effects of government policy on particular people are known, where the government aims directly at such particular effects, it cannot help knowing these effects, and therefore it cannot be impartial. It must, of necessity, take sides, impose its valuations upon people and, instead of assisting them in the advancement of their own ends, choose the ends for them. As soon as the particular effects are foreseen at the time a law is made, it ceases to be a mere instrument to be used by the people and becomes instead an instrument used by the lawgiver upon the people and for his ends. The state ceases to be a piece of utilitarian machinery intended to help individuals in the fullest development of their individual personality and becomes a "moral" institution—where "moral" is not used in contrast to immoral but describes an institution which imposes on its members its views on all moral questions, whether these views be moral or highly immoral. In this sense the Nazi or any other collectivist state is "moral," while the liberal state is not.

Perhaps it will be said that all this raises no serious problem because in the kind of questions which the economic planner would have to decide he need not and should not be guided by his individual prejudices but could rely on the general conviction of what is fair and reasonable. This contention usually receives support from those who have experience of planning in a particular industry and who find that there is no insuperable difficulty about arriving at a decision which all those immediately interested will accept as fair. The reason why this experience proves nothing is, of course, the selection of the "interests" concerned when planning is confined to a particular industry. Those most immediately interested in a particular issue are not necessarily the best judges of the interests of society as a whole. To take only the most characteristic case: when capital and labor in an industry agree on some policy of restriction and thus exploit the consumers, there is usually no difficulty about the division of the spoils in proportion to former earnings or on some similar principle. The loss which is divided between thousands or millions is usually either simply disregarded or quite inadequately considered. If we want to test the usefulness of the principle of "fairness" in deciding the kind of issues which arise in economic planning, we must apply it to some question where the gains and the losses are seen equally clearly. In such instances it is readily recognized that no general principle such as fairness can provide an answer. When we have to choose between higher wages for nurses or doctors and more extensive services for the sick, more milk for children and better wages for agricultural workers, or between employment for the unemployed or better wages for those already employed, nothing short of a complete system of values in which every want of every person or group has a definite place is necessary to provide an answer.

In fact, as planning becomes more and more extensive, it becomes regularly necessary to qualify legal provisions increasingly by reference to what is "fair" or "reasonable"; this means that it becomes necessary to leave the decision of the concrete case more and more to the discretion of the judge or authority in question. One could write a history of the decline of the Rule of Law, the disappearance of the *Rechtsstaat,* in terms of the progressive introduction of these vague formulas into legislation and jurisdiction, and of the increasing arbitrariness and uncertainty of, and the consequent disrespect for, the law and the judicature, which in these circumstances could not but become an instrument of policy.[3] It is important to point out once more in this connection that this process of the decline of the Rule of Law had been going on steadily in Germany for some time before Hitler came into power and that a policy well advanced toward totalitarian planning had already done a great deal of the work which Hitler completed.

There can be no doubt that planning necessarily involves deliberate discrimination between particular needs of different people, and allowing one man to do what another must be prevented from doing. It must lay down by a legal rule how well off particular people shall be and what different people are to be allowed to have and do. It means in effect a return to the rule of status, a reversal of the "movement of progressive societies" which, in the famous phrase of Sir Henry Maine, "has hitherto been a movement from status to contract."[4] Indeed, the Rule of Law, more than the rule of contract, should prob-

[3] [Hayek discusses the decline of the rule of law in *The Constitution of Liberty,* op. cit., chapter 16. —Ed.]

[4] [Sir Henry Maine, *Ancient Law: Its Connection with the Early History of Society and Its Relation to Modern Ideas.* Fourth American edition from the Tenth London edition. (New York: Henry Holt, 1906), p. 165. English jurist and historian Sir Henry Maine (1822–1888), from 1877 the Whewell professor of international law at Cambridge, wrote extensively on the origins and growth of legal and social institutions. The line is taken from the final sentence of chapter 5, titled "Primitive Society and Ancient Law." —Ed.]

ably be regarded as the true opposite of the rule of status. It is the Rule of Law, in the sense of the rule of formal law, the absence of legal privileges of particular people designated by authority, which safeguards that equality before the law which is the opposite of arbitrary government.

A necessary, and only apparently paradoxical, result of this is that formal equality before the law is in conflict, and in fact incompatible, with any activity of the government deliberately aiming at material or substantive equality of different people, and that any policy aiming directly at a substantive ideal of distributive justice must lead to the destruction of the Rule of Law. To produce the same result for different people, it is necessary to treat them differently. To give different people the same objective opportunities is not to give them the same subjective chance. It cannot be denied that the Rule of Law produces economic inequality—all that can be claimed for it is that this inequality is not designed to affect particular people in a particular way. It is very significant and characteristic that socialists (and Nazis) have always protested against "merely" formal justice, that they have always objected to a law which had no views on how well off particular people ought to be,[5] and that they have always demanded a "socialization of the law," attacked the independence of judges, and at the same time given their support to all such movements as the *Freirechtsschule* which undermined the Rule of Law.

It may even be said that for the Rule of Law to be effective it is more important that there should be a rule applied always without exceptions than what this rule is. Often the content of the rule is indeed of minor importance, provided the same rule is universally enforced. To revert to a former example: it does not matter whether we all drive on the left- or on the right-hand side of the road so long as we all do the same. The important thing is that the rule enables us to predict other people's behavior correctly, and this requires that it should apply to all cases—even if in a particular instance we feel it to be unjust.

The conflict between formal justice and formal equality before the law, on the one hand, and the attempts to realize various ideals of substantive justice and equality, on the other, also accounts for the widespread confusion about the

[5] It is therefore not altogether false when the legal theorist of National Socialism, Carl Schmitt, opposes to the liberal *Rechtsstaat* (i.e., the Rule of Law) the National Socialist ideal of the *gerechte Staat* ("the just state")—only that the sort of justice which is opposed to formal justice necessarily implies discrimination between persons. [German jurist Carl Schmitt (1888–1985) was a critic of liberal parliamentarianism and defender of the authoritarian state. In the 1930s he attempted to reconcile his views with those of the Nazis, offering legal justifications of their takeover of the government and defending the Nuremberg Laws that excluded Jews from public and social life. Though he lost favor with the Nazis by 1936, outside of Germany he was often viewed as the legal theorist of National Socialism. Hayek also refers to the *Freirechtsschule*, which is the German term for "legal realism," a doctrine that holds that instinct rather than rule-following is the actual basis of judicial interpretation of the law. —Ed.]

concept of "privilege" and its consequent abuse. To mention only the most important instance of this abuse—the application of the term "privilege" to property as such. It would indeed be privilege if, for example, as has sometimes been the case in the past, landed property were reserved to members of the nobility. And it is privilege if, as is true in our time, the right to produce or sell particular things is reserved to particular people designated by authority. But to call private property as such, which all can acquire under the same rules, a privilege, because only some succeed in acquiring it, is depriving the word "privilege" of its meaning.

The unpredictability of the particular effects, which is the distinguishing characteristic of the formal laws of a liberal system, is also important because it helps us to clear up another confusion about the nature of this system: the belief that its characteristic attitude is inaction of the state. The question whether the state should or should not "act" or "interfere" poses an altogether false alternative, and the term "laissez faire" is a highly ambiguous and misleading description of the principles on which a liberal policy is based. Of course, every state must act and every action of the state interferes with something or other. But that is not the point. The important question is whether the individual can foresee the action of the state and make use of this knowledge as a datum in forming his own plans, with the result that the state cannot control the use made of its machinery and that the individual knows precisely how far he will be protected against interference from others, or whether the state is in a position to frustrate individual efforts. The state controlling weights and measures (or preventing fraud and deception in any other way) is certainly acting, while the state permitting the use of violence, for example, by strike pickets, is inactive. Yet it is in the first case that the state observes liberal principles and in the second that it does not. Similarly with respect to most of the general and permanent rules which the state may establish with regard to production, such as building regulations or factory laws: these may be wise or unwise in the particular instance, but they do not conflict with liberal principles so long as they are intended to be permanent and are not used to favor or harm particular people. It is true that in these instances there will, apart from the long-run effects which cannot be predicted, also be short-run effects on particular people which may be clearly known. But with this kind of laws the short-run effects are in general not (or at least ought not to be) the guiding consideration. As these immediate and predictable effects become more important compared with the long-run effects, we approach the border line where the distinction, however clear in principle, becomes blurred in practice.

The Rule of Law was consciously evolved only during the liberal age and is one of its greatest achievements, not only as a safeguard but as the legal embodiment of freedom. As Immanuel Kant put it (and Voltaire expressed it before him in very much the same terms), "Man is free if he needs to obey no person but solely the laws."[6] As a vague ideal it has, however, existed at least since Roman times, and during the last few centuries it has never been so seriously threatened as it is today. The idea that there is no limit to the powers of the legislator is in part a result of popular sovereignty and democratic government. It has been strengthened by the belief that, so long as all actions of the state are duly authorized by legislation, the Rule of Law will be preserved. But this is completely to misconceive the meaning of the Rule of Law. This rule has little to do with the question whether all actions of government are legal in the juridical sense. They may well be and yet not conform to the Rule of Law. The fact that someone has full legal authority to act in the way he does gives no answer to the question whether the law gives him power to act arbitrarily or whether the law prescribes unequivocally how he has to act. It may well be that Hitler has obtained his unlimited powers in a strictly constitutional manner and that whatever he does is therefore legal in the juridical sense. But who would suggest for that reason that the Rule of Law still prevails in Germany?

To say that in a planned society the Rule of Law cannot hold is, therefore, not to say that the actions of the government will not be legal or that such a society will necessarily be lawless. It means only that the use of the government's coercive powers will no longer be limited and determined by pre-established rules. The law can, and to make a central direction of economic activity possible must, legalize what to all intents and purposes remains arbitrary action. If the law says that such a board or authority may do what it pleases, anything that board or authority does is legal—but its actions are certainly not subject to the Rule of Law. By giving the government unlimited powers, the most arbitrary rule can be made legal; and in this way a democracy may set up the most complete despotism imaginable.[7]

---

[6] [I was unable to locate the quotation attributed to Kant, but for the other, Hayek refers to François Marie Arouet de Voltaire, *Oeuvres Complète de Voltaire*, vol. 23 (Paris: Garnier, 1879), p. 526, where Voltaire writes, "La liberté consiste à ne dépendre que des lois." —Ed.]

[7] The conflict is thus *not*, as it has often been misconceived in nineteenth century discussions, one between liberty and law. As John Locke had already made clear, there can be no liberty without law. The conflict is between different kinds of law—law so different that it should hardly be called by the same name: one is the law of the Rule of Law, general principles laid down beforehand, the "rules of the game" which enable individuals to foresee how the coercive apparatus of the state will be used, or what he and his fellow-citizens will be allowed to do, or made to do, in stated circumstances. The other kind of law gives in effect the authority power to do what it thinks fit to do. Thus the Rule of Law could clearly not be preserved in a democracy that undertook to decide every conflict of interests not according to rules previously laid down but "on its merits." [Locke described the state of nature as "a state of perfect freedom." He went on to say, however, that men form civil societies and submit themselves to laws in order better to preserve their liberty and property. See John Locke, *Two Treatises of Government*, ed. Peter Laslett (Cambridge: Cambridge University Press, 1988), Treatise 2, chapters 4, 9. —Ed.]

If, however, the law is to enable authorities to direct economic life, it must give them powers to make and enforce decisions in circumstances which cannot be foreseen and on principles which cannot be stated in generic form. The consequence is that, as planning extends, the delegation of legislative powers to diverse boards and authorities becomes increasingly common. When before the last war, in a case to which the late Lord Hewart has recently drawn attention, Mr. Justice Darling said that "Parliament had enacted only last year that the Board of Agriculture in acting as they did should be no more impeachable than Parliament itself," this was still a rare thing.[8] It has since become an almost daily occurrence. Constantly the broadest powers are conferred on new authorities which, without being bound by fixed rules, have almost unlimited discretion in regulating this or that activity of the people.

The Rule of Law thus implies limits to the scope of legislation: it restricts it to the kind of general rules known as formal law and excludes legislation either directly aimed at particular people or at enabling anybody to use the coercive power of the state for the purpose of such discrimination. It means, not that everything is regulated by law, but, on the contrary, that the coercive power of the state can be used only in cases defined in advance by the law and in such a way that it can be foreseen how it will be used. A particular enactment can thus infringe the Rule of Law. Anyone ready to deny this would have to contend that whether the Rule of Law prevails today in Germany, Italy, or Russia depends on whether the dictators have obtained their absolute power by constitutional means.[9]

Whether, as in some countries, the main applications of the Rule of Law are laid down in a bill of rights or in a constitutional code, or whether the principle is

[8] [English jurist Charles John, First Baron Darling (1849–1936) served as a conservative MP, a judge, and a member of several royal commissions. For more on Lord Hewart, see the foreword to the 1956 American paperback edition, note 25. —Ed.]

[9] Another illustration of an infringement of the Rule of Law by legislation is the case of the bill of attainder, familiar in the history of England. The form which the Rule of Law takes in criminal law is usually expressed by the Latin tag *nulla poena sine lege*—no punishment without a law expressly prescribing it. The essence of this rule is that the law must have existed as a general rule before the individual case arose to which it is to be applied. Nobody would argue that, when in a famous case in Henry VIII's reign Parliament resolved with respect to the Bishop of Rochester's cook that "the said Richard Rose shall be boiled to death without having the advantage of his clergy," this act was performed under the Rule of Law. But while the Rule of Law had become an essential part of criminal procedure in all liberal countries, it cannot be preserved in totalitarian regimes. There, as E. B. Ashton has well expressed it, the liberal maxim is replaced by the principles *nullum crimen sine poena*—no "crime" must remain without punishment, whether the law explicitly provides for it or not. "The rights of the state do not end with punishing law breakers. The community is entitled to whatever may seem necessary to the protection of its interests—of which observance of the law, as it stands, is only one of the more elementary requirements." See E. B. Ashton, *The Fascist: His State and His Mind*, op. cit., p. 127. What is an infringement of

merely a firmly established tradition, matters comparatively little. But it will readily be seen that, whatever form it takes, any such recognized limitations of the powers of legislation imply the recognition of the inalienable right of the individual, inviolable rights of man.

It is pathetic but characteristic of the muddle into which many of our intellectuals have been led by the conflicting ideals in which they believe that a leading advocate of the most comprehensive central planning like H. G. Wells should at the same time write an ardent defense of the rights of man.[10] The individual rights which Mr. Wells hopes to preserve would inevitably obstruct the planning which he desires. To some extent he seems to realize the dilemma, and we find therefore the provisions of his proposed "Declaration of the Rights of Man" so hedged about with qualifications that they lose all significance. While, for instance, his declaration proclaims that every man "shall have the right to buy and sell without any discriminatory restrictions anything which may be lawfully bought and sold," which is admirable, he immediately proceeds to make the whole provision nugatory by adding that it applies only to buying and selling "in such quantities and with such reservations as are compatible with the common welfare."[11] But since, of course, all restrictions ever imposed upon buying or selling anything are supposed to be necessary in the interest of the "common welfare," there is really no restriction which this clause effectively prevents and no right of the individual that is safeguarded by it.

Or, to take another basic clause, the declaration states that every man "may engage in any lawful occupation" and that "he is entitled to paid employment and to a free choice whenever there is any variety of employment open to him."[12] It is not stated, however, who is to decide whether a particular employment is "open" to a particular person, and the added provision that "he may suggest employment for himself and have his claim publicly considered, accepted or dismissed,"[13] shows that Mr. Wells is thinking in terms of an authority which decides whether a man is "entitled" to a particular position—which certainly

---

"the interests of the community" is, of course, decided by the authorities. [Hayek incorrectly listed Ashton's quote as being found on p. 119, not 127. —Ed.]

[10] [English novelist H. G. Wells (1866–1946) is best remembered today for such science fiction classics as *The Time Machine* and *The War of the Worlds*. In his day he was also known for his biting social satires, contributions to popular history, and involvement with numerous progressive causes. In 1939 he drafted a "Declaration of the Rights of Man" that was published in *The Daily Herald* and other newspapers, and which elicited much commentary. Some of these ideas were later worked into the Universal Declaration of Human Rights that was adopted by the UN General Assembly in December 1948. Wells's "Declaration" was reprinted under the title "Ten Points for World Peace," *Current History*, vol. 51, March 1940, pp. 16–18, from which subsequent citations are taken. —Ed.]

[11] [Wells, "Ten Points for World Peace," op. cit., p. 18. —Ed.]

[12] [*Ibid.* —Ed.]

[13] [*Ibid.* —Ed.]

means the opposite of free choice of occupation. And how in a planned world "freedom of travel and migration" is to be secured when not only the means of communication and currencies are controlled but also the location of industries planned, or how the freedom of the press is to be safeguarded when the supply of paper and all the channels of distribution are controlled by the planning authority, are questions to which Mr. Wells provides as little answer as any other planner.

In this respect much more consistency is shown by the more numerous reformers who, ever since the beginning of the socialist movement, have attacked the "metaphysical" idea of individual rights and insisted that in a rationally ordered world there will be no individual rights but only individual duties. This, indeed, has become the much more common attitude of our so-called "progressives," and few things are more certain to expose one to the reproach of being a reactionary than if one protests against a measure on the grounds that it is a violation of the rights of the individual. Even a liberal paper like the *Economist* was a few years ago holding up to us the example of the French, of all people, who had learned the lesson that "democratic government no less than dictatorship must always [*sic*] have plenary powers *in posse*, without sacrificing their democratic and representative character. There is no restrictive penumbra of individual rights that can never be touched by government in administrative matters whatever the circumstances. There is no limit to the power of ruling which can and should be taken by a government freely chosen by the people and can be fully and openly criticised by an opposition."[14]

This may be inevitable in wartime, when, of course, even free and open criticism is necessarily restricted. But the "always" in the statement quoted does not suggest that the *Economist* regards it as a regrettable wartime necessity. Yet as a permanent institution this view is certainly incompatible with the preservation of the Rule of Law, and it leads straight to the totalitarian state. It is, however, the view which all those who want the government to direct economic life must hold.

How even a formal recognition of individual rights, or of the equal rights of minorities, loses all significance in a state which embarks on a complete control of economic life, has been amply demonstrated by the experience of the various Central European countries. It has been shown there that it is possible to pursue a policy of ruthless discrimination against national minorities by the use of recognized instruments of economic policy without ever infringing the letter of the statutory protection of minority rights. This oppression by means of economic policy was greatly facilitated by the fact that particular industries or activities were largely in the hands of a national minority, so that many a measure

---

[14][Hayek quotes from a leading article entitled, "True Democracy," *The Economist*, vol. 87, November 18, 1939, pp 242–43. —Ed.]

aimed ostensibly against an industry or class was in fact aimed at a national minority. But the almost boundless possibilities for a policy of discrimination and oppression provided by such apparently innocuous principles as "government control of the development of industries" have been amply demonstrated to all those desirous of seeing how the political consequences of planning appear in practice.

SEVEN

ECONOMIC CONTROL AND
TOTALITARIANISM

The control of the production of wealth is the control of human life itself.
—Hilaire Belloc[1]

Most planners who have seriously considered the practical aspects of their task have little doubt that a directed economy must be run on more or less dictatorial lines. That the complex system of interrelated activities, if it is to be consciously directed at all, must be directed by a single staff of experts, and that ultimate responsibility and power must rest in the hands of a commander-in-chief whose actions must not be fettered by democratic procedure, is too obvious a consequence of underlying ideas of central planning not to command fairly general assent. The consolation our planners offer us is that this authoritarian direction will apply "only" to economic matters. One of the most prominent economic planners, Stuart Chase, assures us, for instance, that in a planned society "political democracy can remain if it confines itself to all but economic matters."[2] Such assurances are usually accompanied by the suggestion that, by giving up freedom in what are, or ought to be, the less important aspects of our lives, we shall obtain greater freedom in the pursuit of higher values. On this ground people who abhor the idea of a political dictatorship often clamor for a dictator in the economic field.

The arguments used appeal to our best instincts and often attract the finest minds. If planning really did free us from the less important cares and so made it easier to render our existence one of plain living and high thinking, who would wish to belittle such an ideal? If our economic activities really concerned only the inferior or even more sordid sides of life, of course we ought to endeavor by all means to find a way to relieve ourselves from the excessive care for

---

[1] [Hilaire Belloc, *The Servile State*, op. cit., p. 46. —Ed.]

[2] [The quotation by Chase, but with no mention of its original source, may be found in Walter Lippmann, "The Collectivist Movement in Practice," *Atlantic Monthly*, vol. 158, December 1936, p. 729. Accountant, freelance writer, and prolific author Stuart Chase (1888–1985) was a popular writer in the interwar years. Among his many books on economics were *The Tragedy of Waste* (New York: Macmillan, 1925) and *A New Deal* (New York: Macmillan, 1934). —Ed.]

material ends and, leaving them to be cared for by some piece of utilitarian machinery, set our minds free for the higher things of life.

Unfortunately, the assurance people derive from this belief that the power which is exercised over economic life is a power over matters of secondary importance only, and which makes them take lightly the threat to the freedom of our economic pursuits, is altogether unwarranted. It is largely a consequence of the erroneous belief that there are purely economic ends separate from the other ends of life. Yet, apart from the pathological case of the miser, there is no such thing. The ultimate ends of the activities of reasonable beings are never economic. Strictly speaking, there is no "economic motive" but only economic factors conditioning our striving for other ends. What in ordinary language is misleadingly called the "economic motive" means merely the desire for general opportunity, the desire for power to achieve unspecified ends.[3] If we strive for money, it is because it offers us the widest choice in enjoying the fruits of our efforts. Because in modern society it is through the limitation of our money incomes that we are made to feel the restrictions which our relative poverty still imposes upon us, many have come to hate money as the symbol of these restrictions. But this is to mistake for the cause the medium through which a force makes itself felt. It would be much truer to say that money is one of the greatest instruments of freedom ever invented by man. It is money which in existing society opens an astounding range of choice to the poor man—a range greater than that which not many generations ago was open to the wealthy. We shall better understand the significance of this service of money if we consider what it would really mean if, as so many socialists characteristically propose, the "pecuniary motive" were largely displaced by "noneconomic incentives." If all rewards, instead of being offered in money, were offered in the form of public distinctions or privileges, positions of power over other men, or better housing or better food, opportunities for travel or education, this would merely mean that the recipient would no longer be allowed to choose and that whoever fixed the reward determined not only its size but also the particular form in which it should be enjoyed.

Once we realize that there is no separate economic motive and that an economic gain or economic loss is merely a gain or a loss where it is still in our

---

[3] Cf. Lionel Robbins, *The Economic Causes of War* (London: J. Cape, 1939), Appendix. [British economist Lionel Robbins (1898–1984) was Hayek's close friend and colleague at the London School of Economics. In his appendix, Robbins discusses the meaning of the term "economic causation," and concludes "The causes of war are to be regarded as economic if the objective is purely instrumental to securing for some person or persons a greater command of resources in general. . . . They are to be regarded as non-economic if the objective is not instrumental to anything further—if it is definitely an end in itself rather than means for a number of ends." Op. cit., p. 118. —Ed.]

power to decide which of our needs or desires shall be affected, it is also easier to see the important kernel of truth in the general belief that economic matters affect only the less important ends of life and to understand the contempt in which "merely" economic considerations are often held. In a sense this is quite justified in a market economy—but only in such a free economy. So long as we can freely dispose over our income and all our possessions, economic loss will always deprive us only of what we regard as the least important of the desires we were able to satisfy. A "merely" economic loss is thus one whose effect we can still make fall on our less important needs, while when we say that the value of something we have lost is much greater than its economic value, or that it cannot even be estimated in economic terms, this means that we must bear the loss where it falls. And similarly with an economic gain. Economic changes, in other words, usually affect only the fringe, the "margin," of our needs. There are many things which are more important than anything which economic gains or losses are likely to affect, which for us stand high above the amenities and even above many of the necessities of life which are affected by the economic ups and downs. Compared with them, the "filthy lucre," the question whether we are economically somewhat worse or better off, seems of little importance. This makes many people believe that anything which, like economic planning, affects only our economic interests cannot seriously interfere with the more basic values of life.

This, however, is an erroneous conclusion. Economic values are less important to us than many things precisely because in economic matters we are free to decide what to us is more, and what less, important. Or, as we might say, because in the present society it is *we* who have to solve the economic problems of our lives. To be controlled in our economic pursuits means to be always controlled unless we declare our specific purpose. Or, since when we declare our specific purpose we shall also have to get it approved, we should really be controlled in everything.

The question raised by economic planning is, therefore, not merely whether we shall be able to satisfy what we regard as our more or less important needs in the way we prefer. It is whether it shall be we who decide what is more, and what is less, important for us, or whether this is to be decided by the planner. Economic planning would not affect merely those of our marginal needs that we have in mind when we speak contemptuously about the merely economic. It would, in effect, mean that we as individuals should no longer be allowed to decide what we regard as marginal.

The authority directing all economic activity would control not merely the part of our lives which is concerned with inferior things; it would control the allocation of the limited means for all our ends. And whoever controls all economic activity controls the means for all our ends and must therefore decide which are to be satisfied and which not. This is really the crux of the matter.

Economic control is not merely control of a sector of human life which can be separated from the rest; it is the control of the means for all our ends. And whoever has sole control of the means must also determine which ends are to be served, which values are to be rated higher and which lower—in short, what men should believe and strive for. Central planning means that the economic problem is to be solved by the community instead of by the individual; but this involves that it must also be the community, or rather its representatives, who must decide the relative importance of the different needs.

The so-called economic freedom which the planners promise us means precisely that we are to be relieved of the necessity of solving our own economic problems and that the bitter choices which this often involves are to be made for us. Since under modern conditions we are for almost everything dependent on means which our fellow-men provide, economic planning would involve direction of almost the whole of our life. There is hardly an aspect of it, from our primary needs to our relations with our family and friends, from the nature of our work to the use of our leisure, over which the planner would not exercise his "conscious control."[4]

The power of the planner over our private lives would be no less complete if he chose not to exercise it by direct control of our consumption. Although a planned society would probably to some extent employ rationing and similar devices, the power of the planner over our private lives does not depend on this and would be hardly less effective if the consumer were nominally free to spend his income as he pleased. The source of this power over all consumption which in a planned society the authority would possess would be its control over production.

Our freedom of choice in a competitive society rests on the fact that, if one person refuses to satisfy our wishes, we can turn to another. But if we face a monopolist we are at his mercy. And an authority directing the whole economic system would be the most powerful monopolist conceivable. While we need probably not be afraid that such an authority would exploit this power in the

---

[4]The extent of the control over all life that economic control confers is nowhere better illustrated than in the field of foreign exchanges. Nothing would at first seem to affect private life less than a state control of the dealings in foreign exchange, and most people will regard its introduction with complete indifference. Yet the experience of most Continental countries has taught thoughtful people to regard this step as the decisive advance on the path to totalitarianism and the suppression of individual liberty. It is, in fact, the complete delivery of the individual to the tyranny of the state, the final suppression of all means of escape—not merely for the rich but for everybody. Once the individual is no longer free to travel, no longer free to buy foreign books or journals, once all the means of foreign contact can be restricted to those of whom official opinion approves or for whom it is regarded as necessary, the effective control of opinion is much greater than that ever exercised by any of the absolutist governments of the seventeenth and eighteenth centuries.

manner in which a private monopolist would do so, while its purpose would presumably not be the extortion of maximum financial gain, it would have complete power to decide what we are to be given and on what terms. It would not only decide what commodities and services were to be available and in what quantities; it would be able to direct their distribution between districts and groups and could, if it wished, discriminate between persons to any degree it liked. If we remember why planning is advocated by most people, can there be much doubt that this power would be used for the ends of which the authority approves and to prevent the pursuits of ends which it disapproves?

The power conferred by the control of production and prices is almost unlimited. In a competitive society the prices we have to pay for a thing, the rate at which we can get one thing for another, depend on the quantities of other things of which by taking one, we deprive the other members of society. This price is not determined by the conscious will of anybody. And if one way of achieving our ends proves too expensive for us, we are free to try other ways. The obstacles in our path are not due to someone's disapproving of our ends but to the fact that the same means are also wanted elsewhere. In a directed economy, where the authority watches over the ends pursued, it is certain that it would use its powers to assist some ends and to prevent the realization of others. Not our own view, but somebody else's, of what we ought to like or dislike would determine what we should get. And since the authority would have the power to thwart any efforts to elude its guidance, it would control what we consume almost as effectively as if it directly told us how to spend our income.

Not only in our capacity as consumers, however, and not even mainly in that capacity, would the will of the authority shape and "guide" our daily lives. It would do so even more in our position as producers. These two aspects of our lives cannot be separated; and as for most of us the time we spend at our work is a large part of our whole lives, and as our job usually also determines the place where and the people among whom we live, some freedom in choosing our work is, probably, even more important for our happiness than freedom to spend our income during the hours of leisure.

No doubt it is true that even in the best of worlds this freedom will be very limited. Few people ever have an abundance of choice of occupation. But what matters is that we have some choice, that we are not absolutely tied to a particular job which has been chosen for us, or which we may have chosen in the past, and that if one position becomes quite intolerable, or if we set our heart on another, there is almost always a way for the able, some sacrifice at the price of which he may achieve his goal. Nothing makes conditions more unbearable than the knowledge that no effort of ours can change them; and even if we should never have the strength of mind to make the necessary sacrifice, the knowledge that we could escape if we only strove hard enough makes many otherwise intolerable positions bearable.

This is not to say that in this respect all is for the best in our present world, or has been so in the most liberal past, and that there is not much that could be done to improve the opportunities of choice open to the people. Here as elsewhere the state can do a great deal to help the spreading of knowledge and information and to assist mobility. But the point is that the kind of state action which really would increase opportunity is almost precisely the opposite of the "planning" which is now generally advocated and practiced. Most planners, it is true, promise that in the new planned world free choice of occupation will be scrupulously preserved or even increased. But there they promise more than they can possibly fulfill. If they want to plan, they must control the entry into the different trades and occupations, or the terms of remuneration, or both. In almost all known instances of planning, the establishment of such controls and restrictions was among the first measures taken. If such control were universally practiced and exercised by a single planning authority, one needs little imagination to see what would become of the "free choice of occupation" promised. The "freedom of choice" would be purely fictitious, a mere promise to practice no discrimination where in the nature of the case discrimination must be practiced, and where all one could hope would be that the selection would be made on what the authority believed to be objective grounds.

There would be little difference if the planning authority confined itself to fixing the terms of employment and tried to regulate numbers by adjusting these terms. By prescribing the remuneration, it would no less effectively bar groups of people from entering many trades than by specifically excluding them. A rather plain girl who badly wants to become a saleswoman, a weakly boy who has set his heart on a job where his weakness handicaps him, as well as in general the apparently less able or less suitable are not necessarily excluded in a competitive society; if they value the position sufficiently they will frequently be able to get a start by a financial sacrifice and will later make good through qualities which at first are not so obvious. But when the authority fixes the remunerations for a whole category and the selection among the candidates is made by an objective test, the strength of their desire for the job will count for very little. The person whose qualifications are not of the standard type, or whose temperament is not of the ordinary kind, will no longer be able to come to special arrangements with an employer whose dispositions will fit in with his special needs: the person who prefers irregular hours or even a happy-go-lucky existence with a small and perhaps uncertain income to a regular routine will no longer have the choice. Conditions will be without exception what in some measure they inevitably are in a large organization—or rather worse, because there will be no possibility of escape. We shall no longer be free to be rational or efficient only when and where we think it worth while; we shall all have to conform to the standards which the planning authority must fix in order to simplify its task. To make this immense task manageable, it will have to reduce the diversity of human capacities and inclinations to a few categories of readily interchangeable units and deliberately to disregard minor personal differences.

Although the professed aim of planning would be that man should cease to be a mere means, in fact—since it would be impossible to take account in the plan of individual likes and dislikes—the individual would more than ever become a mere means, to be used by the authority in the service of such abstractions as the "social welfare" or the "good of the community."

That in a competitive society most things can be had at a price—though it is often a cruelly high price we have to pay—is a fact the importance of which can hardly be overrated. The alternative is not, however, complete freedom of choice, but orders and prohibitions which must be obeyed and, in the last resort, the favor of the mighty.

It is significant of the confusion prevailing on all these subjects that it should have become a cause for reproach that in a competitive society almost everything can be had at a price. If the people who protest against having the higher values of life brought into the "cash nexus" really mean that we should not be allowed to sacrifice our lesser needs in order to preserve the higher values, and that the choice should be made for us, this demand must be regarded as rather peculiar and scarcely testifies to great respect for the dignity of the individual. That life and health, beauty and virtue, honor and peace of mind, can often be preserved only at considerable material cost, and that somebody must make the choice, is as undeniable as that we all are sometimes not prepared to make the material sacrifices necessary to protect those higher values against all injury.

To take only one example: We could, of course, reduce casualties by automobile accidents to zero if we were willing to bear the cost—if in no other way—by abolishing automobiles. And the same is true of thousands of other instances in which we are constantly risking life and health and all the fine values of the spirit, of ourselves and of our fellow-men, to further what we at the same time contemptuously describe as our material comfort. Nor can it be otherwise, since all our ends compete for the same means; and we could not strive for anything but these absolute values if they were on no account to be endangered.

That people should wish to be relieved of the bitter choice which hard facts often impose upon them is not surprising. But few want to be relieved through having the choice made for them by others. People just wish that the choice should not be necessary at all. And they are only too ready to believe that the choice is not really necessary, that it is imposed upon them merely by the particular economic system under which we live. What they resent is, in truth, that there is an economic problem.

In their wishful belief that there is really no longer an economic problem people have been confirmed by irresponsible talk about "potential plenty"—which, if it were a fact, would indeed mean that there is no economic problem which makes the choice inevitable. But although this snare has served socialist propaganda under various names as long as socialism has existed, it is still as palpably untrue as it was when it was first used over a hundred years ago. In all this time not one of the many people who have used it has produced a workable plan of how production could be increased so as to abolish even in western Europe what we regard as poverty—not to speak of the world as a whole. The reader may take it that whoever talks about potential plenty is either dishonest or does not know what he is talking about.[5] Yet it is this false hope as much as anything which drives us along the road to planning.

While the popular movement still profits by this false belief, the claim that a planned economy would produce a substantially larger output than the competitive system is being progressively abandoned by most students of the problem. Even a good many economists with socialist views who have seriously studied the problems of central planning are now content to hope that a planned society will equal the efficiency of a competitive system; they advocate planning no longer because of its superior productivity but because it will enable us to secure a more just and equitable distribution of wealth. This is, indeed, the only argument for planning which can be seriously pressed. It is indisputable that if we want to secure a distribution of wealth which conforms to some predetermined standard, if we want consciously to decide who is to have

[5] To justify these strong words, the following conclusions may be quoted at which Colin Clark, one of the best known among the younger economic statisticians and a man of undoubted progressive views and a strictly scientific outlook, has arrived in his *The Conditions of Economic Progress* (London: Macmillan, 1940), pp. 3–4: The "oft-repeated phrases about poverty in the midst of plenty, and the problems of production having already been solved if only we understood the problem of distribution, turn out to be the most untruthful of all modern clichés. . . . The under-utilisation of productive capacity is a question of considerable importance only in the U.S.A., though in certain years also it has been of some importance in Great Britain, Germany and France, but for most of the world it is entirely subsidiary to the more important fact that, with productive resources fully employed, they can produce so little. The age of plenty will still be a long while in coming. . . . If preventable unemployment were eliminated throughout the trade cycle, this would mean a distinct improvement in the standard of living of the population of the U.S.A., but from the standpoint of the world as a whole it would only make a small contribution towards the much greater problem of raising the real income of the bulk of the world population to anything like a civilised standard." [British statistician and economist Colin Clark (1905–1989) taught and held government positions in England, the United States, and Australia. Active in the Labour party in the 1920s and early 1930s (hence his "undoubted progressive views"), he was a pioneer in the estimation of national income statistics. —Ed.]

what, we must plan the whole economic system. But the question remains whether the price we should have to pay for the realization of somebody's ideal of justice is not bound to be more discontent and more oppression than was ever caused by the much-abused free play of economic forces.

We should be seriously deceiving ourselves if for these apprehensions we sought comfort in the consideration that the adoption of central planning would merely mean a return, after a brief spell of a free economy, to the ties and regulations which have governed economic activity through most ages, and that therefore the infringements of personal liberty need not be greater than they were before the age of laissez faire. This is a dangerous illusion. Even during the periods of European history when the regimentation of economic life went furthest, it amounted to little more than the creation of a general and semipermanent framework of rules within which the individual preserved a wide free sphere. The apparatus of control then available would not have been adequate to impose more than very general directions. And even where the control was most complete it extended only to those activities of a person through which he took part in the social division of labor. In the much wider sphere in which he then still lived on his own products, he was free to act as he chose.

The situation is now entirely different. During the liberal era the progressive division of labor has created a situation where almost every one of our activities is part of a social process. This is a development which we cannot reverse, since it is only because of it that we can maintain the vastly increased population at anything like present standards. But, in consequence, the substitution of central planning for competition would require central direction of a much greater part of our lives than was ever attempted before. It could not stop at what we regard as our economic activities, because we are now for almost every part of our lives dependent on somebody else's economic activities.[6] The passion for the "collective satisfaction of our needs," with which our socialists have so well prepared the way for totalitarianism, and which wants us to take our pleasures as well as our necessities at the appointed time and in the prescribed form, is, of course, partly intended as a means of political education. But it is also the result of the exigencies of planning, which consists essentially in depriving us of choice, in order to give us whatever fits best into the plan and that at a time determined by the plan.

It is often said that political freedom is meaningless without economic freedom. This is true enough, but in a sense almost opposite from that in which the

[6]It is no accident that in the totalitarian countries, be it Russia or Germany or Italy, the question of how to organize the people's leisure has become a problem of planning. The Germans have even invented for this problem the horrible and self-contradictory name of *Freizeitgestaltung* (literally: the shaping of the use made of the people's free time), as if it were still "free time" when it has to be spent in the way ordained by authority.

phrase is used by our planners. The economic freedom which is the prerequisite of any other freedom cannot be the freedom from economic care which the socialists promise us and which can be obtained only by relieving the individual at the same time of the necessity and of the power of choice; it must be the freedom of our economic activity which, with the right of choice, inevitably also carries the risk and the responsibility of that right.

EIGHT

WHO, WHOM?

The finest opportunity ever given to the world was thrown away because the passion for equality made vain the hope for freedom. —Lord Acton[1]

It is significant that one of the commonest objections to competition is that it is "blind." It is not irrelevant to recall that to the ancients blindness was an attribute of their deity of justice. Although competition and justice may have little else in common, it is as much a commendation of competition as of justice that it is no respecter of persons. That it is impossible to foretell who will be the lucky ones or whom disaster will strike, that rewards and penalties are not shared out according to somebody's views about the merits or demerits of different people but depend on their capacity and their luck, is as important as that, in framing legal rules, we should not be able to predict which particular person will gain and which will lose by their application. And this is nonetheless true, because in competition chance and good luck are often as important as skill and foresight in determining the fate of different people.

The choice open to us is not between a system in which everybody will get what he deserves according to some absolute and universal standard of right, and one where the individual shares are determined partly by accident or good or ill chance, but between a system where it is the will of a few persons that decides who is to get what, and one where it depends at least partly on the ability and enterprise of the people concerned and partly on unforeseeable circumstances. This is no less relevant because in a system of free enterprise chances are not equal, since such a system is necessarily based on private property and (though perhaps not with the same necessity) on inheritance, with the differences in opportunity which these create. There is, indeed, a strong case for reducing this inequality of opportunity as far as congenital differences permit and as it is possible to do so without destroying the impersonal character of the process by which everybody has to take his chance and no person's view about what is right and desirable overrules that of others.

---

[1] [Lord Acton, "The History of Freedom in Christianity," in *History of Freedom and Other Essays,* op. cit., p. 57. —Ed.]

The fact that the opportunities open to the poor in a competitive society are much more restricted than those open to the rich does not make it less true that in such a society the poor are much more free than a person commanding much greater material comfort in a different type of society. Although under competition the probability that a man who starts poor will reach great wealth is much smaller than is true of the man who has inherited property, it is not only possible for the former, but the competitive system is the only one where it depends solely on him and not on the favors of the mighty, and where nobody can prevent a man from attempting to achieve this result. It is only because we have forgotten what unfreedom means that we often overlook the patent fact that in every real sense a badly paid unskilled worker in this country has more freedom to shape his life than many a small entrepreneur in Germany or a much better paid engineer or manager in Russia. Whether it is a question of changing his job or the place where he lives, of professing certain views or of spending his leisure in a particular manner, although sometimes the price he may have to pay for following his inclinations may be high, and to many appear too high, there are no absolute impediments, no dangers to bodily security and freedom, that confine him by brute force to the task and the environment to which a superior has assigned him.

That the ideal of justice of most socialists would be satisfied if merely private income from property were abolished and the differences between the earned incomes of different people remained what they are now is true.[2] What these people forget is that, in transferring all property in the means of production to the state, they put the state in a position whereby its action must in effect decide all other incomes. The power thus given to the state and the demand that the state should use it to "plan" means nothing else than that it should use it in full awareness of all these effects.

To believe that the power which is thus conferred on the state is merely transferred to it from others is erroneous. It is a power which is newly created and

---

[2] It is probable that we habitually overestimate the extent to which inequality of incomes is mainly caused by income derived from property, and therefore the extent to which the major inequalities would be abolished by abolishing income from property. What little information we have about the distribution of incomes in Soviet Russia does not suggest that the inequalities are substantially smaller there than in a capitalist society. Max Eastman, in *The End of Socialism in Russia* (Boston: Little, Brown, 1937), pp. 30–34, gives some information from official Russian sources which suggest that the difference between the highest and the lowest salaries paid in Russia is of the same order of magnitude (about 50 to 1) as in the United States; and Leon Trotsky, according to an article quoted by James Burnham, *The Managerial Revolution: What Is Happening in the World* (New York: John Day Co., 1941), p. 46, estimated as late as 1939 that "the upper 11 or 12 per cent of the Soviet population now receives approximately 50 per cent of the national income. This differentiation is sharper than in the United States, where the upper 10 per cent of the population receives approximately 35 per cent of the national income." [In the original, Hayek incorrectly listed the passage from Trotsky as appearing on page 43, not 46, of Burnham's book. —Ed.]

which in a competitive society nobody possesses. So long as property is divided among many owners, none of them acting independently has exclusive power to determine the income and position of particular people—nobody is tied to any one property owner except by the fact that he may offer better terms than anybody else.

What our generation has forgotten is that the system of private property is the most important guaranty of freedom, not only for those who own property, but scarcely less for those who do not. It is only because the control of the means of production is divided among many people acting independently that nobody has complete power over us, that we as individuals can decide what to do with ourselves. If all the means of production were vested in a single hand, whether it be nominally that of "society" as a whole or that of a dictator, whoever exercises this control has complete power over us.

Who can seriously doubt that a member of a small racial or religious minority will be freer with no property so long as fellow-members of his community have property and are therefore able to employ him, than he would be if private property were abolished and he became owner of a nominal share in the communal property? Or that the power which a multiple millionaire, who may be my neighbor and perhaps my employer, has over me is very much less than that which the smallest *fonctionnaire* possesses who wields the coercive power of the state and on whose discretion it depends whether and how I am to be allowed to live or to work? And who will deny that a world in which the wealthy are powerful is still a better world than one in which only the already powerful can acquire wealth?

It is pathetic, yet at the same time encouraging, to find as prominent an old communist as Max Eastman rediscovering this truth:

"It seems obvious to me now—though I have been slow, I must say, in coming to the conclusion—that the institution of private property is one of the main things that have given man that limited amount of free-and-equalness that Marx hoped to render infinite by abolishing this institution. Strangely enough Marx was the first to see this. He is the one who informed us, looking backwards, that the evolution of private capitalism with its free market had been a precondition for the evolution of all our democratic freedoms. It never occurred to him, looking forward, that if this was so, these other freedoms might disappear with the abolition of the free market."[3]

It is sometimes said, in answer to such apprehensions, that there is no reason why the planner should determine the incomes of individuals. The social and

[3]Max Eastman, "Socialism Doesn't Jibe with Human Nature," *Reader's Digest*, vol. 38, June 1941, p. 47. [Hayek's original citation, "Max Eastman in the *Reader's Digest*, July, 1941, p. 39" got both the issue and page number wrong, and Hayek neglected to hyphenate "free-and-equalness" as Eastman had done. —Ed.]

political difficulties involved in deciding the shares of different people in the national income are so obvious that even the most inveterate planner may well hesitate before he charges any authority with this task. Probably everybody who realizes what it involves would prefer to confine planning to production, to use it only to secure a "rational organization of industry," leaving the distribution of incomes as far as possible to impersonal forces. Although it is impossible to direct industry without exercising some influence on distribution, and although no planner will wish to leave distribution entirely to the forces of the market, they would probably all prefer to confine themselves to seeing that this distribution conforms to certain general rules of equity and fairness, that extreme inequalities are avoided, and that the relation between the remuneration of the major classes is just, without undertaking the responsibility for the position of particular people within their class or for the gradations and differentiations between smaller groups and individuals.

We have already seen that the close interdependence of all economic phenomena makes it difficult to stop planning just where we wish and that, once the free working of the market is impeded beyond a certain degree, the planner will be forced to extend his controls until they become all-comprehensive. These economic considerations, which explain why it is impossible to stop deliberate control just where we should wish, are strongly reinforced by certain social or political tendencies whose strength makes itself increasingly felt as planning extends.

Once it becomes increasingly true, and is generally recognized, that the position of the individual is determined not by impersonal forces, not as a result of the competitive effort of many, but by the deliberate decision of authority, the attitude of the people toward their position in the social order necessarily changes. There will always exist inequalities which will appear unjust to those who suffer from them, disappointments which will appear unmerited, and strokes of misfortune which those hit have not deserved. But when these things occur in a society which is consciously directed, the way in which people will react will be very different from what it is when they are nobody's conscious choice.

Inequality is undoubtedly more readily borne, and affects the dignity of the person much less, if it is determined by impersonal forces than when it is due to design. In a competitive society it is no slight to a person, no offense to his dignity, to be told by any particular firm that it has no need for his services or that it cannot offer him a better job. It is true that in periods of prolonged mass unemployment the effect on many may be very similar. But there are other and better methods to prevent that scourge than central direction. But the unemployment or the loss of income which will always affect some in any society is certainly less degrading if it is the result of misfortune and not deliberately imposed by authority. However bitter the experience, it would be very much worse in a planned society. There individuals will have to decide not whether a person is needed for a particular job but whether he is of use for anything, and how useful he is. His position in life must be assigned to him by somebody else.

While people will submit to suffering which may hit anyone, they will not so easily submit to suffering which is the result of the decision of authority. It may be bad to be just a cog in an impersonal machine; but it is infinitely worse if we can no longer leave it, if we are tied to our place and to the superiors who have been chosen for us. Dissatisfaction of everybody with his lot will inevitably grow with the consciousness that it is the result of deliberate human decision.

Once government has embarked upon planning for the sake of justice, it cannot refuse responsibility for anybody's fate or position. In a planned society we shall all know that we are better or worse off than others, not because of circumstances which nobody controls, and which it is impossible to foresee with certainty, but because some authority wills it. And all our efforts directed toward improving our position will have to aim, not at foreseeing and preparing as well as we can for the circumstances over which we have no control, but at influencing in our favor the authority which has all the power. The nightmare of English nineteenth-century political thinkers, the state in which "no avenue to wealth and honor would exist save through the government,"[4] would be realized in a completeness which they never imagined—though familiar enough in some countries which have since passed to totalitarianism.

As soon as the state takes upon itself the task of planning the whole economic life, the problem of the due station of the different individuals and groups must indeed inevitably become the central political problem. As the coercive power of the state will alone decide who is to have what, the only power worth having will be a share in the exercise of this directing power. There will be no economic or social questions that would not be political questions in the sense that their solution will depend exclusively on who wields the coercive power, on whose are the views that will prevail on all occasions.

I believe it was Lenin himself who introduced to Russia the famous phrase

[4]The actual words are those of the young Disraeli. [The actual quotation reads, "no public avenues to wealth and honor would *subsist* save through the Government." It is taken from Tory politician and novelist Benjamin Disraeli's (1804–1881) essay, "Vindication of the English Constitution in a Letter to a Noble and Learned Lord" (1835), reprinted in Benjamin Disraeli, *Disraeli on Whigs and Whiggism,* ed. William Hutcheon (New York: Macmillan, 1914), p. 216, a work that established "the young Disraeli" as a political writer and thinker. He used the essay to attack Utilitarians and others who would "form political institutions on abstract principles of theoretic science, instead of permitting them to spring from the natural course of events, and to be naturally created by the necessities of nations" (p. 119). His criticisms of those who would "abrogate the clumsy and chance-born institutions of England, and substitute in their place their own modish inventions, formed on the irrefragable basis of Reason and Utility" (p. 134) bring to mind Hayek's later criticisms of "rationalist constructivism." —Ed.]

"who, whom?"—during the early years of Soviet rule the byword in which the people summed up the universal problem of a socialist society.[5] Who plans whom, who directs and dominates whom, who assigns to other people their station in life, and who is to have his due allotted by others? These become necessarily the central issues to be decided solely by the supreme power.

More recently an American student of politics has enlarged upon Lenin's phrase and asserted that the problem of all government is "who gets what, when, and how."[6] In a way this is not untrue. That all government affects the relative position of different people and that there is under any system scarcely an aspect of our lives which may not be affected by government action is certainly true. In so far as government does anything at all, its action will always have some effect on "who gets what, when, and how."

There are, however, two fundamental distinctions to be made. First, particular measures may be taken without the possibility of knowing how they will affect particular individuals and therefore without aiming at such particular effects. This point we have already discussed. Second, it is the extent of the activities of the government which decides whether everything that any person gets any time depends on the government, or whether its influence is confined to whether some people will get some things in some way at some time. Here lies the whole difference between a free and a totalitarian system.

The contrast between a liberal and a totally planned system is characteristically illustrated by the common complaints of Nazis and socialists of the "artificial separations of economics and politics" and by their equally common demand for the dominance of politics over economics. These phrases presumably mean not only that economic forces are now allowed to work for ends which are not part of the policy of the government but also that economic power can be used independently of government direction and for ends of which the government may not approve. But the alternative is not merely that there should be only one power but that this single power, the ruling group, should have control over all human ends and particularly that it should have complete power over the position of each individual in society.

That a government which undertakes to direct economic activity will have to use its power to realize somebody's ideal of distributive justice is certain. But how can and how will it use that power? By what principles will it or ought it to be guided? Is there a definite answer to the innumerable questions of relative merits that will arise and that will have to be solved deliberately? Is there a scale

[5] Cf. Malcolm Muggeridge, *Winter in Moscow* (Boston: Little, Brown, 1934); Arthur Feiler, *The Experiment of Bolshevism* (London: George Allen and Unwin, 1930).

[6] [The American political scientist Harold Lasswell (1902–1978) provided that classic definition of politics in his book, *Politics: Who Gets What, When and How?* (New York, London: McGraw-Hill, Whittlesey House, 1936). —Ed.]

of values, on which reasonable people can be expected to agree, which would justify a new hierarchical order of society and is likely to satisfy the demands for justice?

There is only one general principle, one simple rule which would indeed provide a definite answer to all these questions: equality, complete and absolute equality of all individuals in all those points which are subject to human control. If this were generally regarded as desirable (quite apart from the question whether it would be practicable, i.e., whether it would provide adequate incentives), it would give the vague idea of distributive justice a clear meaning and would give the planner definite guidance. But nothing is further from the truth than that people in general regard mechanical equality of this kind as desirable. No socialist movement which aimed at complete equality has ever gained substantial support. What socialism promised was not an absolutely equal, but a more just and more equal, distribution. Not equality in the absolute sense but "greater equality" is the only goal which is seriously aimed at.

Though these two ideals sound very similar, they are as different as possible as far as our problem is concerned. While absolute equality would clearly determine the planner's task, the desire for greater equality is merely negative, no more than an expression of dislike of the present state of affairs; and so long as we are not prepared to say that every move in the direction toward complete equality is desirable, it answers scarcely any of the questions the planner will have to decide.

This is not a quibble about words. We face here a crucial issue which the similarity of the terms used is likely to conceal. While agreement on complete equality would answer all the problems of merit the planner must answer, the formula of the approach to greater equality answers practically none. Its content is hardly more definite than the phrases "common good" or "social welfare." It does not free us from the necessity of deciding in every particular instance between the merits of particular individuals or groups, and it gives us no help in that decision. All it tells us in effect is to take from the rich as much as we can. But, when it comes to the distribution of the spoils, the problem is the same as if the formula of "greater equality" had never been conceived.

Most people find it difficult to admit that we do not possess moral standards which would enable us to settle these questions—if not perfectly, at least to greater general satisfaction than is done by the competitive system. Have we not all some idea of what is a "just price" or a "fair wage"? Can we not rely on the strong sense of fairness of the people? And even if we do not now agree fully on what is just or fair in a particular case, would popular ideas not soon consolidate into more definite standards if people were given an opportunity to see their ideals realized?

Unfortunately, there is little ground for such hopes. What standards we have are derived from the competitive regime we have known and would necessarily disappear soon after the disappearance of competition. What we mean by a just price, or a fair wage is either the customary price or wage, the return which past experience has made people expect, or the price or wage that would exist if there were no monopolistic exploitation. The only important exception to this used to be the claim of the workers to the "full produce of their labor," to which so much of socialist doctrine traces back. But there are few socialists today who believe that in a socialist society the output of each industry would be entirely shared by the workers of that industry; for this would mean that workers in industries using a great deal of capital would have a much larger income than those in industries using little capital, which most socialists would regard as very unjust. And it is now fairly generally agreed that this particular claim was based on an erroneous interpretation of the facts. But once the claim of the individual worker to the whole of "his" product is disallowed, and the whole of the return from capital is to be divided among all workers, the problem of how to divide it raises the same basic issue.

What the "just price" of a particular commodity or the "fair" remuneration for a particular service is might conceivably be determined objectively if the quantities needed were independently fixed. If these were given irrespective of cost, the planner might try to find what price or wage is necessary to bring forth this supply. But the planner must also decide how much is to be produced of each kind of goods, and, in so doing, he determines what will be the just price or fair wage to pay. If the planner decides that fewer architects or watchmakers are wanted and that the need can be met by those who are willing to stay in the trade at a lower remuneration, the "fair" wage will be lower. In deciding the relative importance of the different ends, the planner also decides the relative importance of the different groups and persons. As he is not supposed to treat the people merely as a means, he must take account of these effects and consciously balance the importance of the different ends against the effects of his decision. This means, however, that he will necessarily exercise direct control over the conditions of the different people.

This applies to the relative position of individuals no less than to that of the different occupational groups. We are in general far too likely to think of incomes within a given trade or profession as more or less uniform. But the differences between the incomes, not only of the most and the least successful doctor or architect, writer or movie actor, boxer or jockey, but also of the more and the less successful plumber or market gardener, grocer or tailor, are as great as those between the propertied and the propertyless classes. And although, no doubt, there would be some attempt at standardization by creating categories, the necessity of discrimination between individuals would remain the same, whether it were exercised by fixing their individual incomes or by allocating them to particular categories.

141

We need say no more about the likelihood of men in a free society submitting to such control—or about their remaining free if they submitted. On the whole question, what John Stuart Mill wrote nearly a hundred years ago remains equally true today:

"A fixed rule, like that of equality, might be acquiesced in, and so might chance, or an external necessity; but that a handful of human beings should weigh everybody in the balance, and give more to one and less to another at their sole pleasure and judgment, would not be borne unless from persons believed to be more than men, and backed by supernatural terrors."[7]

These difficulties need not lead to open clashes so long as socialism is merely the aspiration of a limited and fairly homogeneous group. They come to the surface only when a socialist policy is actually attempted with the support of the many different groups which together compose the majority of a people. Then it soon becomes the one burning question which of the different sets of ideals shall be imposed upon all by making the whole resources of the country serve it. It is because successful planning requires the creation of a common view on the essential values that the restriction of our freedom with regard to material things touches so directly on our spiritual freedom.

Socialists, the cultivated parents of the barbarous offspring they have produced, traditionally hope to solve this problem by education. But what does education mean in this respect? Surely we have learned that knowledge cannot create new ethical values, that no amount of learning will lead people to hold the same views on the moral issues which a conscious ordering of all social relations raises. It is not rational conviction but the acceptance of a creed which is required to justify a particular plan. And, indeed, socialists everywhere were the first to recognize that the task they had set themselves required the general acceptance of a common Weltanschauung, of a definite set of values. It was in these efforts to produce a mass movement supported by such a single world view that the socialists first created most of the instruments of indoctrination of which Nazis and Fascists have made such effective use.

In Germany and Italy the Nazis and Fascists did, indeed, not have much to invent. The usages of the new political movements which pervaded all aspects of life had in both countries already been introduced by the socialists. The idea of a political party which embraces all activities of the individual from the cradle to the grave, which claims to guide his views on everything, and which delights in making all problems questions of party Weltanschauung, was first put into practice by the socialists. An Austrian socialist writer, speaking of the

[7]John Stuart Mill, *Principles of Political Economy* (London: J. W. Parker, 1848), Book 2, chapter 1, paragraph 4, p. 213. [In the original, Hayek reversed the book and chapter numbers, listing it as Book 1, chapter 2. —Ed.]

socialist movement of his country, reports with pride that it was its "characteristic feature that it created special organizations for every field of activities of
workers and employees."[8]

Though the Austrian socialists may have gone further in this respect than
others, the situation was not very different elsewhere. It was not the Fascists but
the socialists who began to collect children from the tenderest age into political
organizations to make sure that they grew up as good proletarians. It was not
the Fascists but the socialists who first thought of organizing sports and games,
football and hiking, in party clubs where the members would not be infected by
other views. It was the socialists who first insisted that the party member should
distinguish himself from others by the modes of greeting and the forms of address. It was they who by their organization of "cells" and devices for the permanent supervision of private life created the prototype of the totalitarian
party. *Balilla* and *Hitlerjugend*, *Dopolavoro* and *Kraft durch Freude*, political uniforms
and military party formations, are all little more than imitations of older socialist institutions.[9]

So long as the socialist movement in a country is closely bound up with the interests of a particular group, usually the more highly skilled industrial workers,
the problem of creating a common view on the desirable status of the different
members of society is comparatively simple. The movement is immediately
concerned with the status of one particular group, and its aim is to raise that
status relatively to other groups. The character of the problem changes, however, as in the course of the progressive advance toward socialism it becomes
more and more evident to everyone that his income and general position are
determined by the coercive apparatus of the state, that he can maintain or improve his position only as a member of an organized group capable of influencing or controlling the state machine in his interest.

In the tug-of-war between the various pressure groups which arises at this
stage, it is by no means necessary that the interests of the poorest and most numerous groups should prevail. Nor is it necessarily an advantage for the older
socialist parties, who avowedly represented the interests of a particular group,

---

[8] Georg Wieser, *Ein Staat stirbt, Oesterreich 1934–1938* (Paris: Internationale Verlags-Anstalt,
1938), p. 41.

[9] The political "book clubs" in England provide a not unimportant parallel. [*Balilla* was the
Italian Fascist organization for boys, named after the boy who started the insurrection that drove
the Austrians out of Genoa in 1746. The *Hitlerjugend*, or Hitler Youth, was the organization for the
indoctrination of the young in Germany. *Dopolavoro* (from *dopo lavoro*, Italian for "after work"), was
the Italian Fascist recreational program, which included sports, cultural, and tourist events. Its
German counterpart was *Kraft durch Freude* (Strength through Joy). Founded in 1933 within the German Labor Front and modeled after *Dopolavoro*, it was designed to win the working classes to National Socialism, which was particularly important after the trade unions were abolished. —Ed.]

to have been the first in the field and to have designed their whole ideology to appeal to the manual workers in industry. Their very success, and their insistence on the acceptance of the whole creed, is bound to create a powerful countermovement—not by the capitalists but by the very large and equally propertyless classes who find their relative status threatened by the advance of the élite of the industrial workers.

Socialist theory and socialist tactics, even where they have not been dominated by Marxist dogma, have been based everywhere on the idea of a division of society into two classes with common but mutually conflicting interests: capitalists and industrial workers. Socialism counted on a rapid disappearance of the old middle class and completely disregarded the rise of a new middle class, the countless army of clerks and typists, administrative workers and schoolteachers, tradesmen and small officials, and the lower ranks of the professions. For a time these classes often provided many of the leaders of the labor movement. But as it became increasingly clear that the position of those classes was deteriorating relatively to that of the industrial workers, the ideals which guided the latter lost much of their appeal to the others. While they were all socialists in the sense that they disliked the capitalist system and wanted a deliberate sharing-out of wealth according to their ideas of justice, these ideas proved to be very different from those embodied in the practice of the older socialist parties.

The means which the old socialist parties had successfully employed to secure the support of one occupational group—the raising of their relative economic position—cannot be used to secure the support of all. There are bound to arise rival socialist movements that appeal to the support of those whose relative position is worsened. There is a great deal of truth in the often heard statement that fascism and National Socialism are a sort of middle-class socialism—only that in Italy and Germany the supporters of these new movements were economically hardly a middle class any longer. It was to a large extent a revolt of a new underprivileged class against the labor aristocracy which the industrial labor movement had created.

There can be little doubt that no single economic factor has contributed more to help these movements than the envy of the unsuccessful professional man, the university-trained engineer or lawyer, and of the "white-collared proletariat" in general, of the engine driver or compositor and other members of the strongest trade-unions whose income was many times theirs. Nor can there be much doubt that in terms of money income the average member of the rank and file of the Nazi movement in its early years was poorer than the average trade-unionist or member of the older socialist party—a circumstance which only gained poignancy from the fact that the former had often seen better days and were frequently still living in surroundings which were the result of this past.

The expression "class struggle *à rebours,*" current in Italy at the time of the rise of fascism, did point to a very important aspect of the movement. The conflict between the Fascist or National Socialist and the older socialist parties must, indeed, very largely be regarded as the kind of conflict which is bound to arise between rival socialist factions. There was no difference between them about the question of its being the will of the state which should assign to each person his proper place in society. But there were, as there always will be, most profound differences about what are the proper places of the different classes and groups.

The old socialist leaders, who had always regarded their parties as the natural spearhead of the future general movement toward socialism, found it difficult to understand that with every extension in the use of socialist methods the resentment of large poor classes should turn against them. But while the old socialist parties, or the organized labor in particular industries, had usually not found it unduly difficult to come to an understanding for joint action with the employers in their particular industries, very large classes were left out in the cold. To them, and not without some justification, the more prosperous sections of the labor movement seemed to belong to the exploiting rather than to the exploited class.[10]

The resentment of the lower middle class, from which fascism and National Socialism recruited so large a proportion of their supporters, was intensified by the fact that their education and training had in many instances made them aspire to directing positions and that they regarded themselves as entitled to be members of the directing class. While the younger generation, out of that contempt for profit-making fostered by socialist teaching, spurned independent positions which involved risk and flocked in ever increasing numbers into salaried positions which promised security, they demanded a place yielding them the income and power to which in their opinion their training entitled them. While they believed in an organized society, they expected a place in that society very different from that which society ruled by labor seemed to offer. They were quite ready to take over the methods of the older socialism but intended to employ them in the service of a different class. The movement was able to attract

---

[10] It is now twelve years since one of the leading European socialist intellectuals, Hendrik de Man (who has since consistently developed further and made his peace with the Nazis), observed that "for the first time since the beginning of socialism, anti-capitalist resentments are turning against the socialist movement," in *Sozialismus und Nationalfascismus* (Potsdam: A. Protte, 1931), p. 6. [Hendrik de Man (1885–1953) was chairman of the Belgian Socialist party. When Germany invaded in 1940 he disbanded the party and declared that the destruction of parliamentary democracy under the "New Order" imposed by the Nazis would help free the working classes. He was tried and convicted in absentia of collaboration in Belgium in 1946; he spent the remainder of his days in Switzerland. —Ed.]

all those who, while they agreed on the desirability of the state controlling all economic activity, disagreed with the ends for which the aristocracy of the industrial workers used their political strength.

The new socialist movement started with several tactical advantages. Labor socialism had grown in a democratic and liberal world, adapting its tactics to it and taking over many of the ideals of liberalism. Its protagonists still believed that the creation of socialism as such would solve all problems. Fascism and National Socialism, on the other hand, grew out of the experience of an increasingly regulated society's awakening to the fact that democratic and international socialism was aiming at incompatible ideals. Their tactics were developed in a world already dominated by socialist policy and the problems it creates. They had no illusions about the possibility of a democratic solution of problems which require more agreement among people than can reasonably be expected. They had no illusions about the capacity of reason to decide all the questions of the relative importance of the wants of different men or groups which planning inevitably raises, or about the formula of equality providing an answer. They knew that the strongest group which rallied enough supporters in favor of a new hierarchical order of society, and which frankly promised privileges to the classes to which it appealed, was likely to obtain the support of all those who were disappointed because they had been promised equality but found that they had merely furthered the interest of a particular class. Above all, they were successful because they offered a theory, or Weltanschauung, which seemed to justify the privileges they promised to their supporters.

NINE

SECURITY AND FREEDOM

The whole of society will have become a single office and a single factory with equality of work and equality of pay. —Nikolai Lenin (1917)[1]

In a country where the sole employer is the State, opposition means death by slow starvation. The old principle: who does not work shall not eat, has been replaced by a new one: who does not obey shall not eat.
                                                                —Leon Trotsky (1937)[2]

Like the spurious "economic freedom," and with more justice, economic security is often represented as an indispensable condition of real liberty. In a sense this is both true and important. Independence of mind or strength of character is rarely found among those who cannot be confident that they will make their way by their own effort. Yet the idea of economic security is no less vague and ambiguous than most other terms in this field; and because of this the general approval given to the demand for security may become a danger to liberty. Indeed, when security is understood in too absolute a sense, the general striving for it, far from increasing the chances of freedom, becomes the gravest threat to it.

It will be well to contrast at the outset the two kinds of security: the limited one, which can be achieved for all, and which is therefore no privilege but a legitimate object of desire; and absolute security, which in a free society cannot be achieved for all and which ought not to be given as a privilege—except in a few special instances such as that of the judges, where complete independence is of paramount importance. These two kinds of security are, first, security against severe physical privation, the certainty of a given minimum of sustenance for all; and, second, the security of a given standard of life, or of the rel-

---

[1] [The citation is taken from Vladimir Lenin's most important contribution to Marxist political theory, "The State and Revolution: The Marxist Theory of the State and the Tasks of the Proletariat in the Revolution," a translation of which may be found in Robert Tucker, ed., *The Lenin Anthology* (New York: Norton, 1975). The citation may be found in chapter 5, section 4, p. 383. —Ed.]

[2] [Leon Trotsky, *The Revolution Betrayed: What Is the Soviet Union and Where Is It Going?* Translated by Max Eastman. (Garden City, NY: Doubleday, Doran & Company, 1937), p. 283. —Ed.]

ative position which one person or group enjoys compared with others; or, as we may put it briefly, the security of a minimum income and the security of the particular income a person is thought to deserve. We shall presently see that this distinction largely coincides with the distinction between the security which can be provided for all outside of and supplementary to the market system and the security which can be provided only for some and only by controlling or abolishing the market.

There is no reason why in a society which has reached the general level of wealth which ours has attained the first kind of security should not be guaranteed to all without endangering general freedom. There are difficult questions about the precise standard which should thus be assured; there is particularly the important question whether those who thus rely on the community should indefinitely enjoy all the same liberties as the rest.[3] An incautious handling of these questions might well cause serious and perhaps even dangerous political problems; but there can be no doubt that some minimum of food, shelter, and clothing, sufficient to preserve health and the capacity to work, can be assured to everybody. Indeed, for a considerable part of the population of England this sort of security has long been achieved.

Nor is there any reason why the state should not assist the individuals in providing for those common hazards of life against which, because of their uncertainty, few individuals can make adequate provision. Where, as in the case of sickness and accident, neither the desire to avoid such calamities nor the efforts to overcome their consequences are as a rule weakened by the provision of assistance—where, in short, we deal with genuinely insurable risks—the case for the state's helping to organize a comprehensive system of social insurance is very strong. There are many points of detail where those wishing to preserve the competitive system and those wishing to supercede it by something different will disagree on the details of such schemes; and it is possible under the name of social insurance to introduce measures which tend to make competition more or less ineffective. But there is no incompatibility in principle between the state's providing greater security in this way and the preservation of individual freedom. To the same category belongs also the increase of security through the state's rendering assistance to the victims of such "acts of God" as earthquakes and floods. Wherever communal action can mitigate disasters against which the individual can neither attempt to guard himself nor make provision for the consequences, such communal action should undoubtedly be taken.

There is, finally, the supremely important problem of combating general fluctuations of economic activity and the recurrent waves of large-scale unemploy-

[3] There are also serious problems of international relations which arise if mere citizenship of a country confers the right to a standard of living higher than elsewhere and which ought not to be dismissed too lightly.

ment which accompany them. This is, of course, one of the gravest and most pressing problems of our time. But, though its solution will require much planning in the good sense, it does not—or at least need not—require that special kind of planning which according to its advocates is to replace the market. Many economists hope, indeed, that the ultimate remedy may be found in the field of monetary policy, which would involve nothing incompatible even with nineteenth-century liberalism. Others, it is true, believe that real success can be expected only from the skillful timing of public works undertaken on a very large scale.[1] This might lead to much more serious restrictions of the competitive sphere, and, in experimenting in this direction, we shall have carefully to watch our step if we are to avoid making all economic activity progressively more dependent on the direction and volume of government expenditure. But this is neither the only nor, in my opinion, the most promising way of meeting the gravest threat to economic security. In any case, the very necessary efforts to secure protection against these fluctuations do not lead to the kind of planning which constitutes such a threat to our freedom.

The planning for security which has such an insidious effect on liberty is that for security of a different kind. It is planning designed to protect individuals or groups against diminutions of their income, which although in no way deserved yet in a competitive society occur daily, against losses imposing severe hardships having no moral justification yet inseparable from the competitive system. This demand for security is thus another form of the demand for a just remuneration—a remuneration commensurate with the subjective merits and not with the objective results of a man's efforts. This kind of security or justice seems irreconcilable with freedom to choose one's employment.

In any system which for the distribution of men between the different trades and occupations relies on their own choice it is necessary that the remuneration in these trades should correspond to their usefulness to the other members of society, even if this should stand in no relation to subjective merit. Although the results achieved will often be commensurate with efforts and intentions, this cannot always be true in any form of society. It will particularly not be true in the many instances where the usefulness of some trade or special skill is changed by circumstances which could not be foreseen. We all know the tragic plight of the highly trained man whose hard-learned skill has suddenly lost its value because of some invention which greatly benefits the rest of society. The history of the last hundred years is full of instances of this kind, some of them affecting hundreds of thousands of people at a time.

That anyone should suffer a great diminution of his income and bitter dis-

---

[1] [Hayek here refers to policies that would later carry the label "Keynesian" demand management policies. —Ed.]

appointment of all his hopes through no fault of his own, and despite hard work and exceptional skill, undoubtedly offends our sense of justice. The demands of those who suffer in this way, for state interference on their behalf to safeguard their legitimate expectations, are certain to receive popular sympathy and support. The general approval of these demands has had the effect that governments everywhere have taken action, not merely to protect the people so threatened from severe hardship and privation, but to secure to them the continued receipt of their former income and to shelter them from the vicissitudes of the market.[5]

Certainty of a given income can, however, not be given to all if any freedom in the choice of one's occupation is to be allowed. And, if it is provided for some, it becomes a privilege at the expense of others whose security is thereby necessarily diminished. That security of an invariable income can be provided for all only by the abolition of all freedom in the choice of one's employment is easily shown. Yet, although such a general guaranty of legitimate expectation is often regarded as the ideal to be aimed at, it is not a thing which is seriously attempted. What is constantly being done is to grant this kind of security piecemeal, to this group and to that, with the result that for those who are left out in the cold the insecurity constantly increases. No wonder that in consequence the value attached to the privilege of security constantly increases, the demand for it becomes more and more urgent, until in the end no price, not even that of liberty, appears too high.

If those whose usefulness is reduced by circumstances which they could neither foresee nor control were to be protected against undeserved loss, and those whose usefulness has been increased in the same way were prevented from making an unmerited gain, remuneration would soon cease to have any relation to actual usefulness. It would depend on the views held by some authority about what a person ought to have done, what he ought to have foreseen, and how good or bad his intentions were. Such decisions could not but be to a large extent arbitrary. The application of this principle would necessarily bring it about that people doing the same work would receive different remuneration. The differences in remuneration would then no longer present an adequate inducement to people to make the changes which are socially desirable, and it would not even be possible for the individuals affected to judge whether a particular change is worth the trouble it causes.

But if the changes in the distribution of men between different employments, which are constantly necessary in any society, can no longer be brought about

---

[5] Very interesting suggestions of how these hardships might be mitigated within a liberal society have been put forward by Professor W. H. Hutt in a book which will repay careful study, W. H. Hutt, *Plan for Reconstruction: A Project for Victory in War and Peace* (London: Kegan Paul, Trench, Trubner and Co., 1943).

by pecuniary "rewards" and "penalties" (which have no necessary connection with subjective merit), they must be brought about by direct orders. When a person's income is guaranteed, he can neither be allowed to stay in his job merely because he likes it nor to choose what other work he would like to do. As it is not he who makes the gain or suffers the loss dependent on his moving or not moving, the choice must be made for him by those who control the distribution of the available income.

The problem of adequate incentives which arises here is commonly discussed as if it were a problem mainly of the willingness of people to do their best. But this, although important, is not the whole, nor even the most important, aspect of the problem. It is not merely that if we want people to give their best we must make it worth while for them. What is more important is that if we want to leave them the choice, if they are to be able to judge what they ought to do, they must be given some readily intelligible yardstick by which to measure the social importance of the different occupations. Even with the best will in the world it would be impossible for anyone intelligently to choose between various alternatives if the advantages they offered him stood in no relation to their usefulness to society. To know whether as the result of a change a man ought to leave a trade and an environment which he has come to like, and exchange it for another, it is necessary that the changed relative value of these occupations to society should find expression in the remunerations they offer.

The problem is, of course, even more important because in the world as it is men are, in fact, not likely to give their best for long periods unless their own interests are directly involved. At least for great numbers some external pressure is needed if they are to give their best. The problem of incentives in this sense is a very real one, both in the sphere of ordinary labor and in those of the managerial activities. The application of the engineering technique to a whole nation—and this is what planning means—"raises problems of discipline which are hard to solve," as has been well described by an American engineer with great experience in government planning, who has clearly seen the problem.

"In order to do an engineering job," he explains, "there ought to be surrounding the work a comparatively large area of unplanned economic action. There should be a place from which workers can be drawn, and when a worker is fired he should vanish from the job and from the pay-roll. In the absence of such a free reservoir discipline cannot be maintained without corporal punishment, as with slave labor."[6]

In the sphere of executive work the problem of sanctions for negligence arises in a different but no less serious form. It has been well said that, while the last resort of a competitive economy is the bailiff, the ultimate sanction of a planned

[6]David C. Coyle, "The Twilight of National Planning," *Harper's Magazine*, no. 1025, October, 1935, p. 558. [The first passage quoted is found on page 559 of the article. —Ed.]

economy is the hangman.[7] The powers the manager of any plant will have to be given will still be considerable. But no more than in the case of the worker can the manager's position and income in a planned system be made to depend merely on the success or failure of the work under his direction. As neither the risk nor the gain is his, it cannot be his personal judgment, but whether he does what he ought to have done according to some established rule, which must decide. A mistake he "ought" to have avoided is not his own affair; it is a crime against the community and must be treated as such. While so long as he keeps to the safe path of objectively ascertainable duty he may be surer of his income than the capitalist entrepreneur, the danger which threatens him in case of real failure is worse than bankruptcy. He may be economically secure so long as he satisfies his superiors, but this security is bought at the price of the safety of freedom and life.

The conflict with which we have to deal is, indeed, a quite fundamental one between two irreconcilable types of social organization, which, from the most characteristic forms in which they appear, have often been described as the commercial and the military type of society. The terms were, perhaps, unfortunate, because they direct attention to unessentials and make it difficult to see that we face a real alternative and that there is no third possibility. Either both the choice and the risk rest with the individual or he is relieved of both. The army does, indeed, in many ways represent the closest approach familiar to us to the second type of organization, where work and worker alike are allotted by authority and where, if the available means are scanty, everybody is alike put on short-commons. This is the only system in which the individual can be conceded full economic security and through the extension of which to the whole of society it can be achieved for all its members. This security is, however, inseparable from the restrictions on liberty and the hierarchical order of military life—it is the security of the barracks.

It is possible, of course, to organize sections of an otherwise free society on this principle, and there is no reason why this form of life, with its necessary restrictions on individual liberty, should not be open to those who prefer it. Indeed, some voluntary labor service on military lines might well be the best form for the state to provide the certainty of an opportunity for work and a minimum income for all. That proposals of this sort have in the past proved so little acceptable is due to the fact that those who are willing to surrender their freedom for security have always demanded that if they give up their full freedom it should also be taken from those not prepared to do so. For this claim it is difficult to find a justification.

[7] Wilhelm Roepke, *Die Gesellschaftskrisis der Gegenwart* (Zürich: E. Rentsch, 1942), p. 172. [The book was later translated; see Wilhelm Roepke, *The Social Crisis of Our Time* (New Brunswick, NJ: Transaction Publishers, 1992). —Ed.]

The military type of organization as we know it gives us, however, only a very inadequate picture of what it would be like if it were extended to the whole of society. So long as only a part of society is organized on military lines, the un-freedom of the members of the military organization is mitigated by the fact that there is still a free sphere to which they can move if the restrictions become too irksome. If we want to form a picture of what society would be like if, according to the ideal which has seduced so many socialists, it was organized as a single great factory, we have to look to ancient Sparta, or to contemporary Germany, which, after moving for two or three generations in this direction, has now so nearly reached it.

In a society used to freedom it is unlikely that many people would be ready deliberately to purchase security at this price. But the policies which are now followed everywhere, which hand out the privilege of security, now to this group and now to that, are nevertheless rapidly creating conditions in which the striving for security tends to become stronger than the love of freedom. The reason for this is that with every grant of complete security to one group the insecurity of the rest necessarily increases. If you guarantee to some a fixed part of a variable cake, the share left to the rest is bound to fluctuate proportionally more than the size of the whole. And the essential element of security which the competitive system offers, the great variety of opportunities, is more and more reduced.

Within the market system, security can be granted to particular groups only by the kind of planning known as restrictionism (which includes, however, almost all the planning which is actually practiced!). "Control," i.e., limitation of output so that prices will secure an "adequate" return, is the only way in which in a market economy producers can be guaranteed a certain income. But this necessarily involves a reduction of opportunities open to others. If the producer, be he entrepreneur or worker, is to be protected against underbidding by outsiders, it means that others who are worse off are precluded from sharing in the relatively greater prosperity of the controlled industries. Every restriction on the freedom of entry into a trade reduces the security of all those outside it. And, as the number of those whose income is secured in this manner increases, the field of alternative opportunities which are open to anyone who suffers a loss of income is restricted; and for those unfavorably affected by any change the chance of avoiding a fatal diminution of their income is correspondingly diminished. And if, as has become increasingly true, in each trade in which conditions improve, the members are allowed to exclude others in order to secure to themselves the full gain in the form of higher wages or profits, those in the trades where demand has fallen have nowhere to go, and every change becomes the cause of large unemployment. There can be little doubt that it is largely a consequence of the striving for security by these means in the last decades that unemployment and thus insecurity for large sections of the population has so much increased.

In England and America such restrictions, especially those affecting the intermediate strata of society, have assumed important dimensions only in comparatively recent times, and we have scarcely yet realized their full consequences. The utter hopelessness of the position of those who, in a society which has thus grown rigid, are left outside the range of sheltered occupation, and the magnitude of the gulf which separates them from the fortunate possessors of jobs for whom protection against competition has made it unnecessary to budge ever so little to make room for those without, can be appreciated only by those who have experienced it. It is not a question of the fortunate ones' giving up their places, but merely that they should share in the common misfortune by some reduction of their incomes, or frequently even merely by some sacrifice of their prospects of improvement. The protection of their "standard of life," of the "fair price," or the "professional income" to which they regard themselves as entitled, and in the protection of which they receive the support of the state, precludes this. In consequence, instead of prices, wages, and individual incomes, it is now employment and production which have become subject to violent fluctuations. There has never been a worse and more cruel exploitation of one class by another than that of the weaker or less fortunate members of a group of producers by the well-established which has been made possible by the "regulation" of competition. Few catchwords have done so much harm as the ideal of a "stabilization" of particular prices (or wages), which, while securing the income of some, makes the position of the rest more and more precarious.

Thus, the more we try to provide full security by interfering with the market system, the greater the insecurity becomes; and, what is worse, the greater becomes the contrast between the security of those to whom it is granted as a privilege and the ever increasing insecurity of the underprivileged. And the more security becomes a privilege, and the greater the danger to those excluded from it, the higher will security be prized. As the number of the privileged increases and the difference between their security and the insecurity of the others increases, a completely new set of social values gradually arises. It is no longer independence but security which gives rank and status, the certain right to a pension more than confidence in his making good which makes a young man eligible for marriage, while insecurity becomes the dreaded state of the pariah in which those who in their youth have been refused admission to the haven of a salaried position remain for life.

The general endeavor to achieve security by restrictive measures, tolerated or supported by the state, has in the course of time produced a progressive transformation of society—a transformation in which, as in so many other ways,

Germany has led and the other countries have followed. This development has been hastened by another effect of socialist teaching, the deliberate disparagement of all activities involving economic risk and the moral opprobrium cast on the gains which make risks worth taking but which only few can win. We cannot blame our young men when they prefer the safe, salaried position to the risk of enterprise after they have heard from their earliest youth the former described as the superior, more unselfish and disinterested occupation. The younger generation of today has grown up in a world in which in school and press the spirit of commercial enterprise has been represented as disreputable and the making of profit as immoral, where to employ a hundred people is represented as exploitation but to command the same number as honorable. Older people may regard this as an exaggeration of the present state of affairs, but the daily experience of the university teacher leaves little doubt that, as a result of anticapitalist propaganda, values have already altered far in advance of the change in institutions which has so far taken place. The question is whether, by changing our institutions to satisfy the new demands, we shall not unwittingly destroy values which we still rate higher.

The change in the structure of society involved in the victory of the ideal of security over that of independence cannot be better illustrated than by a comparison of what ten or twenty years ago could still be regarded as the English and the German type of society. However great the influence of the army may have been in the latter country, it is a grave mistake to ascribe what the Englishman regarded as the "military" character of German society mainly to that influence. The difference went much deeper than could be explained on that ground, and the peculiar attributes of German society existed no less in circles in which the properly military influence was negligible than in those in which it was strong. It was not so much that at almost all times a larger part of the German people was organized for war than was true in other countries, but that the same type of organization was employed for so many other purposes, which gave German society its peculiar character. It was that a larger part of the civil life of Germany than of any other country was deliberately organized from the top, that so large a proportion of her people did not regard themselves as independent but as appointed functionaries, which gave her social structure its peculiar character. Germany had, as the Germans themselves boasted, for long been a *Beamtenstaat* in which not only in the civil service proper but in almost all spheres of life income and status were assigned and guaranteed by some authority.[8]

While it is doubtful whether the spirit of freedom can anywhere be extirpated by force, it is not certain that any people would successfully withstand the pro-

---

[8][*Beamtenstaat* might be translated as "civil service state," though if used pejoratively, as Hayek here suggests might be appropriate, it might also be rendered "bureaucratic state." —Ed.]

cess by which it was slowly smothered in Germany. Where distinction and rank are achieved almost exclusively by becoming a salaried servant of the state, where to do one's assigned duty is regarded as more laudable than to choose one's own field of usefulness, where all pursuits that do not give a recognized place in the official hierarchy or a claim to a fixed income are regarded as inferior and even somewhat disreputable, it is too much to expect that many will long prefer freedom to security. And where the alternative to security in a dependent position is a most precarious position, in which one is despised alike for success and for failure, only few will resist the temptation of safety at the price of freedom. Once things have gone so far, liberty indeed becomes almost a mockery, since it can be purchased only by the sacrifice of most of the good things of this earth. In this state it is little surprising that more and more people should come to feel that without economic security liberty is "not worth having" and that they are willing to sacrifice their liberty for security. But it is disquieting to find Professor Harold Laski employing the very same argument which has perhaps done more than any other to induce the German people to sacrifice their liberty.[9]

There can be no question that adequate security against severe privation, and the reduction of the avoidable causes of misdirected effort and consequent disappointment, will have to be one of the main goals of policy. But if these endeavors are to be successful and are not to destroy individual freedom, security must be provided outside the market and competition be left to function unobstructed. Some security is essential if freedom is to be preserved, because most men are willing to bear the risk which freedom inevitably involves only so long as that risk is not too great. But while this is a truth of which we must never lose sight, nothing is more fatal than the present fashion among intellectual leaders of extolling security at the expense of freedom. It is essential that we should relearn frankly to face the fact that freedom can be had only at a price and that as individuals we must be prepared to make severe material sacrifices to preserve our liberty. If we want to retain this, we must regain the conviction on which the rule of liberty in the Anglo-Saxon countries has been based and which Benjamin Franklin expressed in a phrase applicable to us in our lives as individuals no less than as nations: "Those who would give up essential liberty to purchase a little temporary safety deserve neither liberty nor safety."[10]

[9]H. J. Laski, *Liberty in the Modern State* (Harmondsworth: Penguin Books Ltd., 1937), Pelican Books ed., p. 51: "Those who know the normal life of the poor, its haunting sense of impending disaster, its fitful search for beauty which perpetually eludes, will realise well enough that, without economic security, liberty is not worth having."

[10][Benjamin Franklin, "Pennsylvania Assembly: Reply to the Governor, November 11, 1755," now available in *The Papers of Benjamin Franklin*, ed. Leonard W. Labaree, vol. 6 (New Haven and London: Yale University Press, 1963), p. 242. —Ed.]

TEN

WHY THE WORST GET ON TOP

Power tends to corrupt, and absolute power corrupts absolutely.

—Lord Acton[1]

We must now examine a belief from which many who regard the advent of totalitarianism as inevitable derive consolation and which seriously weakens the resistance of many others who would oppose it with all their might if they fully apprehended its nature. It is the belief that the most repellent features of the totalitarian regimes are due to the historical accident that they were established by groups of blackguards and thugs. Surely, it is argued, if in Germany the creation of a totalitarian regime brought the Streichers and Killingers, the Leys and Heines, the Himmlers and Heydrichs to power, this may prove the viciousness of the German character but not that the rise of such people is the necessary consequence of a totalitarian system.[2] Why should it not be possible that the same sort of system, if it be necessary to achieve important ends, be run by decent people for the good of the community as a whole?

---

[1] [Lord Acton, *Historical Essays and Studies*, ed. John Neville Figgis and Reginald Vere Laurence (London: Macmillan, 1919), p. 504. —Ed.]

[2] [Hayek's list comprises a rogue's gallery of infamous National Socialist "blackguards and thugs." Journalist and politician Julius Streicher (1885–1946), an early associate of Hitler's, is remembered for the vehemence of his persecution of the Jews in his newspaper *Der Stürmer.* He was convicted of war crimes at Nuremburg and hanged. Manfred von Killinger (1886–1944) made his name in the early 1920s for his role in the assassination of Matthias Erzberger, the politician who signed the armistice. A member of the SA (*Sturmabteilung*), the brown-shirted storm troopers that served as the early army of the Nazi party, he later entered the diplomatic service. Killinger committed suicide in Bucharest as the Soviet army was entering the city. Robert Ley (1890–1945) was the guiding force behind the forced reorganization of the trade unions into a single labor front, as well as the *Kraft durch Freude* recreational movement within it. He hanged himself in Nuremberg before the proceedings there began. Edmund Heines (1897–1934) was a general in the SA and intimate associate of its leader, Ernst Röhm. He was executed in June 1934 during the "Night of the Long Knives" in which Hitler purged elements of the SA. Following the purge, the black-shirted SS (*Schutztaffel*), which began as Hitler's personal bodyguard, was elevated above the SA, and Heinrich Himmler (1900–1945) was put in charge of both the SS and the Gestapo (*Geheime Staatspolizei*), or secret state police. Himmler expanded and transformed the SS into an elite guard that had among its tasks the administration of the concentration and extermination camps. Chief

We must not deceive ourselves into believing that all good people must be democrats or will necessarily wish to have a share in the government. Many, no doubt, would rather entrust it to somebody whom they think more competent. Although this might be unwise, there is nothing bad or dishonorable in approving a dictatorship of the good. Totalitarianism, we can already hear it argued, is a powerful system alike for good and evil, and the purpose for which it will be used depends entirely on the dictators. And those who think that it is not the system which we need fear, but the danger that it might be run by bad men, might even be tempted to forestall this danger by seeing that it is established in time by good men.

No doubt an American or English "Fascist" system would greatly differ from the Italian or German models; no doubt, if the transition were effected without violence, we might expect to get a better type of leader. And, if I had to live under a Fascist system, I have no doubt that I would rather live under one run by Englishmen or Americans than under one run by anybody else. Yet all this does not mean that, judged on our present standards, our Fascist system would in the end prove so very different or much less intolerable than its prototypes. There are strong reasons for believing that what to us appear the worst features of the existing totalitarian systems are not accidental by-products but phenomena which totalitarianism is certain sooner or later to produce. Just as the democratic statesman who sets out to plan economic life will soon be confronted with the alternative of either assuming dictatorial powers or abandoning his plans, so the totalitarian dictator would soon have to choose between disregard of ordinary morals and failure. It is for this reason that the unscrupulous and uninhibited are likely to be more successful in a society tending toward totalitarianism. Who does not see this has not yet grasped the full width of the gulf which separates totalitarianism from a liberal regime, the utter difference between the whole moral atmosphere under collectivism and the essentially individualist Western civilization.

The "moral basis of collectivism" has, of course, been much debated in the past; but what concerns us here is not its moral basis but its moral results. The usual discussions of the ethical aspects of collectivism refer to the question whether collectivism is demanded by existing moral convictions; or what moral convictions would be required if collectivism is to produce the hoped-for results. Our question, however, is what moral views will be produced by a collectivist organization of society, or what views are likely to rule it. The interaction between morals and institutions may well have the effect that the ethics pro-

---

architect of the holocaust, Himmler escaped the executioner by swallowing a cyanide tablet after his capture by the British. Reinhard Heydrich (1904–1942), known as "the hangman," was second in command to Himmler in the Gestapo. He was assassinated by the Czech resistance in 1942; the village of Lidice was razed and all its men executed in reprisal. —Ed.]

duced by collectivism will be altogether different from the moral ideals that lead to the demand for collectivism. While we are likely to think that, since the desire for a collectivist system springs from high moral motives, such a system must be the breeding-ground for the highest virtues, there is, in fact, no reason why any system should necessarily enhance those attitudes which serve the purpose for which it was designed. The ruling moral views will depend partly on the qualities that will lead individuals to success in a collectivist or totalitarian system and partly on the requirements of the totalitarian machinery.

We must here return for a moment to the position which precedes the suppression of democratic institutions and the creation of a totalitarian regime. In this stage it is the general demand for quick and determined government action that is the dominating element in the situation, dissatisfaction with the slow and cumbersome course of democratic procedure which makes action for action's sake the goal. It is then the man or the party who seems strong and resolute enough "to get things done" who exercises the greatest appeal. "Strong" in this sense means not merely a numerical majority—it is the ineffectiveness of parliamentary majorities with which people are dissatisfied. What they will seek is somebody with such solid support as to inspire confidence that he can carry out whatever he wants. It is here that the new type of party, organized on military lines, comes in.

In the Central European countries the socialist parties had familiarized the masses with political organizations of a semi-military character designed to absorb as much as possible of the private life of the members. All that was wanted to give one group overwhelming power was to carry the same principle somewhat further, to seek strength not in the assured votes of huge numbers at occasional elections but in the absolute and unreserved support of a smaller but more thoroughly organized body. The chance of imposing a totalitarian regime on a whole people depends on the leader's first collecting round him a group which is prepared voluntarily to submit to that totalitarian discipline which they are to impose by force upon the rest.

Although the socialist parties had the strength to get anything if they had cared to use force, they were reluctant to do so. They had, without knowing it, set themselves a task which only the ruthless ready to disregard the barriers of accepted morals can execute.

That socialism can be put into practice only by methods which most socialists disapprove is, of course, a lesson learned by many social reformers in the past. The old socialist parties were inhibited by their democratic ideals; they did not possess the ruthlessness required for the performance of their chosen task. It is characteristic that both in Germany and in Italy the success of fascism was preceded by the refusal of the socialist parties to take over the responsibilities of government. They were unwilling wholeheartedly to employ the methods to which they had pointed the way. They still hoped for the miracle of a majority's agreeing on a particular plan for the organization of the whole of society; others had already learned the lesson that in a planned society the question can no longer be on what do a majority of the people agree but what the largest single group is whose members agree sufficiently to make unified direction of all affairs possible; or, if no such group large enough to enforce its views exists, how it can be created and who will succeed in creating it.

There are three main reasons why such a numerous and strong group with fairly homogeneous views is not likely to be formed by the best but rather by the worst elements of any society. By our standards the principles on which such a group would be selected will be almost entirely negative.

In the first instance, it is probably true that, in general, the higher the education and intelligence of individuals become, the more their views and tastes are differentiated and the less likely they are to agree on a particular hierarchy of values. It is a corollary of this that if we wish to find a high degree of uniformity and similarity of outlook, we have to descend to the regions of lower moral and intellectual standards where the more primitive and "common" instincts and tastes prevail. This does not mean that the majority of people have low moral standards; it merely means that the largest group of people whose values are very similar are the people with low standards. It is, as it were, the lowest common denominator which unites the largest number of people. If a numerous group is needed, strong enough to impose their views on the values of life on all the rest, it will never be those with highly differentiated and developed tastes—it will be those who form the "mass" in the derogatory sense of the term, the least original and independent, who will be able to put the weight of their numbers behind their particular ideals.

If, however, a potential dictator had to rely entirely on those whose uncomplicated and primitive instincts happen to be very similar, their number would scarcely give sufficient weight to their endeavors. He will have to increase their numbers by converting more to the same simple creed.

Here comes in the second negative principle of selection: he will be able to obtain the support of all the docile and gullible, who have no strong convictions of their own but are prepared to accept a ready-made system of values if it is only drummed into their ears sufficiently loudly and frequently. It will be those whose vague and imperfectly formed ideas are easily swayed and whose passions and emotions are readily aroused who will thus swell the ranks of the totalitarian party.

It is in connection with the deliberate effort of the skillful demagogue to weld together a closely coherent and homogeneous body of supporters that the third and perhaps most important negative element of selection enters. It seems to be almost a law of human nature that it is easier for people to agree on a negative program—on the hatred of an enemy, on the envy of those better off—

160

than on any positive task. The contrast between the "we" and the "they," the common fight against those outside the group, seems to be an essential ingredient in any creed which will solidly knit together a group for common action. It is consequently always employed by those who seek, not merely support of a policy, but the unreserved allegiance of huge masses. From their point of view it has the great advantage of leaving them greater freedom of action than almost any positive program. The enemy, whether he be internal, like the "Jew" or the "kulak," or external, seems to be an indispensable requisite in the armory of a totalitarian leader.

That in Germany it was the Jew who became the enemy until his place was taken by the "plutocracies" was no less a result of the anticapitalist resentment on which the whole movement was based than the selection of the kulak in Russia. In Germany and Austria the Jew had come to be regarded as the representative of capitalism because a traditional dislike of large classes of the population for commercial pursuits had left these more readily accessible to a group that was practically excluded from the more highly esteemed occupations. It is the old story of the alien race's being admitted only to the less respected trades and then being hated still more for practicing them. The fact that German anti-Semitism and anticapitalism spring from the same root is of great importance for the understanding of what has happened there, but this is rarely grasped by foreign observers.

To treat the universal tendency of collectivist policy to become nationalistic as due entirely to the necessity for securing unhesitating support would be to neglect another and no less important factor. It may, indeed, be questioned whether anyone can realistically conceive of a collectivist program other than in the service of a limited group, whether collectivism can exist in any form other than that of some kind of particularism, be it nationalism, racialism, or classism. The belief in the community of aims and interests with fellow-men seems to presuppose a greater degree of similarity of outlook and thought than exists between men merely as human beings. If the other members of one's group cannot all be personally known, they must at least be of the same kind as those around us, think and talk in the same way and about the same kind of things, in order that we may identify ourselves with them. Collectivism on a world scale seems to be unthinkable—except in the service of a small ruling élite. It would certainly raise not only technical but, above all, moral problems which none of our socialists is willing to face. If the English proletarian, for instance, is entitled to an equal share of the income now derived from his country's capital resources, and of the control of their use, because they are the result of exploitation, so on the same principle all the Indians would be entitled not only to the income from but also to the use of a proportional share of the British capital.

But what socialists seriously contemplate the equal division of existing capital resources among the people of the world? They all regard the capital as belonging not to humanity but to the nation—though even within the nation few would dare to advocate that the richer regions should be deprived of some of "their" capital equipment in order to help the poorer regions. What socialists proclaim as a duty toward the fellow-members of the existing states they are not prepared to grant to the foreigner. From a consistent collectivist point of view the claims of the "have-not" nations for a new division of the world are entirely justified—though, if consistently applied, those who demand it most loudly would lose by it almost as much as the richest nations. They are, therefore, careful not to base their claims on any equalitarian principles but on their pretended superior capacity to organize other peoples.

One of the inherent contradictions of the collectivist philosophy is that, while basing itself on the humanistic morals which individualism has developed, it is practicable only within a relatively small group. That socialism so long as it remains theoretical is internationalist, while as soon as it is put into practice, whether in Russia or in Germany, it becomes violently nationalist, is one of the reasons why "liberal socialism" as most people in the Western world imagine it is purely theoretical, while the practice of socialism is everywhere totalitarian.[3] Collectivism has no room for the wide humanitarianism of liberalism but only for the narrow particularism of the totalitarian.

If the "community" or the state are prior to the individual, if they have ends of their own independent of and superior to those of the individuals, only those individuals who work for the same ends can be regarded as members of the community. It is a necessary consequence of this view that a person is respected only as a member of the group, that is, only if and in so far as he works for the recognized common ends, and that he derives his whole dignity only from this membership and not merely from being a man. Indeed, the very concepts of humanity and therefore of any form of internationalism are entirely products of the individualist view of man, and there can be no place for them in a collectivist system of thought.[4]

Apart from the basic fact that the community of collectivism can extend only as far as the unity of purpose of the individuals exists or can be created, several

---

[3] Cf. now the instructive discussion in Franz Borkenau, *Socialism, National or International?* (London: G. Routledge and Sons, 1942).

[4] It is entirely in the spirit of collectivism when Nietzsche makes his Zarathustra say:

"A thousand goals have existed hitherto, for a thousand people existed. But the fetter for the thousand necks is still lacking, the one goal is still lacking. Humanity has no goal yet.

"But tell me, I pray, my brethren: if the goal be lacking to humanity, is not humanity itself lacking?"

[Hayek quotes from Friedrich Nietzsche's *Thus Spake Zarathustra;* the passage appears at the end of chapter 15. —Ed.]

contributory factors strengthen the tendency of collectivism to become particularist and exclusive. Of these, one of the most important is that the desire of the individual to identify himself with a group is very frequently the result of a feeling of inferiority and that therefore his want will be satisfied only if membership of the group confers some superiority over outsiders. Sometimes, it seems, the very fact that these violent instincts which the individual knows he must curb within the group can be given a free range in the collective action toward the outsider, becomes a further inducement for merging personality in that of the group. There is a profound truth expressed in the title of Reinhold Niebuhr's *Moral Man and Immoral Society*—however little we can follow him in the conclusions he draws from his thesis. There is, indeed, as he says elsewhere, "an increasing tendency among modern men to imagine themselves ethical because they have delegated their vices to larger and larger groups."[5] To act on behalf of a group seems to free people of many of the moral restraints which control their behavior as individuals within the group.

The definitely antagonistic attitude which most planners take toward internationalism is further explained by the fact that in the existing world all outside contacts of a group are obstacles to their effectively planning the sphere in which they can attempt it. It is therefore no accident that, as the editor of one of the most comprehensive collective studies on planning has discovered to his chagrin, "most 'planners' are militant nationalists."[6]

The nationalist and imperialist propensities of socialist planners, much more common than is generally recognized, are not always as flagrant as, for example, in the case of the Webbs and some of the other early Fabians, with whom enthusiasm for planning was characteristically combined with the veneration for the large and powerful political units and a contempt for the small state. The historian Élie Halévy, speaking of the Webbs when he first knew them forty years ago, records that their socialism was profoundly antiliberal. "They did not hate the Tories, indeed they were extraordinarily lenient to them, but they had no mercy for Gladstonian Liberalism. It was the time of the Boer War and both the advanced liberals and the men who were beginning to form the Labour Party had generously sided with the Boers against British

---

[5] Quoted from an article of Dr. Niebuhr's by E. H. Carr, *The Twenty Years' Crisis, 1919–1939: An Introduction to the Study of International Relations* (London: Macmillan, 1940), p. 203. [The article that Carr quotes from was Reinhold Niebuhr, "A Critique of Fascism," *Atlantic Monthly*, vol. 139, May 1927, p. 639. The American protestant theologian Reinhold Niebuhr (1892–1971) was an advocate of Christian realism. In his *Moral Man and Immoral Society*, op cit., Niebuhr examined the implications of the idea that social groups often engage in practices that would be considered repugnant on the individual level. —Ed.]

[6] Findlay MacKenzie, ed. *Planned Society, Yesterday, Today, Tomorrow: A Symposium by Thirty-Five Economists, Sociologists, and Statesmen*, op. cit., p. xx. [Hayek's 1938 review of the MacKenzie volume is reprinted in F. A. Hayek, *Socialism and War*, op. cit., pp. 242–44. —Ed.]

Imperialism, in the name of freedom and humanity. But the two Webbs and their friend, Bernard Shaw, stood apart. They were ostentatiously imperialistic. The independence of small nations might mean something to the liberal individualist. It meant nothing to collectivists like themselves. I can still hear Sidney Webb explaining to me that the future belonged to the great administrative nations, where the officials govern and the police keep order." And elsewhere Halévy quotes George Bernard Shaw, arguing, about the same time, that "the world is to the big and powerful states by necessity; and the little ones must come within their border or be crushed out of existence."[7]

I have quoted at length these passages, which would not surprise one in a description of the German ancestors of National Socialism, because they provide so characteristic an example of that glorification of power which easily leads from socialism to nationalism and which profoundly affects the ethical views of all collectivists. So far as the rights of small nations are concerned, Marx and Engels were little better than most other consistent collectivists, and the views occasionally expressed about Czechs or Poles resemble those of contemporary National Socialists.[8]

While to the great individualist social philosophers of the nineteenth century, to a Lord Acton or a Jacob Burckhardt, down to contemporary socialists, like Bertrand Russell, who have inherited the liberal tradition, power itself has al-

---

[7] Élie Halévy, *L'ère des tyrannies*, op. cit., p. 217, and *A History of the English People*, vol. 1, *Epilogue*, translated by E. I. Watkin (London: Benn, 1929–1934), pp. 105–106. [Halévy's first book was translated as *The Era of Tyrannies: Essays on Socialism and War*, op. cit., and the discussion of the Webbs and Shaw may be found on page 271 of the translation. Irish playwright and essayist George Bernard Shaw (1856–1950) was an early member of the Fabian Society. His most famous work was *Pygmalion*, but he was also known in the interwar period for such tracts as *The Intelligent Woman's Guide to Socialism and Capitalism* (London: Constable, 1928). For more on the Webbs, see chapter 5, note 3. —Ed.]

[8] Cf. Karl Marx, *Revolution and Counter-revolution*, and Engels's letter to Marx, May 23, 1851. [*Revolution and Counter-revolution* is a history of the revolution of 1848, written by Friedrich Engels and originally published as articles in the *New York Tribune* between October 1851 and September 1852. It is reprinted in Friedrich Engels, *The German Revolutions* (Chicago: University of Chicago Press, 1967), and the discussion of the Poles and the "Tschechs" may be found on pp. 174–81. Though written by Engels, the articles were sent to the newspaper through Marx and published under Marx's name, which is why Hayek refers to Marx, rather than Engels, as the author.

Here is part of what Engels wrote to Marx in his letter of May 23, 1851: "The more I think about it, the more obvious it becomes to me that the Poles are *une nation foutue* [a finished nation] who can only continue to serve a purpose until such time as Russia herself becomes caught up into the agrarian revolution. From that moment Poland will have absolutely no raison d'être any more. The Poles' sole contribution to history has been to indulge in foolish pranks at once valiant and provocative. Nor can a single moment be cited when Poland, even if only by comparison with Russia, has successfully represented progress or done anything of historical significance." The Marx-Engels correspondence is available online at http://www.marxists.org/archive/marx/ —Ed.]

ways appeared the archevil, to the strict collectivist it is a goal in itself.[9] It is not only, as Russell has so well described, that the desire to organize social life according to a unitary plan itself springs largely from a desire for power.[10] It is even more the outcome of the fact that, in order to achieve their end, collectivists must create power—power over men wielded by other men—of a magnitude never before known, and that their success will depend on the extent to which they achieve such power.

This remains true even though many liberal socialists are guided in their endeavors by the tragic illusion that by depriving private individuals of the power they possess in an individualist system, and by transferring this power to society, they can thereby extinguish power. What all those who argue in this manner overlook is that, by concentrating power so that it can be used in the service of a single plan, it is not merely transferred but infinitely heightened; that, by uniting in the hands of some single body power formerly exercised independently by many, an amount of power is created infinitely greater than any that existed before, so much more far-reaching as almost to be different in kind. It is entirely fallacious when it is sometimes argued that the great power exercised by a central planning board would be "no greater than the power collectively exercised by private boards of directors."[11] There is, in a competitive society, nobody who can exercise even a fraction of the power which a socialist planning board would possess, and if nobody can consciously use the power, it is just an abuse of words to assert that it rests with all the capitalists put together.[12] It is merely a play upon words to speak of the "power collectively exercised by private boards of directors" so long as they do not combine to concerted action— which would, of course, mean the end of competition and the creation of a planned economy. To split or decentralize power is necessarily to reduce the

[9][Swiss historian Jacob Burckhardt (1818–1897) wrote principally about the Italian renaissance and Greek civilization, hoping that knowledge of the foundations of European culture would serve as a bulwark against the social, political, and cultural upheavals that he witnessed in the nineteenth century. In his book *Force and Freedom: Reflections on History,* trans. James Hastings Nichols (New York: Pantheon, 1943), based on lectures he had delivered just prior to the formation of the German Empire, he presciently warned about coming periods of great national wars and of the dangers of all-powerful states. British philosopher Bertrand Russell (1872–1970), who made important contributions to the foundations of mathematics, logic, and analytic philosophy, was also a public figure famous for his antiwar activities, his frequent marriages and even more numerous affairs, and, later in life, his support of nuclear disarmament. —Ed.]

[10]Bertrand Russell, *The Scientific Outlook* (New York: W. W. Norton, 1931), p. 211.

[11]Benjamin E. Lippincott, in his Introduction to Oscar Lange and F. M. Taylor, *On the Economic Theory of Socialism,* op. cit., p. 35.

[12]We must not allow ourselves to be deceived by the fact that the word "power," apart from the sense in which it is used with respect to human beings, is also used in an impersonal (or rather anthropomorphic) sense for any determining cause. Of course, there will always be something that determines everything that happens, and in this sense the amount of power existing must always be the same. But this is not true of the power consciously wielded by human beings.

absolute amount of power, and the competitive system is the only system designed to minimize by decentralization the power exercised by man over man.

We have seen before how the separation of economic and political aims is an essential guaranty of individual freedom and how it is consequently attacked by all collectivists. To this we must now add that the "substitution of political for economic power" now so often demanded means necessarily the substitution of power from which there is no escape for a power which is always limited. What is called economic power, while it can be an instrument of coercion, is, in the hands of private individuals, never exclusive or complete power, never power over the whole life of a person. But centralized as an instrument of political power it creates a degree of dependence scarcely distinguishable from slavery.

From the two central features of every collectivist system, the need for a commonly accepted system of ends of the group and the all-overriding desire to give to the group the maximum of power to achieve these ends, grows a definite system of morals, which on some points coincides and on others violently contrasts with ours—but differs from it in one point which makes it doubtful whether we can call it morals: that it does not leave the individual conscience free to apply its own rules and does not even know any general rules which the individual is required or allowed to observe in all circumstances. This makes collectivist morals so different from what we have known as morals that we find it difficult to discover any principle in them, which they nevertheless possess.

The difference of principle is very much the same as that which we have already considered in connection with the Rule of Law. Like formal law, the rules of individualist ethics, however unprecise they may be in many respects, are general and absolute; they prescribe or prohibit a general type of action irrespective of whether in the particular instance the ultimate purpose is good or bad. To cheat or steal, to torture or betray a confidence, is held to be bad, irrespective of whether or not in the particular instance any harm follows from it. Neither the fact that in a given instance nobody may be the worse for it, nor any high purpose for which such an act may have been committed, can alter the fact that it is bad. Though we may sometimes be forced to choose between different evils, they remain evils.

The principle that the end justifies the means is in individualist ethics regarded as the denial of all morals. In collectivist ethics it becomes necessarily the supreme rule; there is literally nothing which the consistent collectivist must not be prepared to do if it serves "the good of the whole," because the "good of the whole" is to him the only criterion of what ought to be done. The *raison d'état*, in which collectivist ethics has found its most explicit formulation, knows no other limit than that set by expediency—the suitability of the particular act for the end in view. And what the *raison d'état* affirms with respect to the relations between different countries applies equally to the relations between different individuals within the collectivist state. There can be no limit to what its citizen must be prepared to do, no act which his conscience must prevent him from committing, if it is necessary for an end which the community has set itself or which his superiors order him to achieve.

The absence of absolute formal rules in collectivist ethics does not, of course, mean that there are not some useful habits of the individuals which a collectivist community will encourage and others which it will discourage. Quite the reverse; it will take a much greater interest in the individual's habits of life than an individualist community. To be a useful member of a collectivist society requires very definite qualities which must be strengthened by constant practice. The reason why we designate these qualities as "useful habits" and can hardly describe them as moral virtues is that the individual could never be allowed to put these rules above any definite orders or to let them become an obstacle to the achievement of any of the particular aims of his community. They only serve, as it were, to fill any gaps which direct orders or the designation of particular aims may leave, but they can never justify a conflict with the will of the authority.

The differences between the virtues which will continue to be esteemed under a collectivist system and those which will disappear is well illustrated by a comparison of the virtues which even their worst enemies admit the Germans, or rather the "typical Prussian," to possess, and those of which they are commonly thought lacking and in which the English people, with some justification, used to pride themselves as excelling. Few people will deny that the Germans on the whole are industrious and disciplined, thorough and energetic to the degree of ruthlessness, conscientious and single-minded in any tasks they undertake; that they possess a strong sense of order, duty, and strict obedience to authority; and that they often show great readiness to make personal sacrifices and great courage in physical danger. All these make the German an efficient instrument in carrying out an assigned task, and they have accordingly been carefully nurtured in the old Prussian state and the new Prussian-dominated Reich. What the "typical German" is often thought to lack are the individualist virtues of tolerance and respect for other individuals and their opinions, of independence of mind and that uprightness of character and readiness to defend one's own convictions against a superior which the Germans themselves, usually conscious that they lack it, call *Zivilcourage*, of consideration for the weak and infirm, and of that healthy contempt and dislike of power which only an old tradition of personal liberty creates. Deficient they seem also in most of those little yet so important qualities which facilitate the intercourse between men in a free society: kindliness and a sense of humor, personal modesty, and respect for the privacy and belief in the good intentions of one's neighbor.

After what we have already said it will not cause surprise that these individualist virtues are at the same time eminently social virtues—virtues which smooth social contacts and which make control from above less necessary and at the same time more difficult. They are virtues which flourish wherever the individualist or commercial type of society has prevailed and which are missing according as the collectivist or military type of society predominates—a difference which is, or was, as noticeable between the various regions of Germany as it has now become of the views which rule in Germany and those characteristic of the West. Until recently, at least, in those parts of Germany which have been longest exposed to the civilizing forces of commerce, the old commercial towns of the south and west and the Hanse towns, the general moral concepts were probably much more akin to those of the Western people than to those which have now become dominant all over Germany.

It would, however, be highly unjust to regard the masses of the totalitarian people as devoid of moral fervor because they give unstinted support to a system which to us seems a denial of most moral values. For the great majority of them the opposite is probably true: the intensity of the moral emotions behind a movement like that of National Socialism or communism can probably be compared only to those of the great religious movements of history. Once you admit that the individual is merely a means to serve the ends of the higher entity called society or the nation, most of those features of totalitarian regimes which horrify us follow of necessity. From the collectivist standpoint intolerance and brutal suppression of dissent, the complete disregard of the life and happiness of the individual, are essential and unavoidable consequences of this basic premise, and the collectivist can admit this and at the same time claim that his system is superior to one in which the "selfish" interests of the individual are allowed to obstruct the full realization of the ends the community pursues. When German philosophers again and again represent the striving for personal happiness as itself immoral and only the fulfilment of an imposed duty as praiseworthy, they are perfectly sincere, however difficult this may be to understand for those who have been brought up in a different tradition.

Where there is one common all-overriding end, there is no room for any general morals or rules. To a limited extent we ourselves experience this in wartime. But even war and the greatest peril had led in the democratic countries only to a very moderate approach to totalitarianism, very little setting-aside of all other values in the service of a single purpose. But where a few specific ends dominate the whole of society, it is inevitable that occasionally cruelty may become a duty; that acts which revolt all our feeling, such as the shooting of hostages or the killing of the old or sick, should be treated as mere matters of expediency; that the compulsory uprooting and transportation of hundreds of thousand should become an instrument of policy approved by almost everybody except the victims; or that suggestions like that of a "conscription of woman for breeding purposes" can be seriously contemplated. There is always in the eyes of the collectivist a greater goal which these acts serve and which to him justifies them because the pursuit of the common end of society can know no limits in any rights or values of any individual.

But while for the mass of the citizens of the totalitarian state it is often unselfish devotion to an ideal, although one that is repellent to us, which makes them approve and even perform such deeds, this cannot be pleaded for those who guide its policy. To be a useful assistant in the running of a totalitarian state, it is not enough that a man should be prepared to accept specious justification of vile deeds; he must himself be prepared actively to break every moral rule he has ever known if this seems necessary to achieve the end set for him. Since it is the supreme leader who alone determines the ends, his instruments must have no moral convictions of their own. They must, above all, be unreservedly committed to the person of the leader; but next to this the most important thing is that they should be completely unprincipled and literally capable of everything. They must have no ideals of their own which they want to realize; no ideas about right or wrong which might interfere with the intentions of the leader. There is thus in the positions of power little to attract those who hold moral beliefs of the kind which in the past have guided the European peoples, little which could compensate for the distastefulness of many of the particular tasks, and little opportunity to gratify any more idealistic desires, to recompense for the undeniable risk, the sacrifice of most of the pleasures of private life and of personal independence which the posts of great responsibility involve. The only tastes which are satisfied are the taste for power as such and the pleasure of being obeyed and of being part of a well-functioning and immensely powerful machine to which everything else must give way.

Yet while there is little that is likely to induce men who are good by our standards to aspire to leading positions in the totalitarian machine, and much to deter them, there will be special opportunities for the ruthless and unscrupulous. There will be jobs to be done about the badness of which taken by themselves nobody has any doubt, but which have to be done in the service of some higher end, and which have to be executed with the same expertness and efficiency as any others. And as there will be need for actions which are bad in themselves, and which all those still influenced by traditional morals will be reluctant to perform, the readiness to do bad things becomes a path to promotion and power. The positions in a totalitarian society in which it is necessary to practice cruelty and intimidation, deliberate deception and spying, are numerous. Neither the Gestapo nor the administration of a concentration camp, neither the Ministry of Propaganda nor the SA or SS (or their Italian or Russian counterparts), are suitable places for the exercise of humanitarian feelings.[13] Yet it is through positions like these that the road to the highest positions in the totalitarian state leads. It is only too true when a distinguished American economist concludes from a similar brief enumeration of the duties of the authorities of a collectivist state that "they would have to do these things whether they wanted to or not: and the probability of the people in power being individuals who would dislike the possession and exercise of power is on a level with the probability that an extremely tender-hearted person would get the job of whipping-master in a slave plantation."[14]

We cannot, however, exhaust this subject here. The problem of the selection of the leaders is closely bound up with the wide problem of selection according to the opinions held, or rather according to the readiness with which a person conforms to an ever changing set of doctrines. And this leads us to one of the most characteristic moral features of totalitarianism: its relation to, and its effect on, all the virtues falling under the general heading of truthfulness. This is so big a subject that it requires a separate chapter.

[13][See this chapter, note 2, for more on the Gestapo, the SA, and the SS. —Ed.]
[14]Professor Frank H. Knight, "Book Review: Walter Lippmann's *The Good Society*," *Journal of Political Economy*, vol. 46, December 1938, p. 869.

ELEVEN

THE END OF TRUTH

It is significant that the nationalization of thought has proceeded everywhere pari passu with the nationalization of industry. —E. H. Carr[1]

The most effective way of making everybody serve the single system of ends toward which the social plan is directed is to make everybody believe in those ends. To make a totalitarian system function efficiently, it is not enough that everybody should be forced to work for the same ends. It is essential that the people should come to regard them as their own ends. Although the beliefs must be chosen for the people and imposed upon them, they must become their beliefs, a generally accepted creed which makes the individuals as far as possible act spontaneously in the way the planner wants. If the feeling of oppression in totalitarian countries is in general much less acute than most people in liberal countries imagine, this is because the totalitarian governments succeed to a high degree in making people think as they want them to.

This is, of course, brought about by the various forms of propaganda. Its technique is now so familiar that we need say little about it. The only point that needs to be stressed is that neither propaganda in itself nor the techniques employed are peculiar to totalitarianism and that what so completely changes its nature and effect in a totalitarian state is that all propaganda serves the same goal—that all the instruments of propaganda are coordinated to influence the individuals in the same direction and to produce the characteristic *Gleichschaltung* of all minds.[2] As a result, the effect of propaganda in totalitarian countries is different not only in magnitude but in kind from that of the propaganda made for different ends by independent and competing agencies. If all the sources of current information are effectively under one single control, it is no longer a question of merely persuading the people of this or that. The skillful propagan-

---

[1] [E. H. Carr, *The Twenty Years' Crisis*, op. cit., p. 172. Carr actually uses the term nationalization of *opinion*, rather than nationalization of thought. —Ed.]

[2] [*Gleichschaltung* is usually translated as "coordination," and is the term used to describe the Nazis' efforts to coordinate all political, economic, cultural, and even recreational activities in support of the state. The forced reorganization of the disparate trade unions into a single labor "front" is a standard example. —Ed.]

dist then has power to mold their minds in any direction he chooses, and even the most intelligent and independent people cannot entirely escape that influence if they are long isolated from all other sources of information.

While in the totalitarian states this status of propaganda gives it a unique power over the minds of the people, the peculiar moral effects arise not from the technique but from the object and scope of totalitarian propaganda. If it could be confined to indoctrinating the people with the whole system of values toward which the social effort is directed, propaganda would represent merely a particular manifestation of the characteristic features of collectivist morals which we have already considered. If its object were merely to teach the people a definite and comprehensive moral code, the problem would be solely whether this moral code is good or bad. We have seen that the moral code of a totalitarian society is not likely to appeal to us, that even the striving for equality by means of a directed economy can result only in an officially enforced inequality—an authoritarian determination of the status of each individual in the new hierarchical order—and that most of the humanitarian elements of our morals, the respect for human life, for the weak, and for the individual generally, will disappear. However repellent this may be to most people, and though it involves a change in moral standards, it is not necessarily entirely antimoral. Some features of such a system may even appeal to the sternest moralists of a conservative tint and seem to them preferable to the softer standards of a liberal society.

The moral consequences of totalitarian propaganda which we must now consider are, however, of an even more profound kind. They are destructive of all morals because they undermine one of the foundations of all morals: the sense of and the respect for truth. From the nature of its task, totalitarian propaganda cannot confine itself to values, to questions of opinion and moral convictions in which the individual always will conform more or less to the views ruling his community, but must extend to questions of fact where human intelligence is involved in a different way. This is so, first, because, in order to induce people to accept the official values, these must be justified, or shown to be connected with the values already held by the people, which usually will involve assertions about causal connections between means and ends; and, second, because the distinction between ends and means, between the goal aimed at and the measures taken to achieve it, is in fact never so clear cut and definite as any general discussion of these problems is likely to suggest; and because, therefore, people must be brought to agree not only with the ultimate aims but also with the views about the facts and possibilities on which the particular measures are based.

We have seen that agreement on that complete ethical code, that all-comprehensive system of values which is implicit in an economic plan, does not exist in a free society but would have to be created. But we must not assume that the planner will approach his task aware of that need or that, even if he were aware of it, it would be possible to create such a comprehensive code in advance. He only finds out about the conflicts between different needs as he goes along, and he has to make his decisions as the necessity arises. The code of values guiding his decisions does not exist *in abstracto* before the decisions have to be made; it has to be created with the particular decisions. We have also seen how this inability to separate the general problem of values from the particular decisions makes it impossible that a democratic body, while unable to decide the technical details of a plan, should yet determine the values guiding it.

And while the planning authority will constantly have to decide issues on merits about which there exist no definite moral rules, it will have to justify its decisions to the people—or, at least, have somehow to make the people believe that they are the right decisions. Although those responsible for a decision may have been guided by no more than prejudice, some guiding principle will have to be stated publicly if the community is not merely passively to submit but actively to support the measure. The need to rationalize the likes and dislikes which, for lack of anything else, must guide the planner in many of his decisions, and the necessity of stating his reasons in a form in which they will appeal to as many people as possible, will force him to construct theories, i.e., assertions about the connections between facts, which then become an integral part of the governing doctrine.

This process of creating a "myth" to justify his action need not be conscious. The totalitarian leader may be guided merely by an instinctive dislike of the state of things he has found and a desire to create a new hierarchical order which conforms better to his conception of merit; he may merely know that he dislikes the Jews who seemed to be so successful in an order which did not provide a satisfactory place for him, and that he loves and admires the tall blond man, the "aristocratic" figure of the novels of his youth. So he will readily embrace theories which seem to provide a rational justification for the prejudices which he shares with many of his fellows. Thus a pseudoscientific theory becomes part of the official creed which to a greater or lesser degree directs everybody's action. Or the widespread dislike of the industrial civilization and a romantic yearning for country life, together with a (probably erroneous) idea about the special value of country people as soldiers, provide the basis for another myth: *Blut und Boden* ("blood and soil"), expressing not merely ultimate values but a whole host of beliefs about cause and effect which, once they have become ideals directing the activity of the whole community, must not be questioned.[3]

[3][*Blut und Boden*, a term first introduced by the historian Oswald Spengler, was the doctrine that the state rightly consists of people of a uniform race on their own land. The Nazis used it to justify a number of changes in agricultural policy, including the seizure of the land of non-Germans and the institution of the Hereditary Farm Law, which was meant to preserve an exclusively German peasantry as a source of bloodlines for the German *Volk*. —Ed.]

The need for such official doctrines as an instrument of directing and rallying the efforts of the people has been clearly foreseen by the various theoreticians of the totalitarian system. Plato's "noble lies" and Sorel's "myths" serve the same purpose as the racial doctrine of the Nazis or the theory of the corporative state of Mussolini.[4] They are all necessarily based on particular views about facts which are then elaborated into scientific theories in order to justify a preconceived opinion.

The most effective way of making people accept the validity of the values they are to serve is to persuade them that they are really the same as those which they, or at least the best among them, have always held, but which were not properly understood or recognized before. The people are made to transfer their allegiance from the old gods to the new under the pretense that the new gods really are what their sound instinct had always told them but what before they had only dimly seen. And the most efficient technique to this end is to use the old words but change their meaning. Few traits of totalitarian regimes are at the same time so confusing to the superficial observer and yet so characteristic of the whole intellectual climate as the complete perversion of language, the change of meaning of the words by which the ideals of the new regimes are expressed.

The worst sufferer in this respect is, of course, the word "liberty." It is a word used as freely in totalitarian states as elsewhere. Indeed, it could almost be said—and it should serve as a warning to us to be on our guard against all the tempters who promise us *New Liberties for Old*[5]—that wherever liberty as we understand it has been destroyed, this has almost always been done in the name of some new freedom promised to the people. Even among us we have "planners for freedom" who promise us a "collective freedom for the group," the nature of which may be gathered from the fact that its advocate finds it necessary to assure us that "naturally the advent of planned freedom does not mean that all [*sic*] earlier forms of freedom must be abolished." Dr. Karl Mannheim, from whose work[6] these sentences are taken, at least warns us that "a conception of freedom modelled on the preceding age is an obstacle to any real understanding of the problem." But his use of the word "freedom" is as misleading as

---

[4] [Plato's "noble lies" refers to the lies that the leaders of a republic must tell to get each person to fulfill the function that the leaders thought best suited his nature, thereby ensuring a stable society. The French philosopher Georges Sorel (1847–1922) argued that to be successful political opposition must use violence, and that "social myths" are necessary to inspire the necessary collective action. —Ed.]

[5] This is the title of a recent work by the historian Carl L. Becker. [Hayek refers to Carl Becker, *New Liberties for Old* (New Haven: Yale University Press, 1941). —Ed.]

[6] Karl Mannheim, *Man and Society in an Age of Reconstruction,* op. cit., p. 379. [Hayek incorrectly listed the quotation from Mannheim as appearing on p. 377. —Ed.]

it is in the mouth of totalitarian politicians. Like their freedom, the "collective freedom" he offers us is not the freedom of the members of society but the unlimited freedom of the planner to do with society what he pleases.[7] It is the confusion of freedom with power carried to the extreme.

In this particular case the perversion of the meaning of the word has, of course, been well prepared by a long line of German philosophers and, not least, by many of the theoreticians of socialism. But "freedom" or "liberty" are by no means the only words whose meaning has been changed into their opposites to make them serve as instruments of totalitarian propaganda. We have already seen how the same happens to "justice" and "law," "right" and "equality." The list could be extended until it includes almost all moral and political terms in general use.

If one has not one's self experienced this process, it is difficult to appreciate the magnitude of this change of the meaning of words, the confusion which it causes, and the barriers to any rational discussion which it creates. It has to be seen to be understood how, if one of two brothers embraces the new faith, after a short while he appears to speak a different language which makes any real communication between them impossible. And the confusion becomes worse because this change of meaning of the words describing political ideals is not a single event but a continuous process, a technique employed consciously or unconsciously to direct the people. Gradually, as this process continues, the whole language becomes despoiled, and words become empty shells deprived of any definite meaning, as capable of denoting one thing as its opposite and used solely for the emotional associations which still adhere to them.

It is not difficult to deprive the great majority of independent thought. But the minority who will retain an inclination to criticize must also be silenced. We have already seen why coercion cannot be confined to the acceptance of the ethical code underlying the plan according to which all social activity is directed. Since many parts of this code will never be explicitly stated, since many parts of the guiding scale of values will exist only implicitly in the plan, the plan itself in every detail, in fact every act of the government, must become sacrosanct and exempt from criticism. If the people are to support the common effort without hesitation, they must be convinced that not only the end aimed at but also the means chosen are the right ones. The official creed, to which adherence must be enforced, will therefore comprise all the views about facts on

[7] Peter Drucker, *The End of Economic Man,* op. cit., p. 74, correctly observes that "the less freedom there is, the more there is talk of the 'new freedom.' Yet this new freedom is a mere word which covers the exact contradiction of all that Europe ever understood by freedom. . . . The new freedom which is preached in Europe is, however, the right of the majority against the individual." [The first part of the quotation actually appears on page 79, and the last part on page 80. —Ed.]

which the plan is based. Public criticism or even expressions of doubt must be suppressed because they tend to weaken public support. As the Webbs report of the position in every Russian enterprise: "Whilst the work is in progress, any public expression of doubt, or even fear that the plan will not be successful, is an act of disloyalty and even of treachery because of its possible effects on the will and on the efforts of the rest of the staff."[8] When the doubt or fear expressed concerns not the success of a particular enterprise but of the whole social plan, it must be treated even more as sabotage.

Facts and theories must thus become no less the object of an official doctrine than views about values. And the whole apparatus for spreading knowledge—the schools and the press, radio and motion picture—will be used exclusively to spread those views which, whether true or false, will strengthen the belief in the rightness of the decisions taken by the authority; and all information that might cause doubt or hesitation will be withheld. The probable effect on the people's loyalty to the system becomes the only criterion for deciding whether a particular piece of information is to be published or suppressed. The situation in a totalitarian state is permanently and in all fields the same that it is elsewhere in some fields in wartime. Everything which might cause doubt about the wisdom of the government or create discontent will be kept from the people. The basis of unfavorable comparisons with conditions elsewhere, the knowledge of possible alternatives to the course actually taken, information which might suggest failure on the part of the government to live up to its promises or to take advantage of opportunities to improve conditions—all will be suppressed. There is consequently no field where the systematic control of information will not be practiced and uniformity of views not enforced.

This applies even to fields apparently most remote from any political interests and particularly to all the sciences, even the most abstract. That in the disciplines dealing directly with human affairs and therefore most immediately affecting political views, such as history, law, or economics, the disinterested search for truth cannot be allowed in a totalitarian system, and the vindication of the official views becomes the sole object, is easily seen and has been amply confirmed by experience. These disciplines have, indeed, in all totalitarian countries become the most fertile factories of the official myths which the rulers use to guide the minds and wills of their subjects. It is not surprising that in these spheres even the pretense that they search for truth is abandoned and that the authorities decide what doctrines ought to be taught and published.

Totalitarian control of opinion extends, however, also to subjects which at first seem to have no political significance. Sometimes it is difficult to explain

[8]Sidney and Beatrice Webb, *Soviet Communism: A New Civilization?* op. cit., vol. 2, p. 1038. [Hayek's 1936 review of the Webbs' book is reprinted in F. A. Hayek, *Socialism and War,* op. cit., pp. 239–42. —Ed.]

why particular doctrines should be officially proscribed or why others should be encouraged, and it is curious that these likes and dislikes are apparently somewhat similar in the different totalitarian systems. In particular, they all seem to have in common an intense dislike of the more abstract forms of thought—a dislike characteristically also shown by many of the collectivists among our scientists. Whether the theory of relativity is represented as a "Semitic attack on the foundation of Christian and Nordic physics" or opposed because it is "in conflict with dialectical materialism and Marxist dogma" comes very much to the same thing. Nor does it make much difference whether certain theorems of mathematical statistics are attacked because they "form part of the class struggle on the ideological frontier and are a product of the historical role of mathematics as the servant of the bourgeoisie," or whether the whole subject is condemned because "it provides no guaranty that it will serve the interest of the people." It seems that pure mathematics is no less a victim and that even the holding of particular views about the nature of continuity can be ascribed to "bourgeois prejudices." According to the Webbs, the *Journal for Marxist-Leninist Natural Sciences* has the following slogans: "We stand for Party in Mathematics. We stand for the purity of Marxist-Leninist theory in surgery."[9] The situation seems to be very similar in Germany. The *Journal of the National-Socialist Association of Mathematicians* is full of "party in mathematics," and one of the best-known German physicists, the Nobel prizeman Lenard, has summed up his lifework under the title *German Physics in Four Volumes!*[10]

It is entirely in keeping with the whole spirit of totalitarianism that it condemns any human activity done for its own sake and without ulterior purpose. Science for science's sake, art for art's sake, are equally abhorrent to the Nazis, our socialist intellectuals, and the communists. *Every* activity must derive its justification from a conscious social purpose. There must be no spontaneous, unguided activity, because it might produce results which cannot be foreseen and for which the plan does not provide. It might produce something new, undreamed of in the philosophy of the planner. The principle extends even to games and amusements. I leave it to the reader to guess whether it was in Germany or in Russia that chess-players were officially exhorted that "we must finish once and for all with the neutrality of chess. We must condemn once and for all the formula 'chess for the sake of chess' like the formula 'art for art's sake.'"[11]

[9] [*Ibid.*, p. 1000. —Ed.]

[10] [The German physicist Philipp von Lenard (1862–1947) made a number of contributions to experimental physics, and under the Nazis held the title of Chief of German Physics. The four-volume work to which Hayek refers is *Deutsche Physik in Vier Bänden* (Munich: J. F. Lehmann, 1936–1937). —Ed.]

[11] [The speaker was Nikolai V. Krylenko, the People's Commissar for Justice, and he said this at a 1932 congress of chess players. The quotation is cited in full in Boris Souvarine, *Stalin: A Critical*

Incredible as some of these aberrations may appear, we must yet be on our guard not to dismiss them as mere accidental by-products which have nothing to do with the essential character of a planned or totalitarian system. They are not. They are a direct result of that same desire to see everything directed by a "unitary conception of the whole," of the need to uphold at all costs the views in the service of which people are asked to make constant sacrifices, and of the general idea that the knowledge and beliefs of the people are an instrument to be used for a single purpose. Once science has to serve, not truth, but the interests of a class, a community, or a state, the sole task of argument and discussion is to vindicate and to spread still further the beliefs by which the whole life of the community is directed. As the Nazi minister of justice has explained, the question which every new scientific theory must ask itself is: "Do I serve National Socialism for the greatest benefit of all?"[12]

The word "truth" itself ceases to have its old meaning. It describes no longer something to be found, with the individual conscience as the sole arbiter of whether in any particular instance the evidence (or the standing of those proclaiming it) warrants a belief; it becomes something to be laid down by authority, something which has to be believed in the interest of the unity of the organized effort and which may have to be altered as the exigencies of this organized effort require it.

The general intellectual climate which this produces, the spirit of complete cynicism as regards truth which it engenders, the loss of the sense of even the meaning of truth, the disappearance of the spirit of independent inquiry and of the belief in the power of rational conviction, the way in which differences of opinion in every branch of knowledge become political issues to be decided by authority, are all things which one must personally experience—no short description can convey their extent. Perhaps the most alarming fact is that contempt for intellectual liberty is not a thing which arises only once the totalitarian system is established but one which can be found everywhere among intellectuals who have embraced a collectivist faith and who are acclaimed as intellectual leaders even in countries still under a liberal regime. Not only is even the worst oppression condoned if it is committed in the name of socialism, and the creation of a totalitarian system openly advocated by people who pretend to speak for the scientists of liberal countries; intolerance, too, is openly extolled. Have we not recently seen a British scientific writer defend even Inquisition because in his opinion it "is beneficial to science when it protects

---

Survey of Bolshevism, translated by C. L. R. James (London: Alliance, 1939; reprinted, New York: Octagon, 1972), p. 575. —Ed.]

[12] [Franz Gurtner was the Nazi Minister of Justice from 1933 through 1941. Franz Schlegelberger followed as Acting Minister, and Otto Georg Thierack served as Minister from 1942 to 1945. It is not clear which one is responsible for the statement in the text. —Ed.]

a rising class"?[13] This view is, of course, practically indistinguishable from the views which led the Nazis to the persecution of men of science, the burning of scientific books, and the systematic eradication of the intelligentsia of the subjected people.

The desire to force upon the people a creed which is regarded as salutary for them is, of course, not a thing that is new or peculiar to our time. New, however, is the argument by which many of our intellectuals try to justify such attempts. There is no real freedom of thought in our society, so it is said, because the opinions and tastes of the masses are shaped by propaganda, by advertising, by the example of the upper classes, and by other environmental factors which inevitably force the thinking of the people into well-worn grooves. From this it is concluded that if the ideals and tastes of the great majority are always fashioned by circumstances which we can control, we ought to use this power deliberately to turn the thoughts of the people in what we think is a desirable direction.

Probably it is true enough that the great majority are rarely capable of thinking independently, that on most questions they accept views which they find ready-made, and that they will be equally content if born or coaxed into one set of beliefs or another. In any society freedom of thought will probably be of direct significance only for a small minority. But this does not mean that anyone is competent, or ought to have power, to select those to whom this freedom is to be reserved. It certainly does not justify the presumption of any group of people to claim the right to determine what people ought to think or believe. It shows a complete confusion of thought to suggest that, because under any sort of system the majority of people follow the lead of somebody, it makes no difference if everybody has to follow the same lead. To deprecate the value of intellectual freedom because it will never mean for everybody the same possibility of independent thought is completely to miss the reasons which give intellectual freedom its value. What is essential to make it serve its function as the prime mover of intellectual progress is not that everybody may be able to think or write anything but that any cause or idea may be argued by somebody. So long as dissent is not suppressed, there will always be some who will query the ideas ruling their contemporaries and put new ideas to the test of argument and propaganda.

This interaction of individuals, possessing different knowledge and different views, is what constitutes the life of thought. The growth of reason is a social process based on the existence of such differences. It is of its essence that its results cannot be predicted, that we cannot know which views will assist this growth and which will not—in short, that this growth cannot be governed by any views which we now possess without at the same time limiting it. To "plan" or "organize" the growth of mind, or, for that matter, progress in general, is a

[13]J. G. Crowther, *The Social Relations of Science* (New York: Macmillan, 1941), p. 333.

contradiction in terms. The idea that the human mind ought "consciously" to control its own development confuses individual reason, which alone can "consciously control" anything, with the interpersonal process to which its growth is due. By attempting to control it, we are merely setting bounds to its development and must sooner or later produce a stagnation of thought and a decline of reason.

The tragedy of collectivist thought is that, while it starts out to make reason supreme, it ends by destroying reason because it misconceives the process on which the growth of reason depends. It may indeed be said that it is the paradox of all collectivist doctrine and its demand for "conscious" control or "conscious" planning that they necessarily lead to the demand that the mind of some individual should rule supreme—while only the individualist approach to social phenomena makes us recognize the superindividual forces which guide the growth of reason. Individualism is thus an attitude of humility before this social process and of tolerance to other opinions and is the exact opposite of that intellectual *hubris* which is at the root of the demand for comprehensive direction of the social process.

TWELVE

THE SOCIALIST ROOTS OF NAZIISM

All antiliberal forces are combining against everything that is liberal.
—A. Moeller van den Bruck[1]

It is a common mistake to regard National Socialism as a mere revolt against reason, an irrational movement without intellectual background. If that were so, the movement would be much less dangerous than it is. But nothing could be further from the truth or more misleading. The doctrines of National Socialism are the culmination of a long evolution of thought, a process in which thinkers who have had great influence far beyond the confines of Germany have taken part. Whatever one may think of the premises from which they started, it cannot be denied that the men who produced the new doctrines were powerful writers who left the impress of their ideas on the whole of European thought. Their system was developed with ruthless consistency. Once one accepts the premises from which it starts, there is no escape from its logic. It is simply collectivism freed from all traces of an individualist tradition which might hamper its realization.

Though in this development German thinkers have taken the lead, they were by no means alone. Thomas Carlyle and Houston Stewart Chamberlain, Auguste Comte and Georges Sorel, are as much a part of that continuous development as any Germans.[2] The development of this strand of thought within Germany has been well traced recently by R. D. Butler in his study of *The Roots of National Socialism*.[3] But, although its persistence there through a hundred and fifty years in almost unchanged and ever recurring form, which emerges from that study, is rather frightening, it is easy to exaggerate the importance

[1][Arthur Moeller van den Bruck, *Das dritte Reich* (Hamburg: Hanseatische Verlagsanstalt, 1931), p. 102. An authorized condensed translation appeared in 1934; see Arthur Moeller van den Bruck, *Germany's Third Empire*, trans. E. O. Lorimer (London: G. Allen and Unwin, 1934; reprinted, New York: Fertig, 1971). —Ed.]

[2][For more on Carlyle and Chamberlain, see the author's introduction, note 4. For more on Comte and Sorel, see chapter 1, note 9, and chapter 11, note 4, respectively. —Ed.]

[3][Hayek refers here to Rohan Butler, *The Roots of National Socialism* (New York: E. P. Dutton, 1942). —Ed.]

these ideas had in Germany before 1914. They were only one strand of thought among a people then perhaps more varied in its views than any other. And they were on the whole represented by a small minority and held in as great contempt by the majority of Germans as they were in other countries.

What, then, caused these views held by a reactionary minority finally to gain the support of the great majority of Germans and practically the whole of her youth? It was not merely the defeat, the suffering, and the wave of nationalism which led to their success. Still less was the cause, as so many people wish to believe, a capitalist reaction against the advance of socialism. On the contrary, the support which brought these ideas to power came precisely from the socialist camp. It was certainly not through the bourgeoisie, but rather through the absence of a strong bourgeoisie, that they were helped to power.

The doctrines which had guided the ruling elements in Germany for the past generation were opposed not to the socialism in Marxism but to the liberal elements contained in it, its internationalism and its democracy. And as it became increasingly clear that it was just these elements which formed obstacles to the realization of socialism, the socialists of the Left approached more and more to those of the Right. It was the union of the anticapitalist forces of the Right and of the Left, the fusion of radical and conservative socialism, which drove out from Germany everything that was liberal.

The connection between socialism and nationalism in Germany was close from the beginning. It is significant that the most important ancestors of National Socialism—Fichte, Rodbertus, and Lassalle—are at the same time acknowledged fathers of socialism.[4] While theoretical socialism in its Marxist form was directing the German labor movement, the authoritarian and nationalist element receded for a time into the background. But not for long.[5] From 1914 onward there arose from the ranks of Marxist socialism one teacher after another who led, not the conservatives and reactionaries, but the hardworking laborer and idealist youth into the National Socialist fold. It was only

[4] [German philosopher Johann Gottlieb Fichte (1762–1814) taught at Jena, Berlin, and Erlangen, and in 1810 became the first rector of the new University of Berlin. In 1807–08 he delivered a series of patriotic lectures aimed at fostering German nationalism in opposition to Napoleon; his philosophical categories anticipated the Nazi concept of the *Herrenvolk*. German economist and politician Johann Karl Rodbertus (1805–1875) is known as a founder of scientific socialism; he proposed a program that would gradually lead to a socialist state within the German Empire. German political author and pamphleteer Ferdinand Lassalle (1825–1864) founded the *Allgemeiner Deutscher Arbeiterverein* (Universal German Workingmen's Association), a forerunner of the Social Democratic party. —Ed.]

[5] And only partially. In 1892 one of the leaders of the social-democratic party, August Bebel, was able to tell Bismarck that "the Imperial Chancellor can rest assured that German Social Democracy is a sort of preparatory school for militarism"! [Ferdinand August Bebel (1840–1913) was a leader of the German Social Democratic movement and one of its chief spokesmen in the *Reichstag*. —Ed.]

thereafter that the tide of nationalist socialism attained major importance and rapidly grew into the Hitlerian doctrine. The war hysteria of 1914, which, just because of the German defeat, was never fully cured, is the beginning of the modern development which produced National Socialism, and it was largely with the assistance of old socialists that it rose during this period.

Perhaps the first, and in some ways the most characteristic, representative of this development is the late Professor Werner Sombart, whose notorious *Händler und Helden* ("Merchants and Heroes") appeared in 1915.[6] Sombart had begun as a Marxian socialist and, as late as 1909, could assert with pride that he had devoted the greater part of his life to fighting for the ideas of Karl Marx. He had done as much as any man to spread socialist ideas and anticapitalist resentment of varying shades throughout Germany; and if German thought became penetrated with Marxian elements in a way that was true of no other country until the Russian revolution, this was in a large measure due to Sombart. At one time he was regarded as the outstanding representative of the persecuted socialist intelligentsia, unable, because of his radical views, to obtain a university chair. And even after the last war the influence, inside and outside Germany, of his work as a historian, which remained Marxist in approach after he had ceased to be a Marxist in politics, was most extensive and is particularly noticeable in the works of many of the English and American planners.

In his war book this old socialist welcomed the "German War" as the inevitable conflict between the commercial civilization of England and the heroic culture of Germany. His contempt for the "commercial" views of the English people, who had lost all warlike instincts, is unlimited. Nothing is more contemptible in his eyes than the universal striving after the happiness of the individual; and what he describes as the leading maxim of English morals: be just "that it may be well with thee and that thou mayest prolong thy days upon the land" is to him "the most infamous maxim which has ever been pronounced by a commercial mind."[7] The "German idea of the state," as formulated by Fichte, Lassalle, and Rodbertus, is that the state is neither founded nor formed by individuals, nor an aggregate of individuals, nor is its purpose to serve any interest of individuals. It is a *Volksgemeinschaft* in which the individual has no rights but only duties.[8] Claims of the individual are always an outcome of the commercial spirit. "The ideas of 1789"—liberty, equality, fraternity—are characteristically commercial ideals which have no other purpose but to secure certain advantages to individuals.

[6] [Werner Sombart, *Händler und Helden: patriotische Besinnungen* (Munich and Leipzig: Duncker & Humblot, 1915). For more on Sombart see chapter 1, note 13. —Ed.]

[7] [Sombart, *Händler und Helden*, op. cit., p. 19. —Ed.]

[8] [*Volksgemeinschaft* might be translated as "people's community," though under the Nazis it was carried further to imply something like a "racially pure community." —Ed.]

Before 1914 all the true German ideals of a heroic life were in deadly danger before the continuous advance of English commercial ideals, English comfort, and English sport. The English people had not only themselves become completely corrupted, every trade-unionist being sunk in the "morass of comfort," but they had begun to infect all other peoples. Only the war had helped the Germans to remember that they were really a people of warriors, a people among whom all activities and particularly all economic activities were subordinated to military ends. Sombart knew that the Germans were held in contempt by other people because they regard war as sacred—but he glories in it. To regard war as inhuman and senseless is a product of commercial views. There is a life higher than the individual life, the life of the people and the life of the state, and it is the purpose of the individual to sacrifice himself for that higher life. War is to Sombart the consummation of the heroic view of life, and the war against England is the war against the opposite ideal, the commercial ideal of individual freedom and of English comfort, which in his eyes finds its most contemptible expression in—the safety razors found in the English trenches.

If Sombart's outburst was at the time too much even for most Germans, another German professor arrived at essentially the same ideas in a more moderate and more scholarly, but for that reason even more effective, form. Professor Johann Plenge was as great an authority on Marx as Sombart. His book on *Marx und Hegel* marks the beginning of the modern Hegel renaissance among Marxian scholars; and there can be no doubt about the genuinely socialist nature of the convictions with which he started. Among his numerous war publications the most important is a small but at the time widely discussed book with the significant title, *1789 and 1914: The Symbolic Years in the History of the Political Mind.*[9] It is devoted to the conflict between the "Ideas of 1789," the ideal of freedom, and the "Ideas of 1914," the ideal of organization.

Organization is to him, as to all socialists who derive their socialism from a crude application of scientific ideals to the problems of society, the essence of socialism. It was, as he rightly emphasizes, the root of the socialist movement at its inception in early nineteenth-century France. Marx and Marxism have betrayed this basic idea of socialism by their fanatic but utopian adherence to the abstract idea of freedom. Only now was the idea of organization again com-

---

[9][The two books by Johann Plenge to which Hayek refers are *Marx und Hegel* (Tübingen: H. Laupp, 1911), and *1789 und 1914: die symbolischen Jahre in der Geschichte des politischen Geistes* (Berlin: J. Springer, 1916). Historian and political thinker Johann Plenge (1874–1963) taught at Leipzig and Münster. A proponent of "organizational socialism," Plenge also supported a revival of sociology, a science that he thought could be used to train the executives who would lead large-scale organizations. —Ed.]

ing into its own, elsewhere, as witnessed by the work of H. G. Wells (by whose *Future in America* Professor Plenge was profoundly influenced, and whom he describes as one of the outstanding figures of modern socialism), but particularly in Germany, where it is best understood and most fully realized.[10] The war between England and Germany is therefore really a conflict between two opposite principles. The "Economic World War" is the third great epoch of spiritual struggle in modern history. It is of equal importance with the Reformation and the bourgeois revolution of liberty. It is the struggle for the victory of the new forces born out of the advanced economic life of the nineteenth century: socialism and organization.

"Because in the sphere of ideas Germany was the most convinced exponent of all socialist dreams, and in the sphere of reality she was the most powerful architect of the most highly organized economic system.—In us is the twentieth century. However the war may end, we are the exemplary people. Our ideas will determine the aims of the life of humanity.—World History experiences at present the colossal spectacle that with us a new great ideal of life penetrates to final victory, while at the same time in England one of the World-Historical principles finally collapses."[11]

The war economy created in Germany in 1914 "is the first realization of a socialist society and its spirit the first active, and not merely demanding, appearance of a socialist spirit. The needs of the war have established the socialist idea in German economic life, and thus the defense of our nation produced for humanity the idea of 1914, the idea of German organization, the people's community (*Volksgemeinschaft*) of national socialism.[12] . . . Without our really noticing it the whole of our political life in state and industry has risen to a higher stage. State and economic life form a new unity.[13] . . . The feeling of economic responsibility which characterizes the work of the civil servant pervades all private activity."[14] The new German corporative constitution of economic life, which Professor Plenge admits is not yet ripe or complete, "is the highest form of life of the state which has ever been known on earth."[15]

At first Professor Plenge still hoped to reconcile the ideal of liberty and the ideal of organization, although largely through the complete but voluntary submission of the individual to the whole. But these traces of liberal ideas soon disappear from his writings. By 1918 the union between socialism and ruthless

---

[10] [Hayek refers to H. G. Wells, *Future in America: A Search after Realities* (New York and London: Harper & Brothers, 1906). —Ed.]

[11] [Johann Plenge, *1789 und 1914*, op. cit., p. 20. —Ed.]

[12] [*Ibid.*, p. 82. —Ed.]

[13] [*Ibid.*, p. 120. —Ed.]

[14] [*Ibid.*, p. 121. —Ed.]

[15] [*Ibid.* —Ed.]

power politics had become complete in his mind. Shortly before the end of the war he exhorted his compatriots in the socialist journal *Die Glocke* in the following manner:

"It is high time to recognize the fact that socialism must be power policy, because it is to be organization. Socialism has to win power: it must never blindly destroy power. And the most important and critical question for socialism in the time of war of peoples is necessarily this: what people is pre-eminently summoned to power, because it is the exemplary leader in the organization of peoples?"[16]

And he forecast all the ideas which were finally to justify Hitler's New Order: "Just from the point of view of socialism, which is organization, is not an absolute right of self-determination of the peoples the right of individualistic economic anarchy? Are we willing to grant complete self-determination to the individual in economic life? Consistent socialism can accord to the people a right to incorporation only in accordance with the real distribution of forces historically determined."

The ideals which Plenge expressed so clearly were especially popular among, and perhaps even derive from, certain circles of German scientists and engineers who, precisely as is now so loudly demanded by their English and American counterparts, clamored for the centrally planned organization of all aspects of life. Leading among these was the famous chemist Wilhelm Ostwald, one of whose pronouncements on this point has achieved a certain celebrity. He is reported to have stated publicly that "Germany wants to organize Europe which up to now still lacks organization. I will explain to you now Germany's great secret: we, or perhaps the German race, have discovered the significance of organization. While the other nations still live under the regime of individualism, we have already achieved that of organization."[17]

Ideas very similar to these were current in the offices of the German raw-material dictator, Walther Rathenau, who, although he would have shuddered had he realized the consequences of his totalitarian economics, yet deserves a considerable place in any fuller history of the growth of Nazi ideas.[18] Through

[16] [This and the next quotation apparently appeared in the socialist journal *Die Glocke* shortly before the end of the war. The editors of the German edition of the *Collected Works* could not locate the exact source of the quotation, nor could I. —Ed.]

[17] [The German chemist Friedrich Wilhelm Ostwald (1853–1932) taught principally at Leipzig, where he established a journal and an institute; he also helped found a number of scientific societies. His many discoveries led to his being awarded a Nobel Prize in 1909. —Ed.]

[18] [German industrialist and politician Walther Rathenau (1867–1922) brought his expertise as a former director of the electricity cartel to assist him in setting up raw materials procurement for the German Ministry of War during the First World War. In an influential pamphlet published after the war he argued for the socialization of the economy by the continuation of wartime plan-

his writings he has probably, more than any other man, determined the economic views of the generation which grew up in Germany during and immediately after the last war; and some of his closest collaborators were later to form the backbone of the staff of Göring's Five-Year Plan administration. Very similar also was much of the teaching of another former Marxist, Friedrich Naumann, whose *Mitteleuropa* reached probably the greatest circulation of any war book in Germany.[19]

But it was left to an active socialist politician, a member of the Left wing of the social-democratic party in the Reichstag, to develop these ideas most fully and to spread them far and wide. Paul Lensch had already in earlier books described the war as "the flight of the English bourgeoisie before the advance of socialism" and explained how different were the socialist ideal of freedom and the English conception.[20] But only in his third and most successful war book, his *Three Years of World Revolution*, were his characteristic ideas, under the influence of Plenge, to achieve full development.[21] Lensch bases his argument on an interesting and in many respects accurate historical account of how the adoption of protection by Bismarck had made possible in Germany a development toward that industrial concentration and cartelization which, from his Marxist standpoint, represented a higher state of industrial development.

"The result of Bismarck's decision of the year 1879 was that Germany took on the role of the revolutionary; that is to say, of a state whose position in relation to the rest of the world is that of a representative of a higher and more advanced economic system. Having realized this, we should perceive that *in the present World Revolution Germany represents the revolutionary, and her greatest antagonist, England, the counter-revolutionary side*. This fact proves how little the constitution of

---

ning in peace time. A progressive internationalist, and also a Jew, Rathenau was assassinated in 1922 soon after becoming Foreign Minister. For Rathenau's influence on Hayek, see F. A. Hayek, *Hayek on Hayek*, op. cit., p. 47. —Ed.]

[19]A good summary of Naumann's views, as characteristic of the German combination of socialism and imperialism as any we quote in the text, will be found in R. D. Butler, *The Roots of National Socialism*, op. cit., pp. 203–209. [Hayek refers to Freidrich Naumann, *Mitteleuropa* (Berlin: G. Reimer, 1915). The book was translated by Christabel Meredith as *Central Europe* (New York: A. A. Knopf, 1917; reprinted, Westport, CT: Greenwood, 1971). Journalist, author, and political leader Friedrich Naumann (1860–1919) founded the German Democratic Party at the end of World War I. In his book, Naumann envisioned an economic and political reorganization of central Europe under German-Prussian hegemony. —Ed.]

[20][German economist and journalist Paul Lensch (1873–1926) was, before the war, associated with the Marxist wing of the German Social Democratic party, but he moved increasingly toward the right during the war. His criticisms of the party led to his ouster in 1922. Hayek probably here refers to Lensch's *Die deutsche Sozialdemokratie unter der Weltkrieg: eine politische Studie* (Berlin: Singer, 1915) and *Das englische Weltreich* (Berlin: Singer, 1915). —Ed.]

[21]Paul Lensch, *Three Years of World Revolution*, with a Preface by J. E. M. (London: Constable and Co., Ltd., 1918). The English translation of this work was made available, still during the last war, by some far-seeing person.

a country, whether it be liberal and republican or monarchic and autocratic, affects the question whether, from the point of view of historical development, that country is to be regarded as liberal or not. Or, to put it more plainly, our conceptions of Liberalism, Democracy, and so forth, are derived from the ideas of English Individualism, according to which a state with a weak government is a liberal state, and every restriction upon the freedom of the individual is conceived as the product of autocracy and militarism."[22]

In Germany, the "historically appointed representative" of this higher form of economic life, "the struggle for socialism has been extraordinarily simplified, since all the prerequisite conditions of Socialism had already become established there. And hence it was necessarily a vital concern of any socialist party that Germany should triumphantly hold her own against her enemies, and thereby be able to fulfill her historic mission of revolutionizing the world. Hence the war of the Entente against Germany resembled the attempt of the lower bourgeoisie of the pre-capitalistic age to prevent the decline of their own class."[23]

That organization of capital, Lensch continues, "which began unconsciously before the war, and which during the war has been continued consciously, will be systematically continued after the war. Not through any desire for any arts of organization nor yet because socialism has been recognized as a higher principle of social development. The classes who are today the practical pioneers of socialism are, in theory, its avowed opponents, or, at any rate, were so up to a short time ago. Socialism is coming, and in fact has to some extent already arrived, since we can no longer live without it."[24]

The only people who still oppose this tendency are the liberals. "This class of people, who unconsciously reason from English standards, comprises the whole educated German bourgeoisie. Their political notions of 'freedom' and 'civic right,' of constitutionalism and parliamentarianism, are derived from that individualistic conception of the world, of which English Liberalism is a classical embodiment, and which was adopted by the spokesmen of the German bourgeoisie in the fifties, sixties, and seventies of the nineteenth century. But these standards are old-fashioned and shattered, just as old-fashioned English Liberalism has been shattered by this war. What has to be done now is to get rid of these inherited political ideas and to assist the growth of a new conception of State and Society. In this sphere also Socialism must present a conscious and determined opposition to individualism. In this connection it is an astonishing fact that, in the so-called 'reactionary' Germany, the working

---

[22] [*Ibid.*, pp. 25–26. In this passage Lensch actually said, "from the point of view of historical development, that country is to be regarded as *revolutionary* or not." —Ed.]

[23] [*Ibid.*, pp. 67–68. —Ed.]

[24] [*Ibid.*, p. 204. —Ed.]

classes have won for themselves a much more solid and powerful position in the life of the state than is the case either in England or in France."[25]

Lensch follows this up with a consideration which again contains much truth and which deserves to be pondered:

"Since the Social Democrats, by the aid of this [universal] Suffrage, occupied every post which they could obtain in the Reichstag, the State Parliament, the municipal councils, the courts for the settlement of trade disputes, the sick funds, and so forth, they penetrated very deeply into the organism of the state; but the price which they had to pay for this was that the state, in its turn, exercised a profound influence upon the working classes. To be sure, as the result of strenuous socialistic labors for fifty years, the state is no longer the same as it was in the year 1867, when universal suffrage first came into operation; but then, Social Democracy, in its turn, is no longer the same as it was at the time. *The state has undergone a process of socialization, and Social Democracy has undergone a process of nationalization.*"[26]

Plenge and Lensch in turn have provided the leading ideas for the immediate masters of National Socialism, particularly Oswald Spengler and Arthur Moeller van den Bruck, to mention only the two best-known names.[27] Opin-

---

[25] [*Ibid.*, p. 208. —Ed.]

[26] [*Ibid.*, p. 210. —Ed.]

[27] The same applies to many others of the intellectual leaders of the generation which has produced naziism, such as Othmar Spann, Hans Freyer, Carl Schmitt, and Ernst Jünger. On these compare the interesting study by Aurel Kolnai, *The War against the West* (London: V. Gollancz, 1938), which suffers, however, from the defect that, by confining itself to the postwar period when these ideals had already been taken over by the nationalists, it overlooks their socialist creators. [Historian and critic Arthur Moeller van den Bruck's (1876–1925) book *Das dritte Reich* ("The Third Reich"), originally published in 1923, profoundly influenced Adolf Hitler. In the book, an excerpt from which provided the quotation that introduces this chapter, Moeller van den Bruck criticized such ideologies as socialism, liberalism, and democracy, and called for the formation of a new German self-consciousness and for the institution of an authoritarian state with strict central control of the economy. German philosopher of history Oswald Spengler (1880–1936), another critic of liberal parliamentary democracy, foretold the inevitable decay of European culture, which would be replaced by a new age of Caesarism (analogous to the replacement of Greek culture by Roman, the latter being "uninspired, barbaric, disciplined, practical, Protestant, *Prussian*"—p. 26), in his book *The Decline of the West*, translated by Charles Francis Atkinson, 2 vols. (New York: A. A. Knopf, 1926–1928). The Austrian sociologist-economist Othmar Spann (1878–1950) taught at the University of Vienna, where Hayek was among his students. The prophet of "intuitive universalism," which prepared the way for Austro-Fascism, he attacked democracy, liberalism, socialism, and individualism in his lectures. For more on Spann, and Hayek's reaction to him, see Caldwell, *Hayek's Challenge*, op. cit., pp. 137–39. German philosopher and sociologist Hans Freyer (1887–1969) was another intellectual forerunner of the Nazis. In his book *Revolution von rechts* ("Revolution on the Right"), published in 1931, he called for an end to class struggles and, through educational "reforms," the emergence of a German nationalist "state of the people." In his writings the German author and essayist Ernst Jünger (1895–1998) glorified the aesthetic, spir-

ions may differ in how far the former can be regarded as a socialist. But that in his tract on *Prussianism and Socialism,* which appeared in 1920, he merely gave expression to ideas widely held by German socialists will now be evident.[28] A few specimens of his argument will suffice. "Old Prussian spirit and socialist conviction, which today hate each other with the hatred of brothers, are one and the same."[29] The representatives of Western civilization in Germany, the German liberals, are "the invisible English army which after the Battle of Jena, Napoleon left behind on German soil."[30] To Spengler, men like Hardenberg and Humboldt and all the other liberal reformers were "English."[31] But this "English" spirit will be turned out by the German revolution which began in 1914.

"The three last nations of the Occident have aimed at three forms of existence, represented by famous watchwords: Freedom, Equality, Community. They appear in the political forms of liberal Parliamentarianism, social Democracy, and authoritarian socialism.[32] . . . The German, more correctly, Prussian, instinct is: the power belongs to the whole. . . . Everyone is given his place. One commands or obeys. This is, since the eighteenth century, authoritarian socialism, essentially illiberal and anti-democratic, in so far as English Liberalism and French Democracy are meant.[33] . . . There are in Germany many hated and ill-reputed contrasts, but liberalism alone is contemptible on German soil.[34]

"The structure of the English nation is based on the distinction between rich and poor, that of the Prussian on that between command and obedience. The meaning of class distinction is accordingly fundamentally different in the two countries."[35]

----

itual, and heroic aspects of war, and called for the German nation to embrace a militaristic ethos and organization. His firsthand account of trench warfare during World War I, *In Stahlgewittern,* is available as *Storm of Steel,* translated by Michael Hofmann (New York: Penguin Books, 2004). For more on the jurist Carl Schmitt, see chapter 6, note 5. —Ed.]

[28] [Hayek refers to Oswald Spengler, *Preussentum und Sozialismus* (Munich: Beck, 1920). —Ed.]

[29] [*Ibid.,* p. 4. —Ed.]

[30] [*Ibid.,* p. 7. —Ed.]

[31] [*Ibid.,* p. 62. Under his leadership the Prussian statesman Karl August, Fürst von Hardenberg (1750–1822) oversaw the abolition of serfdom, extensive reform of the Prussian military, and, with Heinrich Stein, reform of the Prussian system of education. For more on Humboldt, see the author's introduction, note 4. —Ed.]

[32] *Ibid.,* p. 14. This Spenglerian formula finds its echo in an often-quoted statement of Schmitt, the leading Nazi expert on constitutional law, according to which the evolution of government proceeds "in three dialectic stages: from the *absolute* state of the seventeenth and eighteenth centuries through the *neutral* state of the liberal nineteenth century to the *totalitarian* state in which state and society are identical." See Carl Schmitt, *Der Hüter der Verfassung* (Tübingen: Mohr, 1931), p. 79.

[33] [Oswald Spengler, *Preussentum und Sozialismus,* op. cit., p. 15. —Ed.]

[34] [*Ibid.,* p. 34. —Ed.]

[35] [*Ibid.,* p. 43–44. —Ed.]

After pointing out the essential difference between the English competitive system and the Prussian system of "economic administration" and after showing (consciously following Lensch) how since Bismarck the deliberate organization of economic activity had progressively assumed more socialist forms, Spengler continues:

"In Prussia there existed a real state in the most ambitious meaning of the word. There could be, strictly speaking, no private persons. Everybody who lived within the system that worked with the precision of a clockwork, was in some way a link in it. The conduct of public business could therefore not be in the hands of private people, as is supposed by Parliamentarianism. It was an *Amt* and the responsible politician was a civil servant, a servant of the whole."[36]

The "Prussian idea" requires that everybody should become a state official—that all wages and salaries be fixed by the state. The administration of all property, in particular, becomes a salaried function. The state of the future will be a *Beamtenstaat*. But "the decisive question not only for Germany, but for the world, which must be solved *by* Germany *for* the world is: Is in the future trade to govern the state, or the state to govern trade? In the face of this question Prussianism and Socialism are the same. . . . Prussianism and Socialism combat the England in our midst."[37]

It was only a step from this for the patron saint of National Socialism, Moeller van den Bruck, to proclaim World War I a war between liberalism and socialism: "We have lost the war against the West. Socialism has lost it against Liberalism."[38] As with Spengler, liberalism is, therefore, the archenemy. Moeller van den Bruck glories in the fact that "there are no liberals in Germany today; there are young revolutionaries, there are young conservatives. But who would be a liberal? . . . Liberalism is a philosophy of life from which German youth now turns with nausea, with wrath, with quite peculiar scorn, for there is none more foreign, more repugnant, more opposed to its philosophy. German youth today recognizes the liberal *as the archenemy*."[39] Moeller van den Bruck's Third Reich was intended to give the Germans a socialism adapted to their nature and undefiled by Western liberal ideas. And so it did.

These writers were by no means isolated phenomena. As early as 1922 a detached observer could speak of a "peculiar and, on a first glance, surprising

---

[36][*Ibid.*, p. 60. —Ed.]

[37][*Ibid.*, p. 97. —Ed.]

[38]Arthur Moeller van den Bruck, *Sozialismus und Aussenpolilik* (Breslau: W. G. Korn, 1933), p. 100. The articles here reprinted, particularly the article on "Lenin and Keynes," which discusses most fully the contention discussed in the text, were first published between 1919 and 1923. [In the original, Hayek references here all three of van den Bruck's quotations, and incorrectly lists them as appearing on pages 87, 90, and 100 respectively, as opposed to where they actually appear, on pages 100–102. —Ed.]

[39][*Ibid.*, pp. 101–2. —Ed.]

phenomenon" then to be observed in Germany: "The fight against the capitalistic order, according to this view, is a continuation of the war against the Entente with the weapons of the spirit and of economic organization, the way which leads to practical socialism, a return of the German people to their best and noblest traditions."[40]

Fight against liberalism in all its forms, liberalism that had defeated Germany, was the common idea which united socialists and conservatives in one common front. At first it was mainly in the German Youth Movement, almost entirely socialist in inspiration and outlook, where these ideas were most readily accepted and the fusion of socialism and nationalism completed. In the later twenties and until the advent to power of Hitler a circle of young men gathered round the journal *Die Tat* and, led by Ferdinand Fried, became the chief exponent of this tradition in the intellectual sphere.[41] Fried's *Ende des Kapitalismus* is perhaps the most characteristic product of this group of *Edelnazis*, as they were known in Germany, and is particularly disquieting because of its resemblance to so much of the literature which we see in England and the United States today, where we can watch the same drawing together of the socialists of the Left and the Right and nearly the same contempt of all that is liberal in the old sense. "Conservative Socialism" (and, in other circles, "Religious Socialism") was the slogan under which a large number of writers prepared the atmosphere in which "National Socialism" succeeded. It is "conservative socialism" which is the dominant trend among us now. Had the war against the Western powers "with the weapons of the spirit and of economic organization" not almost succeeded before the real war began?

[40]Karl Pribram, "Deutscher Nationalismus und deutscher Sozialismus," *Archiv für Sozialwissenschaft und Sozialpolitik*, vol. 49, 1922, 298–99. The writer mentions as further examples the philosopher Max Scheler, preaching "the socialist world mission of Germany," and the Marxist K. Korsch, writing on the spirit of the new *Volksgemeinschaft*, as arguing in the same vein. [German philosopher Max Scheler (1874–1928), who wrote on ethics, religion, metaphysics, and the place of the person in society, was affiliated with Husserl's phenomenological movement. During the First World War he gave propaganda lectures for the government. Marxist journalist and author Karl Korsch (1886–1961) was a leading member of the Communist Party of Germany from 1920–1926, writing frequently for its newspapers and editing its theoretical journal, *Die Internationale*. He was expelled from the party on charges of revisionism in 1926, and left Germany in 1934, eventually settling in the United States. —Ed.]

[41][German journalist Ferdinand Fried (1898–1967) wrote about economics for various newspapers, and was the economic theoretician of the *Tatkreis*, a group of young conservative revolutionaries. In their organ *Die Tat* (translated variously as "Action" or "The Deed") the group opposed parliamentarian democracy and capitalism, and called for an autarkic, planned national economy. —Ed.]

THIRTEEN

THE TOTALITARIANS IN OUR MIDST

When authority presents itself in the guise of organization, it develops charms fascinating enough to convert communities of free people into totalitarian States. —*The Times* (London)[1]

Probably it is true that the very magnitude of the outrages committed by the totalitarian governments, instead of increasing the fear that such a system might one day arise in more enlightened countries, has rather strengthened the assurance that it cannot happen here. When we look to Nazi Germany, the gulf which separates us seems so immense that nothing that happens there can possess relevance for any possible development here. And the fact that the difference has steadily become greater seems to refute any suggestion that we may be moving in a similar direction. But let us not forget that fifteen years ago the possibility of such a thing's happening in Germany would have appeared just as fantastic, not only to nine-tenths of the Germans themselves, but also to the most hostile foreign observers (however wise they may now pretend to have been).

As suggested earlier in these pages, however, it is not the present Germany but the Germany of twenty or thirty years ago to which conditions in the democracies show an ever increasing resemblance. There are many features which were then regarded as "typically German" and which are now equally familiar in England, for instance, and many symptoms that point to a further development in the same direction. We have already mentioned the most significant—the increasing similarity between the economic views of the Right and Left and their common opposition to the liberalism that used to be the common basis of most English politics. We have the authority of Mr. Harold Nicolson for the statement that, during the last Conservative government, among the backbenchers of the Conservative party "the most gifted . . . were all socialists at heart";[2] and there can be little question that, as in the days of the

---

[1] ["The Home Front," *The Times*, February 24, 1937, p. 15. In notes stating the sources of his chapter headings, Hayek mistakenly listed the date as February 24, 1940. —Ed.]

[2] Harold Nicolson, *Spectator*, April 12, 1940, p. 523. [Diplomat and author Sir Harold George Nicolson (1886–1968) was a member of the British delegation to the Versailles peace conference,

Fabians, many socialists have more sympathy with the Conservatives than with the Liberals.[3] There are many other features closely related to this. The increasing veneration for the state, the admiration of power, and of bigness for bigness' sake, the enthusiasm for "organization" of everything (we now call it "planning"), and that "inability to leave anything to the simple power of organic growth," which even von Treitschke deplored in the Germans sixty years ago, are all scarcely less marked in England now than they were in Germany.[4]

How far in the last twenty years England has traveled on the German path is brought home to one with extraordinary vividness if one now reads some of the more serious discussions of the differences between British and German views on political and moral issues which appeared in England during the last war. It is probably true to say that then the British public had, in general, a truer appreciation of these differences than it has now; but while the people of England were then proud of their distinctive tradition, there are few of the political views then regarded as characteristically English of which the majority of her people do not now seem half-ashamed, if they do not positively repudiate them. It is scarcely an exaggeration to say that the more typically English a writer on political or social problems then appeared to the world, the more is he today forgotten in his own country. Men like Lord Morley or Henry Sidgwick, Lord Acton or A. V. Dicey, who were then admired in the world at large as outstanding examples of the political wisdom of liberal England, are to the present generation largely obsolete Victorians.[5] Perhaps nothing shows this change more clearly than that, while there is no lack of sympathetic treatment of Bismarck in contemporary English literature, the name of Gladstone is rarely mentioned by the younger generation without a sneer over his Victorian morality and naïve utopianism.[6]

---

assistant to the first secretary general of the League of Nations, and a National Labour Party MP from 1935–1945. —Ed.]

[3][At the turn of the century many members of the Fabian Society sided with the Conservatives and against the Liberals (as well as other socialists) on such issues as support for the Boer War, education reform, and imperial preference. —Ed.]

[4][Hayek refers to the conservative German nationalist historian Heinrich von Treitschke (1834–1896), who propounded a strong German empire whose interests are advanced by a powerful military. —Ed.]

[5][For more on Morley, see the author's introduction, note 4; on Acton, see the foreword to the 1956 American paperback edition, note 10. Hayek had reason to mention the Oxford jurist A. V. Dicey (1835–1922) in his discussion of the rule of law in chapter 6, note 2. Cambridge philosopher Henry Sidgwick (1838–1900) wrote on both ethics and economics. A quintessential Victorian, his life span roughly coincided with her reign. —Ed.]

[6][In the years following the First World War, Bismarck's diplomatic craftiness was often deemed a virtue: he was thought to have been too smart to have gotten his nation into a position in which war was inevitable. See, for example, the contrast drawn between him and Kaiser Wilhelm II in Esme Howard, "Great Men and Small," *The Atlantic Monthly*, vol. 155, May 1935, pp. 523–33. Liberal politician William Ewart Gladstone (1809–1898), together with his Tory counterpart

I wish I could in a few paragraphs adequately convey the alarming impression gained from the perusal of a few of the English works on the ideas dominating the Germany of the last war, where almost every word could be applied to the views most conspicuous in current English literature. I shall merely quote one brief passage by Lord Keynes, describing in 1915 the "nightmare" which he found expounded in a typical German work of that period: he describes how, according to a German author, "even in peace industrial life must remain mobilised. This is what he means by speaking of the 'militarisation of our industrial life' [the title of the work reviewed]. Individualism must come to an end absolutely. A system of regulations must be set up, the object of which is not the greater happiness of the individual (Professor Jaffé is not ashamed to say this in so many words), but the strengthening of the organised unity of the state for the object of attaining the maximum degree of efficiency (*Leistungsfähigkeit*), the influence of which on individual advantage is only indirect.—This hideous doctrine is enshrined in a sort of idealism. The nation will grow into a 'closed unity' and will become, in fact, what Plato declared it should be—'Der Mensch im Grossen.' In particular, the coming peace will bring with it a strengthening of the idea of State action in industry. . . . Foreign investment, emigration, the industrial policy which in recent years had regarded the whole world as a market, are too dangerous. The old order of industry, which is dying to-day, is based on Profit; and the new Germany of the twentieth-century Power without consideration of Profit is to make an end of that system of Capitalism, which came over from England one hundred years ago."[7] Except that no English author has yet to my knowledge dared openly to disparage individual happiness, is there a passage in this which is not mirrored in much of contemporary English literature?

And, undoubtedly, not merely the ideas which in Germany and elsewhere prepared totalitarianism but also many of the principles of totalitarianism itself are what exercises an increasing fascination in many other countries. Although few people, if anybody, in England would probably be ready to swallow totalitarianism whole, there are few single features which have not yet been advised by somebody or other. Indeed, there is scarcely a leaf out of Hitler's book which somebody or other in England or America has not recommended us to take and

Benjamin Disraeli, dominated British politics during much of the Victorian era. The debunking of all virtues Victorian was most famously undertaken by John Maynard Keynes's Bloomsbury companion Lytton Strachey, whose book *Eminent Victorians* (London: Chatto and Windus, 1918; reprinted, London: Penguin, 1986) became the *locus classicus* of the genre. —Ed.]

[7] John Maynard Keynes, "The Economics of War in Germany," *Economic Journal*, vol. 25, September 1915, p. 450. [Keynes's review is of three issues of the journal *Archiv für Sozialwissenschaft und Sozialpolitik* on the theme of *Krieg und Wirtschaft*, which contained the first articles by German economists on the German economy during the war. Jaffé's article appeared in the March 1915 issue and was titled, "Die Militarisierung unseres Wirtschaftslebens." —Ed.]

use for our own purposes. This applies particularly to many people who are undoubtedly Hitler's mortal enemies because of one special feature in his system. We should never forget that the anti-Semitism of Hitler has driven from his country, or turned into his enemies, many people who in every respect are confirmed totalitarians of the German type.[8]

No description in general terms can give an adequate idea of the similarity of much of current English political literature to the works which destroyed the belief in Western civilization in Germany and created the state of mind in which naziism could become successful. The similarity is even more one of the temper with which the problems are approached than of the specific arguments used—a similar readiness to break all cultural ties with the past and to stake everything on the success of a particular experiment. As was also true in Germany, most of the works which are preparing the way for a totalitarian course in the democracies are the product of sincere idealists and often of men of considerable intellectual distinction. So, although it is invidious to single out particular persons as illustrations where similar views are advocated by hundreds of others, I see no other way of demonstrating effectively how far this development has actually advanced. I shall deliberately choose as illustrations authors whose sincerity and disinterestedness are above suspicion. But though I hope in this way to show how the views from which totalitarianism springs are now rapidly spreading here, I stand little chance of conveying successfully the equally important similarity in the emotional atmosphere. An extensive investigation into all the subtle changes in thought and language would be necessary to make explicit what one readily enough recognizes as symptoms of a familiar development. Through meeting the kind of people who talk about the necessity of opposing "big" ideas to "small" ones and of replacing the old "static" or "partial" thinking by the new "dynamic" or "global" way, one learns to recognize that what at first appears sheer nonsense is a sign of the same intellectual attitude with whose manifestations we can alone concern ourselves here.

My first examples are two works by a gifted scholar which in the past few years have attracted much attention. There are, perhaps, few other instances in contemporary English literature where the influence of the specific German ideas

[8]Especially when we consider the proportion of former socialists who have become Nazis it is important to remember that the true significance of this ratio is seen only if we compare it, not with the total number of former socialists, but with the number of those whose conversion would not in any case have been prevented by their ancestry. In fact, one of the surprising features of the political emigration from Germany is the comparatively small number of refugees from the Left who are not "Jews" in the German sense of the term. How often do we not hear eulogies of the German system prefaced by some statement such as the following with which at a recent conference an enumeration of the "features of the totalitarian technique of economic mobilization which are worth thinking about" was introduced: "Herr Hitler is not my ideal—far from it. There are very pressing personal reasons why Herr Hitler should not be my ideal, but . . ."

with which we are concerned is so marked as in Professor E. H. Carr's books on the *Twenty Years' Crisis* and the *Conditions of Peace*.[9]

In the first of these two books Professor Carr frankly confessed himself an adherent of "the 'historical school' of realists [which] had its home in Germany and [whose] development can be traced through the great names of Hegel and Marx."[10] A realist, he explains, is one "who makes morality a function of politics" and who "cannot logically accept any standard of value save that of fact."[11] This "realism" is contrasted, in truly German fashion, with the "utopian" thought dating from the eighteenth century "which was essentially individualist in that it made the human conscience the final court of appeal."[12] But the old morals with their "abstract general principles" must disappear because "the empiricist treats the concrete case on its individual merits."[13] In other words, nothing but expediency matters, and we are even assured that "the rule *pacta sunt servanda* is not a moral principle."[14] That without abstract general principles merit becomes solely a matter of arbitrary opinion and that international treaties, if they are not morally binding, have no meaning whatever does not seem to worry Professor Carr.

According to Professor Carr, indeed, although he does not explicitly say so, it appears that England fought the last war on the wrong side. Anyone who rereads now the statements of British war aims of twenty-five years ago and compares them with Professor Carr's present views will readily see that what were then believed to be the German views are now those of Professor Carr, who would presumably argue that the different views then professed in this country were merely a product of British hypocrisy. How little difference he is able to see between the ideals held in this country and those practiced by present-day Germany is best illustrated by his assertion that "it is true that when a prominent National Socialist asserts that 'anything that benefits the German people is right, anything that harms them is wrong' he is merely propounding the same identification of national interest with universal right which has already been established for English-speaking countries by [President] Wilson, Professor Toynbee, Lord Cecil, and many others."[15]

[9] [E. H. Carr, *The Twenty Years' Crisis, 1919–1939*, op. cit., and *Conditions of Peace* (New York: Macmillan, 1942). —Ed.]

[10] [E. H. Carr, *The Twenty Years' Crisis, 1919–1939*, op. cit., p. 84. —Ed.]

[11] [The sentence, "The realist cannot logically accept any standard of value save that of fact" is found *ibid.*, p. 28. I could not find the phrase "who makes morality a function of politics," but the phrase "who regard ethics as a function of politics" is found on p. 54. —Ed.]

[12] [*Ibid.*, p. 32. —Ed.]

[13] [*Ibid.*, p. 38. —Ed.]

[14] [*Ibid.*, p. 243. The Latin phrase *pacta sunt servanda*, or "pacts must be respected," refers to a fundamental principle of civil and international law. —Ed.]

[15] [*Ibid.*, p. 100. Twenty-five years earlier, American president Woodrow Wilson (1856–1924) championed the League of Nations at the Paris peace conference. English statesman Robert, First Viscount Cecil of Chelwood (1864–1958) helped to draft the League of Nations covenant and

Since Professor Carr's books are devoted to international problems, it is mainly in that field that their characteristic tendency becomes apparent. But from the glimpses one gets of the character of the future society which he contemplates, it appears also to be quite on the totalitarian model. Sometimes one even wonders whether the resemblance is accidental or deliberate. Does Professor Carr, for example, realize, when he asserts that "we can no longer find much meaning in the distinction familiar to nineteenth-century thought between 'society' and 'state,'" that this is precisely the doctrine of Professor Carl Schmitt, the leading Nazi theoretician of totalitarianism and, in fact, the essence of the definition of totalitarianism which that author has given to that term which he himself had introduced?[16] Or that the view that, "the mass production of opinion is the corollary of the mass production of goods" and that, therefore, "the prejudice which the word propaganda still exerts in many minds today is closely parallel to the prejudice against control of industry and trade"[17] is really an apology for a regimentation of opinion of the kind practiced by the Nazis?

In his more recent *Conditions of Peace* Professor Carr answers with an emphatic affirmative the question with which we concluded the last chapter:

"The victors lost the peace, and Soviet Russia and Germany won it, because the former continued to preach, and in part to apply, the once valid, but now disruptive ideals of the rights of nations and laissez faire capitalism, whereas the latter, consciously or unconsciously borne forward on the tide of the twentieth century, were striving to build up the world in larger units under centralized planning and control."[18]

Professor Carr completely makes his own the German battle cry of the socialist revolution of the East against the liberal West in which Germany was the leader: "The revolution which began in the last war, which has been the driving force of every significant political movement in the last twenty years . . . a revolution against the predominant ideas of the nineteenth century: liberal democracy, national self-determination and laissez faire economics."[19] As he

---

served as the president of the League of Nations Union from 1923 to 1945. He was awarded the Nobel Prize for Peace in 1937. English historian Arnold Joseph Toynbee (1889–1975), also a delegate to the Paris peace conference, expressed his views in such documents as *The World After the Peace Conference, Being an Epilogue to the "History of the Peace Conference of Paris" and a Prologue to the "Survey of International Affairs 1920–1923"* (London: Oxford University Press, 1925). —Ed.]

[16] [*Ibid.*, p. 269. For more on Carl Schmitt, see chapter 6, note 5. Hayek leaves out a clause from Carr's sentence, which reads, "We can no longer find much meaning, within the national community, in the distinction familiar to nineteenth-century thought between 'society' and 'state.'" It may be that Carr was referring to what the national community believed, rather than to what he himself believed. —Ed.]

[17] [Both passages may be found *ibid.*, p. 171. —Ed.]

[18] [E. H. Carr, *Conditions of Peace*, op. cit., p. 8. —Ed.]

[19] [*Ibid.*, pp. 10–11. —Ed.]

himself rightly says, "it was almost inevitable that this challenge to nineteenth-century beliefs which she had never really shared should find in Germany one of its strongest protagonists."[20] With all the fatalistic belief of every pseudo-historian since Hegel and Marx, this development is represented as inevitable: "We know the direction in which the world is moving, and we must bow to it or perish."[21]

The conviction that this trend is inevitable is characteristically based on familiar economic fallacies—the presumed necessity of the general growth of monopolies in consequence of technological developments, the alleged "potential plenty," and all the other popular catchwords which appear in works of this kind. Professor Carr is not an economist, and his economic argument generally will not bear serious examination. But neither this nor his belief characteristically held at the same time, that the importance of the economic factor in social life is rapidly decreasing, prevents him from basing on economic arguments all his predictions about the inevitable developments or from presenting as his main demands for the future "the reinterpretation in predominantly economic terms of the democratic ideals of 'equality' and 'liberty'"![22]

Professor Carr's contempt for all the ideas of liberal economists (which he insists on calling nineteenth-century ideas, though he knows that Germany "had never really shared" them and had already in the nineteenth century practiced most of the principles he now advocates) is as profound as that of any of the German writers quoted in the last chapter. He even takes over the German thesis, originated by Friedrich List, that free trade was a policy dictated solely by, and appropriate only to, the special interests of England in the nineteenth century.[23] Now, however, "the artificial production of some degree of autarchy is a necessary condition of orderly social existence."[24] To bring about a "return to a more dispersed and generalized world trade . . . by a 'removal of trade barriers' or by a resuscitation of the laissez faire principles of the nineteenth century" is "unthinkable."[25] The future belongs to *Grossraumwirtschaft* of the German kind: "The result which we desire can be won only by a deliberate reorganization of European life such as Hitler has undertaken"![26]

[20] [*Ibid.*, p. 218. —Ed.]

[21] [*Ibid.*, p. 131. —Ed.]

[22] [*Ibid.*, p. 30. —Ed.]

[23] [For more on Friedrich List, see chapter 1, note 13. —Ed.]

[24] [E. H. Carr, *The Twenty Years' Crisis, 1919–1939*, op. cit., p. 155. Carr actually said "the artificial *promotion* of some degree of autarchy is a necessary condition of orderly social existence." —Ed.]

[25] [E. H. Carr, *Conditions of Peace*, op. cit., p. 237. —Ed.]

[26] [*Ibid.*, p. 237. *Grossraumwirtschaft* translates literally as "extensive area economy," and refers to the integration of other central and eastern European economies into an expanding German economy, as in the vision of *Mitteleuropa* articulated by Friedrich Naumann that was described in chapter 12, note 19. —Ed.]

After all this one is hardly surprised to find a characteristic section headed "The Moral Functions of War," in which Professor Carr condescendingly pities "the well-meaning people (especially in English-speaking countries) who, steeped in the nineteenth-century tradition, persist in regarding war as senseless and devoid of purpose," and rejoices in the "sense of meaning and purpose" which war, "the most powerful instrument of social solidarity," creates.[27] This is all very familiar—but it was not in the works of English scholars that one expected to find these views.

Possibly we have not yet given enough attention to one feature of the intellectual development in Germany during the last hundred years which is now in an almost identical form making its appearance in the English-speaking countries: the scientists' agitating for a "scientific" organization of society. The ideal of a society organized "through and through" from the top has in Germany been considerably furthered by the quite unique influence which her scientific and technological specialists were allowed to exercise on the formation of social and political opinions. Few people remember that in the modern history of Germany the political professors have played a role comparable to that of the political lawyers in France.[28] The influence of these scientist-politicians was of late years not often on the side of liberty: the "intolerance of reason" so frequently conspicuous in the scientific specialist, the impatience with the ways of the ordinary man so characteristic of the expert, and the contempt for anything which was not consciously organized by superior minds according to a scientific blueprint were phenomena familiar in German public life for generations before they became of significance in England. And perhaps no other country provides a better illustration of the effects on a nation of a general and thorough shift of the greater part of its educational system from the "humanities" to the "realities" than Germany between 1840 and 1940.[29]

The way in which, in the end, with few exceptions, her scholars and scientists put themselves readily at the service of the new rulers is one of the most depressing and shameful spectacles in the whole history of the rise of National Socialism.[30] It is well known that particularly the scientists and engineers, who

[27] [The section on "The Moral Function of War" begins *ibid.*, p. 116, and the three excerpts may be found on pages 116, 119, and 119, respectively. —Ed.]

[28] Cf. Franz Schnabel, *Deutsche Geschichte im neunzehnten Jahrhundert*, vol. 2 (Freiburg im Breisgau: Herder, 1933), p. 204.

[29] I believe it was the author of *Leviathan* who first suggested that the teaching of the classics should be suppressed, because it instilled a dangerous spirit of liberty! [Thomas Hobbes decried the antimonarchical views of the Greeks and Roman in chapter 21 of *Leviathan*, titled "Of the Liberty of Subjects." See Thomas Hobbes, *Leviathan* (1651; Indianapolis: Hackett, 1994), part 2, chapter 21, pp. 140–141. —Ed.]

[30] The servility of the scientists to the powers-that-be appeared early in Germany, hand in hand with the great development of state-organized science, which today is the subject of so much

had so loudly claimed to be the leaders on the march to a new and better world, submitted more readily than almost any other class to the new tyranny.[31]

The role which the intellectuals played in the totalitarian transformation of society was prophetically foreseen in another country by Julien Benda, whose *Trahison des clercs* assumes new significance when one now re-reads it, fifteen years after it has been written.[32] There is particularly one passage in that work which deserves to be well pondered and kept in mind when we come to consider certain examples of the excursions of British scientists into politics. It is the passage in which M. Benda speaks of the "superstition of science held to be competent in all domains, including that of morality; a superstition which, I repeat, is an acquisition of the nineteenth century. It remains to discover whether those who brandish this doctrine believe in it or whether they simply want to give the prestige of a scientific appearance to passions of their hearts, which they perfectly know are nothing but passions. It is to be noted that the dogma that history is obedient to scientific laws is preached especially by partisans of arbitrary authority. This is quite natural, since it eliminates the two

---

eulogy abroad. One of the most famous of German scientists, the physiologist, Emil du Bois-Raymond, was not ashamed, in an oration delivered in 1870 in his double capacity of rector of the University of Berlin and president of the Prussian Academy of Science, to proclaim that "we, the University of Berlin, quartered opposite the King's palace, are, by the deed of our foundation, the intellectual bodyguard of the House of Hohenzollern," in *A Speech on the German War* (London: Bentley, 1870), p. 31.—It is remarkable that du Bois-Reymond should have thought it advisable to issue an English edition of this oration. [German physiologist Emil du Bois-Reymond (1818–1896) taught at Berlin, and is known as the discoverer of neuro-electricity. —Ed.]

[31] It will suffice to quote one foreign witness: Robert A. Brady, in his study of *The Spirit and Structure of German Fascism* (London: V. Gollancz, 1937), pp. 76–77, concludes his detailed account of the development in the German academic world with the statement that "the scientist, per se, is hence, perhaps, the most easily used and 'coordinated' of all the especially trained people in modern society. The Nazis, to be true, fired a good many University professors, and dismissed a good many scientists from research laboratories. But the professors were primarily among the social sciences where there was more common awareness of and a more persistent criticism of the Nazi programmes, and not among the natural sciences where thinking is supposed to be most rigorous. Those dismissed in this latter field were primarily Jewish or exceptions to the generalisations made above, because of the equally uncritical acceptance of beliefs running contrary to Nazi views.— Consequently the Nazis were able to 'coordinate' scholars and scientists with relative ease, and hence to throw behind their elaborate propaganda the seeming weight of the bulk of German learned opinion and support."

[32] [Hayek refers to Julien Benda, *La Trahison des Clercs* (Paris: B. Grasset, 1927). French author and philosopher Julien Benda (1867–1956) began his career writing about the Dreyfuss affair. In his most famous book, Benda argued that in past ages intellectuals (*clercs*) engaged in a disinterested search for universal truths; they searched for ideals that transcended the needs of the state or society in which they lived. In recent times, however, intellectuals have become more and more the handmaiden of political and national causes. As a result of this betrayal of the *clercs*, extremist political passions had recently become more universal, coherent, continuous, and preponderant. —Ed.]

realities they most hate, i.e., human liberty and the historical action of the individual."[33]

We have already had occasion to mention one English product of this kind, a work in which, on a Marxist background, all the characteristic idiosyncrasies of the totalitarian intellectual, a hatred of almost everything which distinguishes Western civilization since the Renaissance, is combined with an approval of the methods of Inquisition.[34] We do not wish to consider here such an extreme case and shall take a work which is more representative and which has achieved considerable publicity. C. H. Waddington's little book under the characteristic title, *The Scientific Attitude*, is as good an example as any of a class of literature which is actively sponsored by the influential British weekly *Nature* and which combines claims for greater political power for the scientists with an ardent advocacy of wholesale "planning."[35] Though not quite so outspoken in his contempt for freedom as Mr. Crowther, Dr. Waddington is hardly more reassuring. He differs from most of the writers of the same kind in that he clearly sees and even emphasizes that the tendencies he describes and supports inevitably lead to a totalitarian system. Yet apparently this appears to him preferable to what he describes as "the present ferocious monkey-house civilization."[36]

Dr. Waddington's claim that the scientist is qualified to run a totalitarian society is based mainly on his thesis that "science can pass ethical judgment on human behavior"—a claim to the elaboration of which by Dr. Waddington *Nature* has given considerable publicity.[37] It is, of course, a thesis which has long been familiar to the German scientist-politicians and which has justly been singled out by J. Benda.[38] For an illustration of what this means we do not

[33] [Hayek quotes from the English translation of Benda's book. See Julien Benda, *The Betrayal of the Intellectuals*, trans. Richard Aldington (New York: William Morrow, 1928; reprinted, Boston: Beacon, 1955), p. 182. The original 1928 translation carried the title, *The Treason of the Intellectuals*, but "betrayal," chosen for the reprinted version, conveys Benda's argument better than the more literal "treason." —Ed.]

[34] [See the statement of J. G. Crowther, chapter 11, note 13. —Ed.]

[35] [Hayek refers to C. H. Waddington, *The Scientific Attitude* (Harmondsworth: Penguin, 1941). English embryologist and geneticist Conrad Hal Waddington (1905–1975) made contributions to evolutionary theory and also authored a number of popular texts on science. During the early days of the war the editors of *Nature* frequently endorsed the use of scientific planning both for the war effort and beyond, as I noted in my introduction, pp. 11–12. —Ed.]

[36] [C. H. Waddington, *The Scientific Attitude*, op. cit., p. 101. —Ed.]

[37] [*Ibid.*, p. 27. The September 6, 1941, issue of *Nature* contained an essay by Waddington titled "The Relations between Science and Ethics," together with comments on the article by eight others. Subsequent issues contained further exchanges between Waddington and various others. All of this was ultimately collected in the book by C. H. Waddington et al., *Science and Ethics* (London: George Allen and Unwin, 1942). —Ed.]

[38] [Julien Benda, *The Betrayal of the Intellectuals*, op. cit., more than once blames German scholars for initiating the betrayal of the *clercs* and for making it more likely that others would follow.

need to go outside Dr. Waddington's book. Freedom, he explains, "is a very troublesome concept for the scientist to discuss, partly because he is not convinced that, in the last analysis, there is such a thing."[39] Nevertheless, we are told that "science recognizes" this and that kind of freedom, but "the freedom to be odd and unlike one's neighbor is not . . . a scientific value."[40] Apparently the "harlot humanities," about which Dr. Waddington has to say many uncomplimentary things, have gravely misled us in teaching us tolerance![41]

That when it comes to social and economic questions this book on the "scientific attitude" is anything but scientific is what one has learned to expect of this kind of literature. We find again all the familiar clichés and baseless generalizations about "potential plenty" and the inevitable tendency toward monopoly, though the "best authorities" quoted in support of these contentions prove on examination to be mostly political tracts of questionable scientific standing, while the serious studies of the same problems are conspicuously neglected.[42]

As in almost all works of this type, Dr. Waddington's convictions are largely determined by his belief in "inevitable historical tendencies" which science is presumed to have discovered and which he derives from "the profound scientific philosophy" of Marxism, whose basic notions are "almost, if not quite, identical with those underlying the scientific approach to nature"[43] and which his "competence to judge" tells Dr. Waddington are an advance on anything which has gone before.[44] Thus Dr. Waddington, though he finds it "difficult to deny that England now is a worse country to live in than it was" in 1913,[45] looks forward to an economic system which "will be centralized and totalitarian in the sense that all aspects of the economic development of large regions are consciously planned as an integrated whole."[46] And for his facile optimism that in this totalitarian system freedom of thought will be preserved, his "scientific attitude" has no better counsel than the conviction that "there must be

Thus he states, on pp. 42–43, "The nationalist 'clerk' is essentially a German invention. . . . It is undeniable that from the moment when Germany had a Mommsen, France especially was bound to have a Barrès, under penalty of finding herself in a position of great inferiority in nationalist fanaticism. . . ." —Ed.]

[39] [C. H. Waddington, *The Scientific Attitude*, op. cit., p. 110. —Ed.]

[40] [*Ibid.*, p. 112. —Ed.]

[41] [*Ibid.*, p. 125. —Ed.]

[42] [Among the references that Waddington cited *ibid.*, pp. 89–91, are social surveys from *Time* magazine, and such books as Frank Verulam, *Production for the People* (London: Gollancz, 1940) and John Boyd Orr, *Food, Health and Income: Report on a Survey of Adequacy of Diet in Relation to Income* (London: Macmillan, 1936). —Ed.]

[43] [C. H. Waddington, *The Scientific Attitude*, op. cit., p. 81. —Ed.]

[44] [*Ibid.*, p. 84. —Ed.]

[45] [*Ibid.*, p. 14. —Ed.]

[46] [*Ibid.*, p. 124. —Ed.]

very valuable evidence about questions which one does not need to be an expert to understand," such as, for example, whether it is possible "to combine totalitarianism with freedom of thought."[47]

A fuller survey of the various tendencies toward totalitarianism in England would have to give considerable attention to the various attempts to create some kind of middle-class socialism bearing, no doubt unknown to their authors, an alarming resemblance to similar developments in pre-Hitler Germany.[48] If we were concerned here with political movements proper, we should have to consider such new organizations as the "Forward-March" or "Common-Wealth" movement of Sir Richard Acland, the author of *Unser Kampf*, or the activities of the "1941 Committee" of Mr. J. B. Priestley, at one time associated with the former.[49] But, though it would be unwise to disregard the symptomatic significance of such phenomena as these, they can hardly yet be counted as important political forces. Apart from the intellectual influences which we have illustrated by two instances, the impetus of the movement toward totalitarianism comes mainly from the two great vested interests: organized capital and organized labor. Probably the greatest menace of all is the fact that the policies of these two most powerful groups point in the same direction.

They do this through their common, and often concerted, support of the monopolistic organization of industry; and it is this tendency which is the great immediate danger. While there is no reason to believe that this movement is

---

[47] [*Ibid.*, p. 19. —Ed.]

[48] Another element which after this war is likely to strengthen the tendencies in this direction will be some of the men who during the war have tasted the powers of coercive control and will find it difficult to reconcile themselves with the humbler roles they will then have to play. Though after the last war men of this kind were not so numerous as they will probably be in the future, they exercised even then a not inconsiderable influence on the economic policy of this country. It was in the company of some of these men that as long as ten or twelve years ago I first experienced in this country the then still unusual sensation of being suddenly transported into what I had learned to regard as a thoroughly "German" intellectual atmosphere. ["Ten or twelve years" earlier Hayek had just joined the faculty at the London School of Economics. As noted in my introduction, pp. 3–4, Hayek expanded on the claim that certain then-common views among the British public were reminiscent of those held earlier in Germany in his inaugural lecture, "The Trend of Economic Thinking," op. cit. —Ed.]

[49] [Sir Richard Acland, Bt. (1906–1990) formed the socialist Commonwealth Party in 1942 together with the English writer and political commentator John Boynton Priestly (1894–1984). The party found little success at the polls and was dissolved in 1945. Priestly was the chairman of the "Committee of 1941," of which Acland was a member. The Committee called for more comprehensive central planning during the war effort, and for its continuation after the war concluded. Acland was the author of both *Unser Kampf: Our Struggle* (Harmondsworth: Penguin, 1940) and *The Forward March* (London: George Allen and Unwin, 1941). In the latter he argued that, in the new age of plenty toward which we are marching, men feel that they must serve a higher cause and participate in something greater than themselves. Acland outlined a new "service economy" in which this can occur. —Ed.]

inevitable, there can be little doubt that if we continue on the path we have been treading, it will lead us to totalitarianism.

This movement is, of course, deliberately planned mainly by the capitalist organizers of monopolies, and they are thus one of the main sources of this danger. Their responsibility is not altered by the fact that their aim is not a totalitarian system but rather a sort of corporative society in which the organized industries would appear as semi-independent and self-governing "estates." But they are as shortsighted as were their German colleagues in believing that they will be allowed not only to create but also for any length of time to run such a system. The decisions which the managers of such an organized industry would constantly have to make are not decisions which any society will long leave to private individuals. A state which allows such enormous aggregations of power to grow up cannot afford to let this power rest entirely in private control. Nor is the belief any less illusory that in such conditions the entrepreneurs will be long allowed to enjoy the favored position which in a competitive society is justified by the fact that, of the many who take the risks, only a few achieve the success the chances of which make the risk worth taking. It is not surprising that entrepreneurs should like to enjoy both the high income which in a competitive society the successful ones among them gain and the security of the civil servant. So long as a large sector of private industry exists side by side with the government-run industry, great industrial talent is likely to command high salaries even in fairly secure positions. But while the entrepreneurs may well see their expectations borne out during a transition stage, it will not be long before they will find, as their German colleagues did, that they are no longer masters but will in every respect have to be satisfied with whatever power and emoluments the government will concede them.

Unless the argument of this book has been completely misunderstood, the author will not be suspected of any tenderness toward the capitalists if he stresses here that it would nevertheless be a mistake to put the blame for the modern movement toward monopoly exclusively or mainly on that class. Their propensity in this direction is neither new nor would it by itself be likely to become a formidable power. The fatal development was that they have succeeded in enlisting the support of an ever increasing number of other groups and, with their help, in obtaining the support of the state.

In some measure the monopolists have gained this support either by letting other groups participate in their gains or, and perhaps even more frequently, by persuading them that the formation of monopolies was in the public interest. But the change in public opinion, which through its influence on legislation and judicature[50] has been the most important factor to make this development

[50] Cf. on this the instructive article by W. Arthur Lewis, "Monopoly and the Law: An Economist's Reflections on the Crofter Case," *Modern Law Review*, vol. 6, April 1943, pp. 97–111.

THE ROAD TO SERFDOM

possible, is more than anything the result of the propaganda against competition by the Left. Very frequently even measures aimed against the monopolists in fact serve only to strengthen the power of monopoly. Every raid on the gains of monopoly, be it in the interest of particular groups or of the state as a whole, tends to create new vested interests which will help to bolster up monopoly. A system in which large privileged groups profit from the gains of monopoly may be politically much more dangerous, and monopoly in such a system certainly is much more powerful, than in one where the profits go to a limited few. But though it should be clear that, for example, the higher wages which the monopolist is in a position to pay are just as much the result of exploitation as his own profit, and are just as certain to make poorer not only all the consumers but still more all other wage-earners, not merely those who benefit from it but the public generally nowadays accept the ability to pay higher wages as a legitimate argument in favor of monopoly.[51]

There is serious reason for doubt whether even in those cases where monopoly is inevitable the best way of controlling it is to put it in the hands of the state. If only a single industry were in question, this might well be so. But, when we have to deal with many different monopolistic industries, there is much to be said for leaving them in different private hands rather than combining them under the single control of the state. Even if railways, road and air transport, or the supply of gas and electricity were all inevitably monopolies, the consumer is unquestionably in a much stronger position so long as they remain separate monopolies than when they are "coordinated" by a central control. Private monopoly is scarcely ever complete and even more rarely of long duration or able to disregard potential competition. But a state monopoly is always a state-protected monopoly—protected against both potential competition and effective criticism. It means in most instances that a temporary monopoly is given the power to secure its position for all time—a power almost certain to be used. Where the power which ought to check and control monopoly becomes interested in sheltering and defending its appointees, where for the government to remedy an abuse is to admit responsibility for it, and where criticism of the actions of monopoly means criticism of the government, there is little hope of monopoly becoming the servant of the community. A state which is entangled in all directions in the running of monopolistic enterprise, while it would possess

---

[51] Even more surprising, perhaps, is the remarkable tenderness which many socialists are likely to show toward the *rentier* bondholders to whom monopolist organization of industry frequently guarantees secure incomes. That their blind enmity to profits should lead people to represent effortless fixed income as socially or ethically more desirable than profits, and to accept even monopoly to secure such a guaranteed income to, for example, railway bondholders, is one of the most extraordinary symptoms of the perversion of values which has taken place during the last generation.

crushing power over the individual, would yet be a weak state in so far as its freedom in formulating policy is concerned. The machinery of monopoly becomes identical with the machinery of the state, and the state itself becomes more and more identified with the interests of those who run things than with the interests of the people in general.

The probability is that wherever monopoly is really inevitable the plan which used to be preferred by Americans, of a strong state control over private monopolies, if consistently pursued, offers a better chance of satisfactory results than state management. This would at least seem to be so where the state enforces a stringent price control which leaves no room for extraordinary profits in which others than the monopolists can participate. Even if this should have the effect (as it sometimes had with American public utilities) that the services of the monopolistic industries would become less satisfactory than they might be, this would be a small price to pay for an effective check on the powers of monopoly. Personally, I should much prefer to have to put up with some such inefficiency than have organized monopoly control my ways of life. Such a method of dealing with monopoly, which would rapidly make the position of the monopolist the least eligible among entrepreneurial positions, would also do as much as anything to reduce monopoly to the spheres where it is inevitable and to stimulate the invention of substitutes which can be provided competitively. Only make the position of the monopolist once more that of the whipping boy of economic policy, and you will be surprised how quickly most of the abler entrepreneurs will rediscover their taste for the bracing air of competition!

The problem of monopoly would not be difficult as it is if it were only the capitalist monopolist whom we have to fight. But, as has already been said, monopoly has become the danger that it is, not through the efforts of a few interested capitalists, but through the support they have obtained from those whom they have let share in their gains, and from the many more whom they have persuaded that in supporting monopoly they assist in the creation of a more just and orderly society. The fatal turning-point in the modern development was when the great movement which can serve its original ends only by fighting all privilege, the labor movement, came under the influence of anti-competition doctrines and became itself entangled in the strife for privilege. The recent growth of monopoly is largely the result of a deliberate collaboration of organized capital and organized labor where the privileged groups of labor share in the monopoly profits at the expense of the community and particularly at the expense of the poorest, those employed in the less-well-organized industries and the unemployed.

It is one of the saddest spectacles of our time to see a great democratic movement support a policy which must lead to the destruction of democracy and which meanwhile can benefit only a minority of the masses who support it.[52] Yet it is this support from the Left of the tendencies toward monopoly which make them so irresistible and the prospects of the future so dark. So long as labor continues to assist in the destruction of the only order under which at least some degree of independence and freedom has been secured to every worker, there is indeed little hope for the future. The labor leaders who now proclaim so loudly that they have "done once and for all with the mad competitive system"[53] are proclaiming the doom of the freedom of the individual. There is no other possibility than either the order governed by the impersonal discipline of the market or that directed by the will of a few individuals; and those who are out to destroy the first are wittingly or unwittingly helping to create the second. Even though some workmen will perhaps be better fed, and all will no doubt be more uniformly dressed in that new order, it is permissible to doubt whether the majority of English workmen will in the end thank the intellectuals among their leaders who have presented them with a socialist doctrine which endangers their personal freedom.

To anyone who is familiar with the history of the major Continental countries in the last twenty-five years, the study of the recent program of the Labour party in England, now committed to the creation of a "planned society," is a most depressing experience. To "any attempt to restore traditional Britain" there is opposed a scheme which not only in general outline but also in detail

---

[52] [Hayek refers here to the British Labour Party's policies as enunciated in the Labour Party pamphlet, *The Old World and the New Society: A Report on the Problems of War and Peace Reconstruction*, op. cit., or in Harold Laski's address before the Labour Party Conference in 1942. —Ed.]

[53] Professor H. J. Laski, "A Planned Economic Democracy," *The Labour Party Report of the 41st Annual Conference*, op. cit., p. 111. It deserves to be noted that, according to Professor Laski, it is "this mad competitive system which spells poverty for all peoples, and war as outcome of that poverty"—a curious reading of the history of the last hundred and fifty years. [Hayek refers to Laski's address on May 26, 1942, in support of a resolution, found on p. 110, that reads, "This Conference affirms that there must be no return after the war to an unplanned competitive society, which inevitably produces economic insecurity, industrial inefficiency, and social inequality. It notes that the pressure of war has already necessitated far-reaching Government control of industry, central planning of the nation's economic life, and the subordination of many private interests to the common good, and urges that this process be carried further in order to achieve swift and total victory. It declares that measures of Government control needed for mobilising the national resources in war are no less necessary for securing their best use in peace, and must therefore be maintained after final victory is won. It regards the socialisation of the basic industries and services of the country, and the planning of production for community consumption, as the only lasting foundation for a just and prosperous economic order in which political democracy and personal liberty can be combined with a reasonable standard of living for all citizens.

"The Conference therefore affirms that it is urgent to undertake without delay the necessary preparation for the vital changes here proposed." The resolution as stated was passed by the assembly. —Ed.]

and even wording is indistinguishable from the socialist dreams which dominated German discussion twenty-five years ago. Not only demands, like those of the resolution, adopted on Professor Laski's motion, which requires the retention in peacetime of the "measures of government control needed for mobilizing the national resources in war" but all the characteristic catchwords, such as the "balanced economy," which Professor Laski now demands for Great Britain, or the "community consumption" toward which production is to be centrally directed, are bodily taken over from the German ideology.

Twenty-five years ago there was perhaps still some excuse for holding the naïve belief that "a planned society can be a far more free society than the competitive laissez faire order it has come to replace."[54] But to find it once more held after twenty-five years of experience and the re-examination of the old beliefs to which this experience has led, and at a time when we are fighting the results of those very doctrines, is tragic beyond words. That the great party which in Parliament and public opinion has largely taken the place of the progressive parties of the past should have ranged itself with what, in the light of all past development, must be regarded as a reactionary movement, is the decisive change which has taken place in our time and the source of the mortal danger to everything a liberal must value. That the advances of the past should be threatened by the traditionalist forces of the Right is a phenomenon of all ages which need not alarm us. But if the place of the opposition, in public discussion as well as in Parliament, should become lastingly the monopoly of a second reactionary party, there would, indeed, be no hope left.

[54] *The Old World and the New Society*, op. cit., pp. 12 and 16.

FOURTEEN

MATERIAL CONDITIONS AND IDEAL ENDS

Is it just or reasonable, that most voices against the main end of government should enslave the less number that would be free? More just it is, doubtless, if it come to force, that a less number compel a greater to retain, which can be no wrong to them, their liberty, than that a greater number, for the pleasure of their baseness, compel a less most injuriously to be their fellow slaves. They who seek nothing but their own just liberty, have always the right to win it, whenever they have the power, be the voices never so numerous that oppose it.

—John Milton[1]

Our generation likes to flatter itself that it attaches less weight to economic considerations than did its parents or grandparents. The "End of Economic Man" bids fair to become one of the governing myths of our age.[2] Before we accept this claim, or treat the change as praiseworthy, we must inquire a little further how far it is true. When we consider the claims for social reconstruction which are most strongly pressed, it appears that they are almost all economic in character: we have seen already that the "reinterpretation in economic terms" of the political ideals of the past, of liberty, equality, and security, is one of the main demands of people who at the same time proclaim the end of economic man. Nor can there be much doubt that in their beliefs and aspirations men are today more than ever before governed by economic doctrines, by the carefully

[1] [John Milton, "The Ready and Easy Way to Establish a Free Commonwealth," in *Areopagitica and Other Prose Works* (London: J. M. Dent and Sons, Everyman's Edition, 1927), p. 181. —Ed.]

[2] [In this paragraph Hayek refers to themes found in Peter Drucker's *The End of Economic Man: A Study of the New Totalitarianism*, op. cit. Drucker argued that Europeans have searched for freedom and equality over the centuries, first in spiritual, and subsequently in intellectual, political, and economic spheres. Fascism emerged due to the failures of both capitalism and socialism to deliver on their promises of freedom and equality in the economic sphere. "Fascist Noneconomic Societies" have arisen in which the authority of command substitutes for economic privilege and where all hopes for economic growth and wealth creation are abandoned. Under fascism, the individual serves the larger corporate society, and though equality is achieved, individual freedom and initiative are foregone. Drucker forecast a confrontation between the totalitarian states and the western democracies, and recommended that the latter create their own noneconomic societies, but ones that retain the quest for the freedom and equality of individuals. —Ed.]

fostered belief in the irrationality of our economic system, by the false assertions about "potential plenty," pseudo-theories about the inevitable trend toward monopoly, and the impression created by certain much-advertised occurrences such as the destruction of stocks of raw materials or the suppression of inventions, for which competition is blamed, though they are precisely the sort of thing which could not happen under competition and which are made possible only by monopoly and usually by government-aided monopoly.[3]

In a different sense, however, it is no doubt true that our generation is less willing to listen to economic considerations than was true of its predecessors. It is most decidedly unwilling to sacrifice any of its demands to what are called economic arguments; it is impatient and intolerant of all restraints on their immediate ambitions and unwilling to bow to economic necessities. It is not any contempt for material welfare, or even any diminished desire for it, but, on the contrary, a refusal to recognize any obstacles, any conflict with other aims which might impede the fulfillment of their own desires, which distinguishes our generation. Economophobia would be a more correct description of this attitude than the doubly misleading "End of Economic Man," which suggests a change from a state of affairs which has never existed in a direction in which we are not moving. Man has come to hate, and to revolt against, the impersonal forces to which in the past he submitted, even though they have often frustrated his individual efforts.

This revolt is an instance of a much more general phenomenon, a new unwillingness to submit to any rule or necessity the rationale of which man does not understand; it makes itself felt in many fields of life, particularly in that of morals; and it is often a commendable attitude. But there are fields where this craving for intelligibility cannot be fully satisfied and where at the same time a refusal to submit to anything we cannot understand must lead to the destruction of our civilization. Though it is natural that, as the world around us becomes more complex, our resistance grows against the forces which, without our understanding them, constantly interfere with individual hopes and plans, it is just in these circumstances that it becomes less and less possible for anyone fully to understand these forces. A complex civilization like ours is necessarily based on the individual's adjusting himself to changes whose cause and nature he cannot understand: why he should have more or less, why he should have to move to another occupation, why some things he wants should become more

[3] The frequent use that is made of the occasional destruction of wheat, coffee, etc., as an argument against competition is a good illustration of the intellectual dishonesty of much of this argument, since a little reflection will show that in a competitive market no owner of such stocks can gain by their destruction. The case of the alleged suppression of useful patents is more complicated and cannot be adequately discussed in a note; but the conditions in which it would be profitable to put into cold storage a patent *which in the social interest ought to be used* are so exceptional that it is more than doubtful whether this has happened in any important instance.

difficult to get than others, will always be connected with such a multitude of circumstances that no single mind will be able to grasp them; or, even worse, those affected will put all the blame on an obvious immediate and avoidable cause, while the more complex interrelationships which determine the change remain inevitably hidden to them. Even the director of a completely planned society, if he wanted to give an adequate explanation to anyone why he has to be directed to a different job, or why his remuneration has to be changed, could not fully do so without explaining and vindicating his whole plan—which means, of course, that it could not be explained to more than a few.

It was men's submission to the impersonal forces of the market that in the past has made possible the growth of a civilization which without this could not have developed; it is by thus submitting that we are every day helping to build something that is greater than any one of us can fully comprehend. It does not matter whether men in the past did submit from beliefs which some now regard as superstitious: from a religious spirit of humility or an exaggerated respect for the crude teachings of the early economists. The crucial point is that it is infinitely more difficult rationally to comprehend the necessity of submitting to forces whose operation we cannot follow in detail than to do so out of the humble awe which religion, or even the respect for the doctrines of economics, did inspire. It may, indeed, be the case that infinitely more intelligence on the part of everybody would be needed than anybody now possesses, if we were even merely to maintain our present complex civilization without anyone's having to do things of which he does not comprehend the necessity. The refusal to yield to forces which we neither understand nor can recognize as the conscious decisions of an intelligent being is the product of an incomplete and therefore erroneous rationalism. It is incomplete because it fails to comprehend that the coordination of the multifarious individual efforts in a complex society must take account of facts no individual can completely survey. And it fails to see that, unless this complex society is to be destroyed, the only alternative to submission to the impersonal and seemingly irrational forces of the market is submission to an equally uncontrollable and therefore arbitrary power of other men. In his anxiety to escape the irksome restraints which he now feels, man does not realize that the new authoritarian restraints which will have to be deliberately imposed in their stead will be even more painful.

Those who argue that we have to an astounding degree learned to master the forces of nature but are sadly behind in making successful use of the possibilities of social collaboration are quite right so far as this statement goes. But they are mistaken when they carry the comparison further and argue that we must learn to master the forces of society in the same manner in which we have learned to master the forces of nature. This is not only the path to totalitarianism but the path to the destruction of our civilization and a certain way to block future progress. Those who demand it show by their very demands that they have not yet comprehended the extent to which the mere preservation of what we have so far achieved depends on the coordination of individual efforts by impersonal forces.

We must now return briefly to the crucial point—that individual freedom cannot be reconciled with the supremacy of one single purpose to which the whole society must be entirely and permanently subordinated. The only exception to the rule that a free society must not be subjected to a single purpose is war and other temporary disasters when subordination of almost everything to the immediate and pressing need is the price at which we preserve our freedom in the long run. This explains also why so many of the fashionable phrases about doing for the purposes of peace what we have learned to do for the purposes of war are so very misleading: it is sensible temporarily to sacrifice freedom in order to make it more secure in the future; but the same cannot be said for a system proposed as a permanent arrangement.

That no single purpose must be allowed in peace to have absolute preference over all others applies even to the one aim which everybody now agrees comes in the front rank: the conquest of unemployment. There can be no doubt that this must be the goal of our greatest endeavor; even so, it does not mean that such an aim should be allowed to dominate us to the exclusion of everything else, that, as the glib phrase runs, it must be accomplished "at any price." It is, in fact, in this field that the fascination of vague but popular phrases like "full employment" may well lead to extremely shortsighted measures, and where the categorical and irresponsible "it must be done at all cost" of the single-minded idealist is likely to do the greatest harm.

It is of very great importance that we should approach with open eyes the task which in this field we shall have to face after the war and that we should clearly realize what we may hope to achieve. One of the dominant features of the immediate postwar situation will be that the special needs of war have drawn hundreds of thousands of men and women into specialized jobs where during the war they have been able to earn relatively high wages. There will, in many instances, be no possibility of employing the same numbers in these particular trades. There will be an urgent need for the transfer of large numbers to other jobs, and many of them will find that the work they can then get is less favorably remunerated than was true of their war job. Even retraining, which certainly ought to be provided on a liberal scale, cannot entirely overcome this problem. There will still be many people who, if they are to be paid according to what their services will then be worth to society, would under any system have to be content with a lowering of their material position relative to that of others.

If, then, the trade unions successfully resist any lowering of the wages of the particular groups in question, there will be only two alternatives open: either coercion will have to be used (i.e., certain individuals will have to be selected for compulsory transfer to other and relatively less well paid positions) or those who can no longer be employed at the relatively high wages they have earned during the war must be allowed to remain unemployed until they are willing to accept work at a relatively lower wage. This is a problem which would arise in a socialist society no less than in any other; and the great majority of workmen would probably be just as little inclined to guarantee in perpetuity their present wages to those who were drawn into specially well-paid employments because of the special need of war. A socialist society would certainly use coercion in this position. The point that is relevant for us is that if we are determined not to allow unemployment at any price, and are not willing to use coercion, we shall be driven to all sorts of desperate expedients, none of which can bring any lasting relief and all of which will seriously interfere with the most productive use of our resources. It should be specially noted that monetary policy cannot provide a real cure for this difficulty except by a general and considerable inflation, sufficient to raise all other wages and prices relatively to those which cannot be lowered, and that even this would bring about the desired result only by effecting in a concealed and underhand fashion that reduction of real wages which could not be brought about directly. Yet to raise all other wages and incomes to an extent sufficient to adjust the position of the group in question would involve an inflationary expansion on such a scale that the disturbances, hardships, and injustices caused would be much greater than those to be cured.

This problem, which will arise in a particularly acute form after the war, is one which will always be with us so long as the economic system has to adopt itself to continuous changes. There will always be a possible maximum of employment in the short run which can be achieved by giving all people employment where they happen to be and which can be achieved by monetary expansion. But not only can this maximum be maintained solely by progressive inflationary expansion and with the effect of holding up those redistributions of labor between industries made necessary by the changed circumstances, and which so long as workmen are free to choose their jobs will always come about only with some delays and thereby cause some unemployment: to aim always at the maximum of employment achievable by monetary means is a policy which is certain in the end to defeat its own purposes. It tends to lower the productivity of labor and thereby constantly increases the proportion of the working population which can be kept employed at present wages only by artificial means.

There is little doubt that after the war wisdom in the management of our economic affairs will be even more important than before and that the fate of our civilization will ultimately depend on how we solve the economic problems we shall then face. The British, at least, will at first be poor, very poor indeed—and the problem of regaining and improving former standards may in fact prove for Great Britain more difficult than for many other countries. If they act wisely, there is little question that by hard work and by devoting a considerable part of their efforts to overhauling and renewing their industrial apparatus and organization, they will in the course of a few years be able to return to and even surpass the level they had reached. But this presupposes that they will be satisfied to consume currently no more than is possible without impairing the task of reconstruction, that no exaggerated hopes create irresistible claims for more than this, and that they regard it as more important to use their resources in the best manner and for the purposes which contribute most to well-being than that we should use all their resources somehow.[4] Perhaps no less important is that they should not, by shortsighted attempts to cure poverty by a redistribution instead of by an increase in our income, so depress large classes as to turn them into determined enemies of the existing political order. It should never be forgotten that the one decisive factor in the rise of totalitarianism on the Continent, which is yet absent in England and America, is the existence of a large recently dispossessed middle class.

Our hopes of avoiding the fate which threatens must indeed to a large extent rest on the prospect that we can resume rapid economic progress which, however low we may have to start, will continue to carry us upward; and the main condition for such progress is that we should all be ready to adapt ourselves quickly to a very much changed world, that no considerations for the accustomed standard of particular groups must be allowed to obstruct this adaptation, and that we learn once more to turn all our resources to wherever they contribute most to make us all richer. The adjustments that will be needed if we are to recover and surpass our former standards will be greater than any similar adjustments we had to make in the past; and only if every one of us is ready individually to obey the necessities of this readjustment shall we be able to get through a difficult period as free men who can choose their own way of life. Let a uniform minimum be secured to everybody by all means; but let us admit at the same time that with this assurance of a basic minimum all claims for a privileged security of particular classes must lapse, that all excuses disappear for allowing groups to exclude newcomers from sharing their relative prosperity in order to maintain a special standard of their own.

It may sound noble to say, "Damn economics, let us build up a decent

---

[4]This is perhaps the place to emphasize that, however much one may wish a speedy return to a free economy, this cannot mean the removal at one stroke of most of the wartime restrictions. Nothing would discredit the system of free enterprise more than the acute, though probably short-lived, dislocation and instability such an attempt would produce. The problem is at what kind of system we should aim in the process of demobilization, not whether the wartime system should be transformed into more permanent arrangements by a carefully thought-out policy of gradual relaxation of controls, which may have to extend over several years.

world"—but it is, in fact, merely irresponsible. With our world as it is, with everyone convinced that the material conditions here or there must be improved, our only chance of building a decent world is that we can continue to improve the general level of wealth. The one thing modern democracy will not bear without cracking is the necessity of a substantial lowering of the standards of living in peacetime or even prolonged stationariness of its economic conditions.

People who admit that present political trends constitute a serious threat to our economic prospects, and through their economic effects endanger much higher values, are yet likely to deceive themselves that we are making material sacrifices to gain ideal ends. It is, however, more than doubtful whether a fifty years' approach toward collectivism has raised our moral standards, or whether the change has not rather been in the opposite direction. Though we are in the habit of priding ourselves on our more sensitive social conscience, it is by no means clear that this is justified by the practice of our individual conduct. On the negative side, in its indignation about the inequities of the existing social order, our generation probably surpasses most of its predecessors. But the effect of that movement on our positive standards in the proper field of morals, individual conduct, and on the seriousness with which we uphold moral principles against the expediencies and exigencies of social machinery, is a very different matter.

Issues in this field have become so confused that it is necessary to go back to fundamentals. What our generation is in danger of forgetting is not only that morals are of necessity a phenomenon of individual conduct but also that they can exist only in the sphere in which the individual is free to decide for himself and is called upon voluntarily to sacrifice personal advantage to the observance of a moral rule. Outside the sphere of individual responsibility there is neither goodness nor badness, neither opportunity for moral merit nor the chance of proving one's conviction by sacrificing one's desires to what one thinks right. Only where we ourselves are responsible for our own interests and are free to sacrifice them has our decision moral value. We are neither entitled to be unselfish at someone else's expense nor is there any merit in being unselfish if we have no choice. The members of a society who in all respects are *made* to do the good thing have no title to praise. As Milton said: "If every action which is good or evil in a man of ripe years were under pittance and prescription and compulsion, what were virtue but a name, what praise should then be due to well-doing, what gramercy to be sober, just, or continent?"[5]

Freedom to order our own conduct in the sphere where material circumstances force a choice upon us, and responsibility for the arrangement of our

---

[5] [John Milton, "Areopagitica," reprinted in *Areopagitica and Other Prose Works*, op. cit., p. 18. —Ed.]

own life according to our own conscience, is the air in which alone moral sense grows and in which moral values are daily re-created in the free decision of the individual. Responsibility, not to a superior, but to one's conscience, the awareness of a duty not exacted by compulsion, the necessity to decide which of the things one values are to be sacrificed to others, and to bear the consequences of one's own decision, are the very essence of any morals which deserve the name.

That in this sphere of individual conduct the effect of collectivism has been almost entirely destructive is both inevitable and undeniable. A movement whose main promise is the relief from responsibility[6] cannot but be antimoral in its effect, however lofty the ideals to which it owes its birth. Can there be much doubt that the feeling of personal obligation to remedy inequities, where our individual power permits, has been weakened rather than strengthened, that both the willingness to bear responsibility and the consciousness that it is our own individual duty to know how to choose have been perceptibly impaired? There is all the difference between demanding that a desirable state of affairs should be brought about by the authorities, or even being willing to submit provided everyone else is made to do the same, and the readiness to do what one thinks right one's self at the sacrifice of one's own desires and perhaps in the face of hostile public opinion. There is much to suggest that we have in fact become more tolerant toward particular abuses and much more indifferent to inequities in individual cases, since we have fixed our eyes on an entirely different system in which the state will set everything right. It may even be, as has been suggested, that the passion for collective action is a way in which we now without compunction collectively indulge in that selfishness which as individuals we had learned a little to restrain.

It is true that the virtues which are less esteemed and practiced now—independence, self-reliance, and the willingness to bear risks, the readiness to back one's own conviction against a majority, and the willingness to voluntary cooperation with one's neighbors—are essentially those on which the working of an individualist society rests. Collectivism has nothing to put in their place, and in so far as it already has destroyed them it has left a void filled by nothing but the demand for obedience and the compulsion of the individual to do what is col-

[6] This becomes more and more clearly expressed as socialism approaches totalitarianism, and in England is most explicitly stated in the program of that latest and most totalitarian form of English socialism, Sir Richard Acland's "Common-Wealth" movement. The main feature of the new order he promises is that in it the community will "say to the individual 'Don't *you* bother about the business of getting your *own* living.'" In consequence, of course, "it must be the community as a whole which must decide whether or not a man shall be employed upon our resources, and how and when and in what manner he shall work," and that the community will have "to run camps for shirkers in very tolerable conditions." Is it surprising that the author discovers that Hitler "has stumbled across (or has needed to make use of) a small part, or perhaps one should say one particular aspect of, what will ultimately be required of humanity." See Sir Richard Acland, Bt., *The Forward March*, op. cit., pp. 127, 126, 135, and 32.

lectively decided to be good. The periodical election of representatives, to which the moral choice of the individual tends to be more and more reduced, is not an occasion on which his moral values are tested or where he has constantly to reassert and prove the order of his values and to testify to the sincerity of his profession by the sacrifice of those of his values he rates lower to those he puts higher.

As the rules of conduct evolved by individuals are the source from which collective political action derives what moral standards it possesses, it would indeed be surprising if the relaxation of the standards of individual conduct were accompanied by a raising of the standards of social action. That there have been great changes is clear. Every generation, of course, puts some values higher and some lower than its predecessors. Which, however, are the aims which take a lower place now, which are the values which we are now warned may have to give way if they come into conflict with others? Which kind of values figure less prominently in the picture of the future held out to us by the popular writers and speakers than they did in the dreams and hopes of our fathers?

It is certainly not material comfort, certainly not a rise in our standard of living or the assurance of a certain status in society which ranks lower. Is there a popular writer or speaker who dares to suggest to the masses that they might have to make sacrifices of their material prospects for the enhancement of an ideal end? Is it not, in fact, entirely the other way round? Are not the things which we are more and more frequently taught to regard as "nineteenth-century illusions" all moral values—liberty and independence, truth and intellectual honesty, peace and democracy, and the respect for the individual *qua* man instead of merely as the member of an organized group?

What are the fixed poles now which are regarded as sacrosanct, which no reformer dare touch, since they are treated as the immutable boundaries which must be respected in any plan for the future? They are no longer the liberty of the individual, his freedom of movement, and scarcely that of speech. They are the protected standards of this or that group, their "right" to exclude others from providing their fellowmen with what they need. Discrimination between members and nonmembers of closed groups, not to speak of nationals of different countries, is accepted more and more as a matter of course; injustices inflicted on individuals by government action in the interest of a group are disregarded with an indifference hardly distinguishable from callousness; and the grossest violations of the most elementary rights of the individual, such as are involved in the compulsory transfer of populations, are more and more often countenanced even by supposed liberals.

All this surely indicates that our moral sense has been blunted rather than sharpened. When we are reminded, as more and more frequently happens, that one cannot make omelettes without breaking eggs, the eggs which are broken are almost all of the kind which a generation or two ago were regarded as the essential bases of civilized life. And what atrocities committed by powers with whose professed principles they sympathize have not been readily condoned by many of our so-called "liberals"?

There is one aspect of the change in moral values brought about by the advance of collectivism which at the present time provides special food for thought. It is that the virtues which are held less and less in esteem and which consequently become rarer are precisely those on which Anglo-Saxons justly prided themselves and in which they were generally recognized to excel. The virtues these people possessed—in a higher degree than most other people, excepting only a few of the smaller nations, like the Swiss and the Dutch—were independence and self-reliance, individual initiative and local responsibility, the successful reliance on voluntary activity, noninterference with one's neighbor and tolerance of the different and queer, respect for custom and tradition, and a healthy suspicion of power and authority. Almost all the traditions and institutions in which democratic moral genius has found its most characteristic expression, and which in turn have molded the national character and the whole moral climate of England and America, are those which the progress of collectivism and its inherently centralistic tendencies are progressively destroying.

A foreign background is sometimes helpful in seeing more clearly to what circumstances the peculiar excellencies of the moral atmosphere of a nation are due. And if one who, whatever the law may say, must forever remain a foreigner, may be allowed to say so, it is one of the most disheartening spectacles of our time to see to what extent some of the most precious things which England, for example, has given to the world are now held in contempt in England herself. The English hardly know to what degree they differ from most other people in that they all, irrespective of party, hold to a greater or less extent the ideas which in their most pronounced form are known as liberalism. Compared with most other peoples only twenty years ago almost all Englishmen were liberals—however much they may have differed from party liberalism. And even today the English conservative or socialist, no less than the liberal, if he travels abroad, though he may find the ideas and writings of Carlyle or Disraeli, of the Webbs or H. G. Wells, exceedingly popular in circles with which he has little in common, among Nazis and other totalitarians, if he finds an intellectual island where the tradition of Macaulay and Gladstone, of J. S. Mill or John Morley, lives, will find kindred spirits who "talk the same language" as himself—however much he himself may differ from the ideals for which these men specifically stood.[7]

---

[7] [In this passage Hayek is contrasting the writings of conservative thinkers like Carlyle and Disraeli, and those of socialists like the Webbs and H. G. Wells, with those of writers in the English

Nowhere is the loss of the belief in the specific values of British civilization more manifest, and nowhere has it had a more paralyzing effect on the pursuit of our immediate great purpose, than in the fatuous ineffectiveness of most British propaganda. The first prerequisite for success in propaganda directed to other people is the proud acknowledgment of the characteristic values and distinguishing traits for which the country attempting it is known to the other peoples. The main cause of the ineffectiveness of British propaganda is that those directing it seem to have lost their own belief in the peculiar values of English civilization or to be completely ignorant of the main points on which it differs from that of other people. The Left intelligentsia, indeed, have so long worshiped foreign gods that they seem to have become almost incapable of seeing any good in the characteristic English institutions and traditions. That the moral values on which most of them pride themselves are largely the product of the institutions they are out to destroy, these socialists cannot, of course, admit. And this attitude is unfortunately not confined to avowed socialists. Though one must hope that this is not true of the less vocal but more numerous cultivated Englishmen, if one were to judge by the ideas which find expression in current political discussion and propaganda, the Englishmen who not only "the language speak that Shakespeare spake" but also "the faith and morals hold that Milton held" seem to have almost vanished.[8]

---

liberal tradition. We have earlier met some of these men: Carlyle and Morley in the author's introduction, note 4; the Webbs in chapter 5, note 3; Wells in chapter 6, note 10, Disraeli in chapter 8, note 4, and Gladstone in chapter 13, note 6, though it might be added that Carlyle's most relevant works in the present context are probably his lectures on heroes and hero worship (in which the need for strong leaders to shape a nation's history was advocated), and his multivolume history of the Prussian king Frederick the Great. On the Liberal side, author, historian, and MP Thomas Babington Macauley's (1800–1859) *History of England* is often taken as an exemplar of "Whig history." In his book *On Liberty*, philosopher John Stuart Mill (1806–1873) defended the freedom of the individual in the face of political and social control. —Ed.]

[8]Though the subject of this chapter has already invited more than one reference to Milton, it is difficult to resist the temptation to add here one more quotation, a very familiar one, though one, it seems, which nowadays nobody but a foreigner would dare to cite: "Let not England forget her precedence of teaching nations how to live." It is, perhaps, significant that our generation has seen a host of American and English detractors of Milton—and that the first of them, Ezra Pound, was during this war broadcasting from Italy! [The quotation in the text is from a poem by William Wordsworth that begins, "It Is Not To Be Thought Of," which may be found in *The Poetical Works of William Wordsworth*, ed. E. Selincourt and Helen Darbishire (Oxford: Clarendon Press, 1946), volume 3, p. 117. The full passage reads, "we must be free or die, who speak the tongue that Shakspeare spake; the faith and morals hold which Milton held." The quotation from Milton is from his "The Doctrine and Discipline of Divorce," reprinted in *Areopagitica and Other Prose Works*, op. cit., p. 193. The American poet and critic Ezra Pound (1885–1972) was credited by T. S. Eliot as being the motivating force behind "modern" poetry. Pound lived in Italy from 1924 to 1945, where he became enamored with fascist ideas. In the early part of the war he issued broadcasts critical of democracy. He was indicted for treason after the war, but instead of being tried he was judged insane and spent over a decade in an asylum. He was released in 1958. —Ed.]

To believe, however, that the kind of propaganda produced by this attitude can have the desired effect on our enemies and particularly on the Germans, is a fatal blunder. The Germans know England and America, not well, perhaps, yet sufficiently to know what are the characteristic traditional values of democratic life, and what for the last two or three generations has increasingly separated the minds of the countries. If we wish to convince them, not only of our sincerity, but also that we have to offer a real alternative to the way they have gone, it will not be by concessions to their system of thought. We shall not delude them with a stale reproduction of the ideas of their fathers which we have borrowed from them—be it state socialism, *Realpolitik*, "scientific" planning, or corporativism. We shall not persuade them by following them half the way which leads to totalitarianism. If the democracies themselves abandon the supreme ideal of the freedom and happiness of the individual, if they implicitly admit that their civilization is not worth preserving, and that they know nothing better than to follow the path along which the Germans have led, they have indeed nothing to offer. To the Germans all these are merely belated admissions that the liberals have been wrong all the way through and that they themselves are leading the way to a new and better world, however appalling the period of transition may be. The Germans know that what they still regard as the British and American traditions and their own new ideals are fundamentally opposed and irreconcilable views of life. They might be convinced that the way they have chosen was wrong—but nothing will ever convince them that the British or Americans will be better guides on the German path.

Least of all will that type of propaganda appeal to those Germans on whose help we must ultimately count in rebuilding Europe because their values are nearest to our own. For experience has made them wiser and sadder men: they have learned that neither good intentions nor efficiency of organization can preserve decency in a system in which personal freedom and individual responsibility are destroyed. What the German and Italian who have learned the lesson want above all is protection against the monster state—not grandiose schemes for organization on a colossal scale, but opportunity peacefully and in freedom to build up once more their own little worlds. It is not because they believe that to be ordered about by British or Americans is preferable to being ordered about by the Prussians, but because they believe that in a world where democratic ideals have been victorious they will be less ordered about and left in peace to pursue their own concerns, that we can hope for support from some of the nationals of the enemy countries.

If we are to succeed in the war of ideologies and to win over the decent elements in the enemy countries, we must, first of all, regain the belief in the traditional values for which we have stood in the past and must have the moral courage stoutly to defend the ideals which our enemies attack. Not by shamefaced apologies and by assurances that we are rapidly reforming, not by explaining that we are seeking some compromise between the traditional liberal values and the new totalitarian ideas, shall we win confidence and support. Not the latest improvements we may have effected in our social institutions, which count but little compared with the basic differences of two opposed ways of life, but our unwavering faith in those traditions which have made England and America countries of free and upright, tolerant and independent, people is the thing that counts.

FIFTEEN

THE PROSPECTS OF
INTERNATIONAL ORDER

Of all checks on democracy, federation has been the most efficacious and the most congenial. . . . The federal system limits and restrains the sovereign power by dividing it and by assigning to Government only certain defined rights. It is the only method of curbing not only the majority but the power of the whole people. —Lord Acton[1]

In no other field has the world yet paid so dearly for the abandonment of nineteenth-century liberalism as in the field where the retreat began: in international relations. Yet only a small part of the lesson which experience ought to have taught us has been learned. Perhaps even more than elsewhere current notions of what is desirable and practicable are here still of a kind which may well produce the opposite of what they promise.

The part of the lesson of the recent past which is slowly and gradually being appreciated is that many kinds of economic planning, conducted independently on a national scale, are bound in their aggregate effect to be harmful even from a purely economic point of view and, in addition, to produce serious international friction. That there is little hope of international order or lasting peace so long as every country is free to employ whatever measures it thinks desirable in its own immediate interest, however damaging they may be to others, needs little emphasis now. Many kinds of economic planning are indeed practicable only if the planning authority can effectively shut out all extraneous influences; the result of such planning is therefore inevitably the piling-up of restrictions on the movements of men and goods.

Less obvious but by no means less real are the dangers to peace arising out of the artificially fostered economic solidarity of all the inhabitants of any one country and from the new blocs of opposed interests created by planning on a national scale. It is neither necessary nor desirable that national boundaries should mark sharp differences in standards of living, that membership of a

---

[1] [Lord Acton, "Review of Sir Erskine May's *Democracy in Europe*," op. cit., p. 98. Acton actually said, "Of all checks on democracy, *federalism* has been the most efficacious and the most congenial." —Ed.]

national group should entitle one to a share in a cake altogether different from that in which members of other groups share. If the resources of different nations are treated as exclusive properties of these nations as wholes, if international economic relations, instead of being relations between individuals, become increasingly relations between whole nations organized as trading bodies, they inevitably become the source of friction and envy between whole nations. It is one of the most fatal illusions that, by substituting negotiations between states or organized groups for competition for markets or for raw materials, international friction would be reduced. This would merely put a contest of force in the place of what can only metaphorically be called the "struggle" of competition and would transfer to powerful and armed states, subject to no superior law, the rivalries which between individuals had to be decided without recourse to force. Economic transactions between national bodies who are at the same time the supreme judges of their own behavior, who bow to no superior law, and whose representatives cannot be bound by any considerations but the immediate interest of their respective nations, must end in clashes of power.[2]

If we were to make no better use of victory than to countenance existing trends in this direction, only too visible before 1939, we might indeed find that we have defeated National Socialism merely to create a world of many national socialisms, differing in detail, but all equally totalitarian, nationalistic, and in recurrent conflict with each other. The Germans would appear as the disturbers of peace, as they already do to some people,[3] merely because they were the first to take the path along which all the others were ultimately to follow.

Those who at least partly realize these dangers usually draw the conclusion that economic planning must be done "internationally," i.e., by some supernational authority. But though this would avert some of the obvious dangers raised by planning on a national scale, it seems that those who advocate such ambitious schemes have little conception of the even greater difficulties and dangers which their proposals create. The problems raised by a conscious direction of economic affairs on a national scale inevitably assume even greater dimensions when the same is attempted internationally. The conflict between planning and freedom cannot but become more serious as the similarity of standards and values among those submitted to a unitary plan diminishes. There need be little difficulty in planning the economic life of a family, comparatively little in a small community. But, as the scale increases, the amount of agreement on the order of ends decreases and the necessity to rely on force and compulsion grows. In a small community common views on the relative importance of the

---

[2]On all these and on the following points, which can be touched upon only very briefly, see Professor Lionel Robbins's *Economic Planning and International Order* (London: Macmillan, 1937), *passim*.
[3]See particularly the significant book by James Burnham, *The Managerial Revolution*, op. cit.

main tasks, agreed standards of value, will exist on a great many subjects. But their number will become less and less the wider we throw the net; and, as there is less community of views, the necessity to rely on force and coercion increases.

The people of any one country may easily be persuaded to make a sacrifice in order to assist what they regard as "their" iron industry or "their" agriculture, or in order that in their country nobody should sink below a certain level. So long as it is a question of helping people whose habits of life and ways of thinking are familiar to us, of correcting the distribution of incomes among, or the working conditions of, people we can well imagine and whose views on their appropriate status are fundamentally similar to ours, we are usually ready to make some sacrifices. But one has only to visualize the problems raised by economic planning of even an area such as western Europe to see that the moral bases for such an undertaking are completely lacking. Who imagines that there exist any common ideals of distributive justice such as will make the Norwegian fisherman consent to forgo the prospect of economic improvement in order to help his Portuguese fellow, or the Dutch worker to pay more for his bicycle to help the Coventry mechanic, or the French peasant to pay more taxes to assist the industrialization of Italy?

If most people are not willing to see the difficulty, this is mainly because, consciously or unconsciously, they assume that it will be they who will settle these questions for the others, and because they are convinced of their own capacity to do this justly and equitably. The English people, for instance, perhaps even more than others, begin to realize what such schemes mean only when it is presented to them that they might be a minority in the planning authority and that the main lines of the future economic development of Great Britain might be determined by a non-British majority. How many people in England would be prepared to submit to the decision of an international authority, however democratically constituted, which had power to decree that the development of the Spanish iron industry must have precedence over similar development in South Wales, that the optical industry had better be concentrated in Germany to the exclusion of Great Britain, or that only fully refined gasoline should be imported to Great Britain and all the industries connected with refining reserved for the producer countries?

To imagine that the economic life of a vast area comprising many different people can be directed or planned by democratic procedure betrays a complete lack of awareness of the problems such planning would raise. Planning on an international scale, even more than is true on a national scale, cannot be anything but a naked rule of force, an imposition by a small group on all the rest of that sort of standard and employment which the planners think suitable for the rest. If anything is certain, it is that *Grossraumwirtschaft* of the kind at which the Germans have been aiming can be successfully realized only by a master-race, a *Herrenvolk*, ruthlessly imposing its aims and ideas on the rest. It is a mistake to regard the brutality and the disregard of all the wishes and ideals of the smaller people shown by the Germans simply as a sign of their special wickedness; it is the nature of the task they have assumed which makes these things inevitable. To undertake the direction of the economic life of people with widely divergent ideals and values is to assume responsibilities which commit one to the use of force; it is to assume a position where the best intentions cannot prevent one from being forced to act in a way which to some of those affected must appear highly immoral.[4]

This is true even if we assume the dominant power to be as idealistic and unselfish as we can possibly conceive. But how small is the likelihood that it will be unselfish, and how great are the temptations! I believe the standards of decency and fairness, particularly with regard to international affairs, to be as high, if not higher, in England than in any other country. Yet even now we can hear people in England arguing that victory must be used to create conditions in which British industry will be able to utilize to the full the particular equipment which it has built up during the war, that the reconstruction of Europe must be so directed as to fit in with the special requirements of the industries of England, and to secure to everybody in the country the kind of employment for which he thinks himself most fit. The alarming thing about these suggestions is not that they are made but that they are made in all innocence and regarded as a matter of course by decent people who are completely unaware of the moral enormity which the use of force for such purposes involves.[5]

Perhaps the most powerful agent in creating the belief in the possibility of a single central direction by democratic means of the economic life of many different peoples is the fatal delusion that if the decisions were left to the "people," the community of interest of the working classes would readily overcome the differences which exist between the ruling classes. There is every reason to ex-

[4]The experience in the colonial sphere, of Great Britain as much as of any other, has amply shown that even the mild forms of planning which Englishmen know as colonial development involve, whether they wish it or not, the imposition of certain values and ideals on those whom they try to assist. It is, indeed, this experience which has made even the most internationally minded of colonial experts so very skeptical of the practicability of an "international" administration of colonies.
[5]If anyone should still fail to see the difficulties, or cherish the belief that with a little good will they can all be overcome, it will help if he tries to follow the implications of central direction of economic activity applied on a world scale. Can there be much doubt that this would mean a more or less conscious endeavor to secure the dominance of the white man, and would rightly be so regarded by all other races? Until I find a sane person who seriously believes that the European races will voluntarily submit to their standard of life and rate of progress being determined by a world parliament, I cannot regard such plans as anything but absurd. But this does unfortunately not preclude that particular measures, which could be justified only if the principle of world direction were a feasible ideal, are seriously advocated.

pect that with world planning the clash of economic interests which arises now about the economic policy of any one nation would in fact appear in even fiercer form as a clash of interests between whole peoples which could be decided only by force. On the questions which an international planning authority would have to decide, the interests and opinions of the working classes of the different people will inevitably be as much in conflict, and there will be even less of a commonly accepted basis for an equitable settlement than there is with respect to different classes in any one country. To the worker in a poor country the demand of his more fortunate colleague to be protected against his low-wage competition by minimum-wage legislation, supposedly in his interest, is frequently no more than a means to deprive him of his only chance to better his conditions by overcoming natural disadvantages by working at wages lower than his fellows in other countries. And to him the fact that he has to give the product of ten hours of his labor for the product of five hours of the man elsewhere who is better equipped with machinery is as much "exploitation" as that practiced by any capitalist.

It is fairly certain that in a planned international system the wealthier and therefore most powerful nations would to a very much greater degree than in a free economy become the object of hatred and envy of the poorer ones: and the latter, rightly or wrongly, would all be convinced that their position could be improved much more quickly if they were only free to do what they wished. Indeed, if it comes to be regarded as the duty of the international authority to bring about distributive justice between the different peoples, it is no more than a consistent and inevitable development of socialist doctrine that class strife would become a struggle between the working classes of the different countries.

There is at present a great deal of muddleheaded talk about "planning to equalize standards of life." It is instructive to consider in a little more detail one of these proposals to see what precisely it involves. The area for which at the present moment our planners are particularly fond of drawing up such schemes is the Danube Basin and southeastern Europe.[6] There can be no doubt about the urgent need for amelioration of economic conditions in this region, from humanitarian and economic considerations as well as in the interest of the future peace of Europe, nor that this can be achieved only in a political setting different from that of the past. But this is not the same thing as to wish to see economic life in this region directed according to a single master-plan, to foster the development of the different industries according to a schedule laid down beforehand in a way which makes the success of local initiative dependent on being approved by the central authority and being incorporated in its

---

[6][Hayek may have had in mind such studies as C. A. Macartney, *Problems of the Danube Basin* (Cambridge: Cambridge University Press, 1942), or Antonin Basch, *The Danube Basin and the German Economic Sphere* (New York: Columbia University Press, 1943). —Ed.]

plan. One cannot, for example, create a kind of Tennessee Valley Authority for the Danube Basin without thereby determining beforehand for many years to come the relative rate of progress of the different races inhabiting this area or without subordinating all their individual aspirations and wishes to this task.[7]

Planning of this kind must of necessity begin by fixing an order of priorities of the different claims. To plan for the deliberate equalization of standards of living means that the different claims must be ranked according to merit, that some must be given precedence over others, and that the latter must wait their turn—even though those whose interests are thus relegated may be convinced, not only of their better right, but also of their ability to reach their goal sooner if they were only given freedom to act on their own devices. There exists no basis which allows us to decide whether the claims of the poor Rumanian peasant are more or less urgent than those of the still poorer Albanian, or the needs of the Slovakian mountain shepherd greater than those of his Slovenian colleague. But if the raising of their standards of life is to be effected according to a unitary plan, somebody must deliberately balance the merits of all these claims and decide between them. And once such a plan is put into execution, all the resources of the planned area must serve that plan—there can be no exemption for those who feel they could do better for themselves. Once their claim has been given a lower rank, they will have to work for the prior satisfaction of the needs of those who have been given preference.

In such a state of affairs *everybody* will rightly feel that he is worse off than he might be if some other plan had been adopted and that it is the decision and the might of the dominant powers which have condemned him to a place less favorable than he thinks is due to him. To attempt such a thing in a region peopled by small nations, each of which believes equally fervently in its own superiority over the others, is to undertake a task which can be performed only by the use of force. What it would amount to in practice is that the decisions and power of the large nations would have to settle whether the standards of the Macedonian or the Bulgarian peasant should be raised faster, whether the Czech or the Hungarian miner should more rapidly approach Western standards. It does not need much knowledge of human nature, and certainly only a little knowledge of the people of Central Europe, to see that, whatever the decision imposed, there will be many, probably a majority, to whom the particular order chosen will appear supreme injustice and that their common hatred will soon turn against the power which, however disinterestedly, in fact decides their fate.

Though there are no doubt many people who honestly believe that if they were allowed to handle the job they would be able to settle all those problems

---

[7][The Tennessee Valley Authority was an agency set up during the New Deal to generate electricity and control flooding in a seven-state region around the Tennessee River Valley. —Ed.]

justly and impartially, and who would be genuinely surprised to find suspicion and hatred turning against them, they would probably be the first to apply force when those whom they mean to benefit prove recalcitrant, and to show themselves quite ruthless in coercing people in what is presumed to be their own interests. What these dangerous idealists do not see is that where the assumption of a moral responsibility involves that one's moral views should by force be made to prevail over those dominant in other communities, the assumption of such responsibility may place one in a position in which it becomes impossible to act morally. To impose such an impossible moral task on the victorious nations is a certain way morally to corrupt and discredit them.

By all means let us assist the poorer people as much as we can in their own efforts to build up their lives and to raise their standards of living. An international authority can be very just and contribute enormously to economic prosperity if it merely keeps order and creates conditions in which the people can develop their own life; but it is impossible to be just or to let people live their own life if the central authority doles out raw materials and allocates markets, if every spontaneous effort has to be "approved" and nothing can be done without the sanction of the central authority.

After the discussions in earlier chapters it is hardly necessary to stress that these difficulties cannot be met by conferring on the various international authorities "merely" specific economic powers. The belief that this is a practical solution rests on the fallacy that economic planning is merely a technical task, which can be solved in a strictly objective manner by experts, and that the really vital things would still be left in the hands of the political authorities. Any international economic authority, not subject to a superior political power, even if strictly confined to a particular field, could easily exercise the most tyrannical and irresponsible power imaginable. Exclusive control of an essential commodity or service (as, for example, air transport) is in effect one of the most far-reaching powers which can be conferred on any authority. And as there is scarcely anything which could not be justified by "technical necessities" which no outsider could effectively question—or even by humanitarian and possibly entirely sincere arguments about the needs of some specially ill-favored group which could not be helped in any other way—there is little possibility of controlling that power. The kind of organization of the resources of the world under more or less autonomous bodies, which now so often finds favor in the most surprising quarters, a system of comprehensive monopolies recognized by all the national governments, but subject to none, would inevitably become the worst of all conceivable rackets—even if those entrusted with their administration should prove the most faithful guardians of the particular interests placed in their care.

One need only seriously consider the full implications of such apparently innocuous proposals, widely regarded as the essential basis of the future economic order, such as the conscious control and distribution of the supply of essential raw materials, in order to see what appalling political difficulties and moral dangers they create. The controller of the supply of any such raw material as gasoline or timber, rubber or tin, would be the master of the fate of whole industries and countries. In deciding whether to allow the supply to increase and the price or the income of the producers to fall, he would decide whether some country is to be allowed to start some new industry or whether it is to be precluded from doing so. While he "protects" the standards of life of those he regards as specially entrusted to his care, he will deprive many who are in a much worse position of their best and perhaps only chance to improve it. If all essential raw materials were thus controlled, there would indeed be no new industry, no new venture on which the people of a country could embark without the permission of the controllers, no plan for development or improvement which could not be frustrated by their veto. The same is true of international arrangement for "sharing" of markets and even more so of the control of investment and the development of natural resources.

It is curious to observe how those who pose as the most hard-boiled realists, and who lose no opportunity of casting ridicule on the "utopianism" of those who believe in the possibility of an international political order, yet regard as more practicable the much more intimate and irresponsible interference with the lives of the different peoples which economic planning involves; and believe that, once hitherto undreamed-of power is given to an international government, which has just been represented as not even capable of enforcing a simple Rule of Law, this greater power will be used in so unselfish and so obviously just a manner as to command general consent. If anything is evident, it should be that, while nations might abide by formal rules on which they have agreed, they will never submit to the direction which international economic planning involves—that while they may agree on the rules of the game, they will never agree on the order of preference in which the rank of their own needs and the rate at which they are allowed to advance is fixed by majority vote. Even if, at first, the peoples should, under some illusion about the meaning of such proposals, agree to transfer such powers to an international authority, they would soon find out that what they have delegated is not merely a technical task but the most comprehensive power over their very lives.

What is evidently at the back of the minds of the not altogether unpracticable "realists" who advocate these schemes is that, while the great powers will be unwilling to submit to any superior authority, they will be able to use those "international" authorities to impose their will on the smaller nations within the area in which they exercise hegemony. There is so much "realism" in this that by thus camouflaging the planning authorities as "international" it might be easier to achieve the condition under which international planning is alone practicable, namely, that it is in effect done by one single predominant power. This disguise would, however, not alter the fact that for all the smaller states it would mean a much more complete subjection to an external power, to which no real resistance would any longer be possible, than would be involved in the renunciation of a clearly defined part of political sovereignty.

It is significant that the most passionate advocates of a centrally directed economic New Order for Europe should display, like their Fabian and German prototypes, the most complete disregard of the individuality and of the rights of small nations. The views of Professor Carr, who in this sphere even more than in that of internal policy is representative of the trend toward totalitarianism in England, have already made one of his professional colleagues ask the very pertinent question: "If the Nazi way with small sovereign states is indeed to become the common form, what is the war about?"[8] Those who have observed how much disquiet and alarm some recent utterances on these questions in papers as different as the London *Times* and the *New Statesman*[9] have caused among our smaller Allies will have little doubt how much this attitude is even now resented among our closest friends, and how easy it will be to dissipate the stock of good will which has been laid up during the war if these advisers are followed.

Those who are so ready to ride roughshod over the rights of small states are, of course, right in one thing: we cannot hope for order or lasting peace after this war if states, large or small, regain unfettered sovereignty in the economic sphere. But this does not mean that a new superstate must be given powers which we have not learned to use intelligently even on a national scale, that an international authority ought to be given power to direct individual nations how to use their resources. It means merely that there must be a power which can restrain the different nations from action harmful to their neighbors, a set of rules which defines what a state may do, and an authority capable of enforcing these rules. The powers which such an authority would need are mainly of a negative kind; it must, above all, be able to say "No" to all sorts of restrictive measures.

Far from its being true that, as is now widely believed, we need an international economic authority while the states can at the same time retain their unrestricted political sovereignty, almost exactly the opposite is true. What we

[8] Professor C. A. W. Manning, in a review of Professor Carr's *Conditions of Peace* in the *International Affairs Review Supplement*, vol. 19, June 1942, p. 443.

[9] It is significant in more than one respect that, as was once observed in one of the weekly journals, "one had already begun to expect a touch of the Carr flavour in the *New Statesman* pages as well as in those of *The Times*." The quotation is found in the article titled "Four Winds," *Time and Tide*, February 20, 1943. [*Time and Tide* began as a magazine and then became an independent weekly paper. Published at No. 38 Bloomsbury Street, it was run by and written for women. —Ed.]

need and can hope to achieve is not more power in the hands of irresponsible international economic authorities but, on the contrary, a superior political power which can hold the economic interests in check, and in the conflict between them can truly hold the scales, because it is itself not mixed up in the economic game. The need is for an international political authority which, without power to direct the different people what they must do, must be able to restrain them from action which will damage others.

The powers which must devolve on an international authority are not the new powers assumed by the states in recent times but that minimum of powers without which it is impossible to preserve peaceful relationships, i.e., essentially the powers of the ultra-liberal "laissez faire" state. And, even more than in the national sphere, it is essential that these powers of the international authority should be strictly circumscribed by the Rule of Law. The need for such a supernational authority becomes indeed greater as the individual states more and more become units of economic administration, the actors rather than merely the supervisors of the economic scene, and as therefore any friction is likely to arise not between individuals but between states as such.

The form of international government under which certain strictly defined powers are transferred to an international authority, while in all other respects the individual countries remain responsible for their internal affairs, is, of course, that of federation. We must not allow the numerous ill-considered and often extremely silly claims made on behalf of a federal organization of the whole world during the height of the propaganda for "Federal Union" to obscure the fact that the principle of federation is the only form of association of different peoples which will create an international order without putting an undue strain on their legitimate desire for independence.[10] Federalism is, of course, nothing but the application to international affairs of democracy, the only method of peaceful change man has yet invented. But it is a democracy with definitely limited powers. Apart from the more impracticable ideal of fusing different countries into a single centralized state (the desirability of which is far from obvious), it is the only way in which the ideal of international law can be made a reality. We must not deceive ourselves that, in the past, in calling the rules of international behavior international law, we were doing more than expressing a pious wish. When we want to prevent people from killing each other,

---

[10] It is a great pity that the flood of federalist publications which in recent years has descended upon us has deprived the few important and thoughtful works among them of the attention they deserved. One which in particular ought to be carefully consulted when the time comes for the framing of a new political structure of Europe is Dr. W. Ivor Jennings's small book on *A Federation for Western Europe* (New York: Macmillan, and Cambridge: Cambridge University Press, 1940). [Both Hayek and Lionel Robbins were in favor of some form of federation for Europe; see Hayek's letters to *The Spectator* titled "War Aims" and "An Anglo-French Federation," reprinted in F. A. Hayek, *Socialism and War*, op. cit., pp. 161–64. —Ed.]

we are not content to issue a declaration that killing is undesirable, but we give an authority power to prevent it. In the same way there can be no international law without a power to enforce it. The obstacle to the creation of such an international power was very largely the idea that it need command all the practically unlimited powers which the modern state possesses. But with the division of power under the federal system this is by no means necessary.

This division of power would inevitably act at the same time also as a limitation of the power of the whole as well as of the individual state. Indeed, many of the kinds of planning which are now fashionable would probably become altogether impossible.[11] But it would by no means constitute an obstacle to all planning. It is, in fact, one of the main advantages of federation that it can be so devised as to make most of the harmful planning difficult while leaving the way free for all desirable planning. It prevents, or can be made to prevent, most forms of restrictionism. And it confines international planning to the fields where true agreement can be reached—not only between the "interests" immediately concerned but among all those affected. The desirable forms of planning which can be effected locally and without the need of restrictive measures are left free and in the hands of those best qualified to undertake it. It is even to be hoped that within a federation, where there will no longer exist the same reasons for making the individual states as strong as possible, the process of centralization of the past may in some measure be reversed and some devolution of powers from the state to the local authorities become possible.

It is worth recalling that the idea of the world at last finding peace through the absorption of the separate states in large federated groups and ultimately perhaps in one single federation, far from being new, was indeed the ideal of almost all the liberal thinkers of the nineteenth century. From Tennyson, whose much-quoted vision of the "battle of the air" is followed by a vision of the federation of the people which will follow their last great fight, right down to the end of the century the final achievement of a federal organization remained the ever recurring hope of a next great step in the advance of civilization.[12]

[11]See on this the author's article on "The Economic Conditions of Inter-state Federalism," *New Commonwealth Quarterly*, vol. 5, September 1939, pp. 131–49. [This article was subsequently reprinted in F. A. Hayek, *Individualism and Economic Order*, op. cit., pp. 255–72. —Ed.]

[12][Hayek refers to Alfred, Lord Tennyson's poem "Locksley Hall." See *The Poetical Works of Alfred Lord Tennyson* (Boston and New York: Houghton Mifflin, 1892), p. 60, where a battle in the heavens is concluded with the following lines:

Till the war-drum throbb'd no longer,
And the battle flags were furl'd
In the Parliament of man, the Federation
Of the world.

The poem begins with the bitter lament of a young man who had been separated from his first love, his cousin, who had then gone on to marry another. There are parallels with Hayek's own life; see Bruce Caldwell, *Hayek's Challenge*, op. cit., p. 133, note 1. —Ed.]

Nineteenth-century liberals may not have been fully aware *how* essential a complement of their principles a federal organization of the different states formed;[13] but there were few among them who did not express their belief in it as an ultimate goal.[14] It was only with the approach of our twentieth century that before the triumphant rise of *Realpolitik* these hopes came to be regarded as unpracticable and utopian.

We shall not rebuild civilization on the large scale. It is no accident that on the whole there was more beauty and decency to be found in the life of the small peoples, and that among the large ones there was more happiness and content in proportion as they had avoided the deadly blight of centralization. Least of all shall we preserve democracy or foster its growth if all the power and most of the important decisions rest with an organization far too big for the common man to survey or comprehend. Nowhere has democracy ever worked well without a great measure of local self-government, providing a school of political training for the people at large as much as for their future leaders. It is only where responsibility can be learned and practiced in affairs with which most people are familiar, where it is the awareness of one's neighbor rather than some theoretical knowledge of the needs of other people which guides action, that the ordinary man can take a real part in public affairs because they concern the world he knows. Where the scope of the political measures becomes so large that the necessary knowledge is almost exclusively possessed by the bureaucracy, the creative impulses of the private person must flag. I believe that here the experience of the small countries like Holland and Switzerland contains much from which even the most fortunate larger countries like Great Britain can learn. We shall all be the gainers if we can create a world fit for small states to live in.

But the small can preserve their independence in the international as in the national sphere only within a true system of law which guarantees both that certain rules are invariably enforced and that the authority which has the power to enforce these cannot use it for any other purpose. While for its task of enforcing the common law the supernational authority must be very powerful,

---

[13] See on this Professor Robbins's already quoted book, *Economic Planning and Economic Order*, op. cit., pp. 240–57.

[14] As late as the closing years of the nineteenth century Henry Sidgwick thought it "not beyond the limits of a sober forecast to conjecture that some future integration may take place in the West European states: and if it should take place, it seems probable that the example of America will be followed, and that the new political aggregate will be formed on the basis of a federal polity." See Henry Sidgwick, *The Development of European Polity* (London: Macmillan, 1903), p. 439, published posthumously. [Sidgwick actually said that it is "not beyond the limits of a sober forecast to conjecture that some *further* integration may take place in the West European states. . . ." —Ed.]

its constitution must at the same time be so designed that it prevents the international as well as the national authorities from becoming tyrannical. We shall never prevent the abuse of power if we are not prepared to limit power in a way which occasionally may also prevent its use for desirable purposes. The great opportunity we shall have at the end of this war is that the great victorious powers, by themselves first submitting to a system of rules which they have the power to enforce, may at the same time acquire the moral right to impose the same rules upon others.

An international authority which effectively limits the powers of the state over the individual will be one of the best safeguards of peace. The international Rule of Law must become a safeguard as much against the tyranny of the state over the individual as against the tyranny of the new superstate over the national communities. Neither an omnipotent superstate nor a loose association of "free nations" but a community of nations of free men must be our goal. We have long pleaded that it had become impossible to behave in international affairs as we thought it desirable because others would not play the game. The coming settlement will be the opportunity to show that we have been sincere and that we are prepared to accept the same restrictions on our freedom of action which in the common interest we think it necessary to impose upon others.

Wisely used, the federal principle of organization may indeed prove the best solution of some of the world's most difficult problems. But its application is a task of extreme difficulty, and we are not likely to succeed if in an overambitious attempt we strain it beyond its capacity. There will probably exist a strong tendency to make any new international organization all-comprehensive and world-wide; and there will, of course, be an imperative need for some such comprehensive organization, some new League of Nations. The great danger is that, if in the attempt to rely exclusively on this world organization it is charged with all the tasks which it seems desirable to place in the hands of an international organization, they will not in fact be adequately performed. It has always been my conviction that such ambitions were at the root of the weakness of the League of Nations: that in the (unsuccessful) attempt to make it world-wide it had to be made weak and that a smaller and at the same time more powerful League might have been a better instrument to preserve peace. I believe that these considerations still hold and that a degree of cooperation could be achieved between, say, the British Empire and the nations of western Europe and probably the United States which would not be possible on a world scale. The comparatively close association which a federal union represents will not at first be practicable beyond perhaps even as narrow a region as part of western Europe, though it may be possible gradually to extend it.

It is true that with the formation of such regional federations the possibility of war between the different blocs still remains and that, to reduce this risk as much as possible, we must rely on a larger and looser association. My point is that the need for some such other organization should not form an obstacle to a closer association of those countries which are more similar in their civilization, outlook, and standards. While we must aim at preventing future wars as much as possible, we must not believe that we can at one stroke create a permanent organization which will make all war in any part of the world entirely impossible. Not only would we be unsuccessful in such an attempt but we would thereby probably spoil our chances of achieving success in a more limited sphere. As is true with respect to other great evils, the measures by which war might be made altogether impossible for the future may well be worse than even war itself. If we can reduce the risk of friction likely to lead to war, this is probably all we can reasonably hope to achieve.

SIXTEEN

CONCLUSION

The purpose of this book has not been to sketch a detailed program of a desirable future order of society. If with regard to international affairs we have gone a little beyond its essentially critical task, it was because in this field we may soon be called upon to create a framework within which future growth may have to proceed for a long time to come. A great deal will depend on how we use the opportunity we shall then have. But, whatever we do, it can only be the beginning of a new, long, and arduous process in which we all hope we shall gradually create a world very different from that which we knew during the last quarter of a century.

It is at least doubtful whether at this stage a detailed blueprint of a desirable internal order of society would be of much use—or whether anyone is competent to furnish it. The important thing now is that we shall come to agree on certain principles and free ourselves from some of the errors which have governed us in the recent past. However distasteful such an admission may be, we must recognize that we had before this war once again reached a stage where it is more important to clear away the obstacles with which human folly has encumbered our path and to release the creative energy of individuals than to devise further machinery for "guiding" and "directing" them—to create conditions favorable to progress rather than to "plan progress." The first need is to free ourselves of that worst form of contemporary obscurantism which tries to persuade us that what we have done in the recent past was all either wise or inevitable. We shall not grow wiser before we learn that much that we have done was very foolish.

If we are to build a better world, we must have the courage to make a new start—even if that means some *reculer pour mieux sauter.*[1] It is not those who believe in inevitable tendencies who show this courage, not those who preach a "New Order" which is no more than a projection of the tendencies of the last forty years, and who can think of nothing better than to imitate Hitler. It is,

---

[1] [The phrase "*reculer pour mieux sauter*" is the recommendation to back up a little before renewing one's attack. The advice to "Drop back and punt" might serve as a rough American equivalent. —Ed.]

indeed, those who cry loudest for the New Order who are most completely under the sway of the ideas which have created this war and most of the evils from which we suffer. The young are right if they have little confidence in the ideas which rule most of their elders. But they are mistaken or misled when they believe that these are still the liberal ideas of the nineteenth century, which, in fact, the younger generation hardly knows. Though we neither can wish nor possess the power to go back to the reality of the nineteenth century, we have the opportunity to realize its ideals—and they were not mean. We have little right to feel in this respect superior to our grandfathers; and we should never forget that it is we, the twentieth century, and not they, who have made a mess of things. If they had not yet fully learned what was necessary to create the world they wanted, the experience we have since gained ought to have equipped us better for the task. If in the first attempt to create a world of free men we have failed, we must try again. The guiding principle that a policy of freedom for the individual is the only truly progressive policy remains as true today as it was in the nineteenth century.

BIBLIOGRAPHICAL NOTE

The exposition of a point of view which for many years has been decidedly out of favor suffers from the difficulty that, within the compass of a few chapters, it is not possible to discuss more than some aspects of it. For the reader whose outlook has been formed entirely by the views that have been dominant during the last twenty years this will scarcely be sufficient to provide the common ground required for profitable discussion. But although unfashionable, the views of the author of the present book are not so singular as they may appear to some readers. His basic outlook is the same as that of a steadily growing number of writers in many countries whose studies have led them independently to similar conclusions. The reader who would like to acquaint himself further with what he may have found an unfamiliar but not uncongenial climate of opinion may find useful the following list of some of the more important works of this kind, including several in which the essentially critical character of the present essay is supplemented by a fuller discussion of the structure of a desirable future society. The earliest and still the most important of these works is that by von Mises, originally published in 1922.

Cassel, Gustav. *From Protectionism through Planned Economy to Dictatorship*. Cobden Memorial Lecture, London: Cobden-Sanderson, 1934.

Chamberlin, William H. *A False Utopia: Collectivism in Theory and Practice*. London: Duckworth, 1937.

Graham, Frank D. *Social Goals and Economic Institutions*. Princeton: Princeton University Press, 1942.

Gregory, T. E. *Gold, Unemployment, and Capitalism*. London: P. S. King and Son, 1933.

Halévy, Élie. *L'ère des tyrannies: Études sur le socialisme et la guerre*. (Paris: Gallimard, 1938). (English versions of two of the most important essays in this volume will be found in *Economica*, February, 1941, and in *International Affairs*, 1934.)[1]

Hayek, F. A., ed. *Collectivist Economic Planning: Critical Studies on the Possibilities of Socialism*. London: Routledge, 1935.

[1] [Hayek refers here to Élie Halévy, "The Age of Tyrannies" (trans. May Wallas), *Economica, N.S.*, vol. 4, February 1941, pp. 77–93, and Élie Halévy, "Socialism and the Problem of Democratic Parliamentarianism," *International Affairs*, vol. 13, July–August 1934, pp. 490–507. —Ed.]

Hutt, W. H. *Economists and the Public: A Study of Competition and Opinion.* London: Cape, 1936.

Lippmann, Walter. *An Inquiry into the Principles of the Good Society.* London: Allen & Unwin, 1937.

Mises, Ludwig von. *Socialism: An Economic and Sociological Analysis,* translated by Jacques Kahane, London: Cape, 1936.

———. *Omnipotent Government: The Rise of the Total State and Total War.* New Haven: Yale University Press, 1944.

Muir, Ramsay. *Civilization and Liberty.* London: Cape, 1940.

Polanyi, Michael. *The Contempt of Freedom: The Russian Experiment and After.* London: Watts and Co., 1940.

Queeny, Edgar M. *The Spirit of Enterprise.* New York: Scribner's, 1943.

Rappard, William. *The Crisis of Democracy.* Chicago: University of Chicago Press, 1938.

Robbins, Lionel. *Economic Planning and International Order.* London: Macmillan, 1937.

———. *The Economic Basis of Class Conflict and Other Essays in Political Economy.* London: Macmillan, 1939.

———. *The Economic Causes of War.* London: Cape, 1939.

Roepke, Wilhelm. *Die Gesellschaftskrisis der Gegenwart.* Zürich: Eugen Rentsch, 1942.

———. *Civitas Humana.* Zurich: Eugen Rentsch, 1944.

Rougier, Louis. *Les mystiques économiques: comment l'on passe des démocraties libérales aux états totalitaires.* Paris: Librairie de Médicis, 1938.

Voigt, Fritz. *Unto Caesar.* London: Constable, 1938.

The following of the "Public Policy Pamphlets" published by the University of Chicago Press:

Simons, Henry. *A Positive Program for Laissez Faire: Some Proposals for a Liberal Economic Policy.* Public Policy Pamphlet no. 15. Chicago: University of Chicago Press, 1934.

Gideonse, Harry D. *Organized Scarcity and Public Policy: Monopoly and Its Implications.* Public Policy Pamphlet no. 30. Chicago: University of Chicago Press, 1939.

Hermens, Ferdinand. *Democracy and Proportional Representation.* Public Policy Pamphlet no. 31. Chicago: University of Chicago Press, 1940.

Sulzbach, Walter. *"Capitalistic Warmongers": A Modern Superstition.* Public Policy Pamphlet no. 35. Chicago: University of Chicago Press, 1942.

Heilperin, Michael A. *Economic Policy and Democracy.* Public Policy Pamphlet no. 37. Chicago: University of Chicago Press, 1943.

There are also important German and Italian works of a similar character which, in consideration for their authors, it would be unwise at present to mention by name.

To this list I add the titles of three books which more than any others known to me help one to understand the system of ideas ruling our enemies and the differences which separate their minds from ours,

Ashton, E. B. *The Fascist: His State and Mind.* London: Putnam, 1937.

Foerster, Friedrich W. *Europe and the German Question.* London: Sheed and Ward, 1940.

Kantorowicz, H. *The Spirit of British Policy and the Myth of the Encirclement of Germany.* New York: Oxford University Press, 1932.

and that of a remarkable recent work on the modern history of Germany which is not so well known abroad as it deserves:

Schnabel, Franz. *Deutsche Geschichte im 19. Jahrhundert.* 4 vols. Freiburg im Breisgau, 1929–37.

Perhaps the best guides through some of our contemporary problems will still be found in the works of some of the great political philosophers of the liberal age, Tocqueville or Lord Acton, and, to go even further back, Benjamin Constant, Edmund Burke, and *The Federalist* papers of Madison, Hamilton, and Jay—generations to whom liberty was still a problem and a value to be defended, where ours at the same time takes it for granted and neither realizes whence the danger threatens nor has the courage to emancipate itself from the doctrines which endanger it.

APPENDIX:
RELATED DOCUMENTS

Nazi-Socialism[1]

Spring 1933

Incomprehensible as the recent events in Germany must seem to anyone who has known that country chiefly in the democratic post-war years, any attempt fully to understand these developments must treat them as the culmination of tendencies which date back to a period long before the Great War. Nothing could be more superficial than to consider the forces which dominate the Germany of today as reactionary—in the sense that they want a return to the social and economic order of 1914. The persecution of the Marxists, and of democrats in general, tends to obscure the fundamental fact that National Socialism is a genuine socialist movement, whose leading ideas are the final fruit of the anti-liberal tendencies which have been steadily gaining ground in Germany since the later part of the Bismarckian era, and which led the majority of the German intelligentsia first to "socialism of the chair" and later to Marxism in its social-democratic or communist form.

One of the main reasons why the socialist character of National Socialism has been quite generally unrecognized, is, no doubt, its alliance with the nationalist groups which represent the great industries and the great landowners. But this merely proves that these groups too—as they have since learnt to their bitter disappointment—have, at least partly, been mistaken as to the nature of the movement. But only partly because— and this is the most characteristic feature of modern Germany—many capitalists are themselves strongly influenced by socialistic ideas, and have not sufficient belief in capitalism to defend it with a clear conscience. But, in spite of this, the German entrepreneur class have manifested almost incredible short-sightedness in allying themselves with a movement of whose strong anti-capitalistic tendencies there should never have been any doubt.

A careful observer must always have been aware that the opposition of the Nazis to the established socialist parties, which gained them the sympathy of the entrepreneur, was only to a very small extent directed against their economic policy. What the Nazis mainly objected to was their internationalism and all the aspects of their cultural programme which were still influenced by liberal ideas. But the accusations against the social-democrats and the communists which were most effective in their propaganda were not so much directed against their programme as against their supposed practice—their corruption and nepotism, and even their alleged alliance with "the golden International of Jewish Capitalism."

It would, indeed, hardly have been possible for the Nationalists to advance fundamental objections to the economic policy of the other socialist parties when their own

---

[1][The memorandum may be found in the Hayek Papers, box 105, folder 10, Hoover Institution Archives. In the original memo quotation marks enclose "Nazi" in the German style, and Socialism was originally spelled "Sozialism" but was corrected. —Ed.]

published programme differed from these only in that its socialism was much cruder and less rational. The famous 25 points drawn up by Herr Feder,[2] one of Hitler's early allies, repeatedly endorsed by Hitler and recognised by the by-laws of the National-Socialist party as the immutable basis of all its actions, which together with an extensive commentary is circulating throughout Germany in many hundreds of thousands of copies, is full of ideas resembling those of the early socialists. But the dominant feature is a fierce hatred of anything capitalistic—individualistic profit seeking, large scale enterprise, banks, joint-stock companies, department stores, "international finance and loan capital," the system of "interest slavery" in general; the abolition of these is described as the "[indecipherable] of the programme, around which everything else turns." It was to this programme that the masses of the German people, who were already completely under the influence of collectivist ideas, responded so enthusiastically.

That this violent anti-capitalistic attack is genuine—and not a mere piece of propaganda becomes as clear from the personal history of the intellectual leaders of the movement as from the general *milieu* from which it springs. It is not even denied that many of the young men who today play a prominent part in it have previously been communists or socialists. And to any observer of the literary tendencies which made the German intelligentsia ready to join the ranks of the new party, it must be clear that the common characteristic of all the politically influential writers—in many cases free from definite party affiliations—was their anti-liberal and anti-capitalist trend. Groups like that formed around the review "Die Tat" have made the phrase "the end of capitalism" an accepted dogma to most young Germans.[3]

That the movement is more anti-liberal than anything else is closely connected with another important aspect of it—the anti-rational, mystical and romantic sentiment, which has been growing for years among the youth of Germany. The protest against "liberal intellectualism" which was recently so strongly voiced by the students of the University of Berlin, was not an isolated aberration but a true expression of the feeling of great masses of the people.[4] It would be too long a story to go into all the different intellectual sources of these anti-rational tendencies in art and literature which have all converged—often to the amazement and consternation of their originators—in the Nazi movement. But it must be said that here again the main influence which destroyed the belief in the universality and unity of human reason was Marx' teaching of the class-conditioned nature of our thinking, of the difference between bourgeois and proletarian logic, which needed only to be applied to other social groups such as nations or races, to supply the weapon now used against rationalism as such. How completely this

[2] [Gottfried Feder (1883–1941) was an early economic advisor to Hitler. A fundamental element of his economic teaching was the concept of "interest slavery" and his recommendation that interest be abolished. Once he came to power Hitler abandoned Feder's program in order better to attract the support of German industrialists. —Ed.]

[3] [For more on *Die Tat*, see chapter 12, note 41. —Ed.]

[4] [The student protests in Berlin culminated in a book-burning in the Opernplatz on the night of May 10, 1933. —Ed.]

Marxian idea has permeated German thought can be seen from the fact that, during the past few years, it has actually been promoted, as "sociology of knowledge" to the rank of a new branch of learning.[5] It is obvious that, from this intellectual relativism, which denied the existence of truths which could be recognised independently of race, nation, or class, there was only a step to the position which puts sentiment above rational thinking.

That anti-liberalism and anti-rationalism are so intimately bound up with one another is easy to understand, and is, in fact, inevitable. If rule by force by some privileged group is to be justified, its superiority has to be accepted for it cannot be proved. But what is less easily understood—thought of immense importance—is the fact illustrated by German and Russian developments that the anti-liberalism which, when confined to the economic field, today has the sympathy of almost all the rest of the world, leads inevitably to a reign of universal compulsion, to intolerance and the suppression of intellectual freedom. The inherent logic of collectivism makes it impossible to confine it to a limited sphere. Beyond certain limits collective action in the interest of all can only be made possible if all can be coerced into accepting as their common interest what those in power take it to be. At that point, coercion must extend to the individuals' ultimate aims and ideas and must attempt to bring everyone's *Weltanschauung* into line with the ideas of the rulers.

The collectivist and anti-individualist character of German National Socialism is not much modified by the fact that it is not a proletarian but a middle class socialism, and that it is, in consequence, inclined to favour the small artisan and shop keeper and to set the limit up to which it recognises private property somewhat higher than does communism. In the first instance, it will probably nominally recognise private property in general. But private initiative will probably be hedged about with restrictions on competition so that little freedom will remain. Artisans, shop-keepers and professional men will, in all likelihood, be organised in guilds, like those of the mediaeval crafts, which will regulate their activities. In the case of the wealthier capitalists, state control and restriction of income will leave little more than the name of property, even while the intention of correcting the undue accumulation of wealth in the hands of individuals has not yet been carried out. Even at the present moment, state commissioners have been put in charge of many important industries and, if the more radical wing of the party has its way, the same is likely to happen in many other cases.[6] At the present time, when the National Socialist party has grown to such an enormous size, and accordingly em-

---

[5] [Karl Mannheim was one of the leading proponents of "the sociology of knowledge," see especially his *Ideology and Utopia: An Introduction to the Sociology of Knowledge*, trans. Louis Wirth and Edward Shils, a volume in the series *The International Library of Psychology, Philosophy, and Scientific Method* (New York: Harcourt, Brace, 1936). —Ed.]

[6] [In the first few months of Nazi rule self-appointed Nazi party radicals simply marched into certain enterprises and took them over, usually granting themselves and their accomplices large salaries and other perks. Goering and the other Nazi leaders considered these self-styled *Kommisars* dangerous and by late 1933 had rooted most of them out. —Ed.]

braces elements with very divergent views, it is, of course, difficult to say which view will predominate. But if, as seems increasingly probable, the more radical views on economic policy hold the field, it will mean that the scare of Russian communism has driven the German people unawares into something which differs from communism in little but name. Indeed, it is more than probable that the real meaning of the German revolution is that the long dreaded expansion of communism into the heart of Europe has taken place but is not recognised because the fundamental similarity of methods and ideas is hidden by the difference in the phraseology and the privileged groups. For the present, the German people have reacted against the treatment received from the community of democratic and capitalistic countries by leaving that community.

Nothing, however, would be less justifiable than that the nations of western Europe should look down on the German people because they have fallen victims to which, in this country, seems a kind of barbarism. What must be realised is that this is only the ultimate and necessary outcome of a process of development in which the other nations have been for a long time steadily following Germany—albeit at a considerable distance. The gradual extension of the field of state activity, the increase in restrictions on international movements of both men and goods, sympathy with central economic planning and the widespread playing with dictatorship ideas, all tend in this direction. In Germany, where these things had gone furthest, an intellectual reaction, which will now hardly survive, had been definitely under way. The fact that the character of the present movement is so generally misjudged makes it seem likely that the reaction in other countries will speed up, rather than weaken, the operation of these tendencies which lead in the direction in which Germany is now going. So far, there seems little prospect that the reversal of these intellectual tendencies elsewhere will come in time to prevent other countries from following Germany in this last step also.

Reader's Report by Frank Knight[7]

December 10, 1943
To: General Editor and Committee on Publication, University of Chicago Press
From: Frank H. Knight

The Road to Serfdom, by F. A. Hayek, is a masterly performance of the job it undertakes. That job is to show by general and historical reasoning, the latter primarily with reference to the course of events in Germany, two things: first, that any such policy as socialism, or planned economy, will inevitably lead to totalitarianism and dictatorship; and second that such a social order will inevitably fall under the control of "the worst" individuals. The argument is naturally political rather than economic, except in the indirect sense that the problems solved, the functions performed, by the open-market system of organization are economic and they cannot be solved, or performed by government under a free political order, nor the open-market system itself maintained under a democratic political regime. There is little or no economic theory in the book. The fifteen short chapters ably describe the old liberalism and contrast it with current tendencies which are virtually antithetical and discuss such problems as individualism, democracy, the rule of law, security and freedom, the place of truth in political and social life, the relation between material conditions and ideal ends, and the problem of international order.

When I say that the argument is well stated, compact and conclusive, I should add that the position defended is in accord with my conviction before reading this work. Highly intelligent opinion can be found against this view and it might be well to get a report from someone who holds this contrary position. Such persons are to be found in this faculty and in the Economics Department.

From the standpoint of desirability of publishing the book in this country, I may note some grounds for doubt. The author is an Austrian refugee, a very able economist, who has been a professor at the London School of Economics since the middle thirties. He writes from a distinctly English point of view, and frequently uses the expression "this country" with that reference. While there is some treatment of American conditions, and citation of American writings, this is secondary in scope and emphasis. This fact in itself might limit the appeal in "this country" to a fairly cultivated, even academic, circle of readers. Moreover, the whole discussion is pitched at a quite high intellectual and scholarly level and the amount of knowledge of central European conditions and history assumed is rather large for even the educated American audience. It is hardly a "popular" book from this point of view.

In addition, there are limitations in connection with the treatment itself, both as to the theoretical and the historical argument. In the latter connection, the work is essen-

[7][Frank Knight, reader's report, December 10, 1943, may be found in the University of Chicago Press collection, box 230, folder 1, University of Chicago Library. —Ed.]

tially negative. It hardly considers the problem of alternatives, and inadequately recognizes the necessity, as well as political inevitability, of a wide range of governmental activity in relation to economic life in the future. It deals only with the simpler fallacies, unreasonable demands and romantic prejudices which underlie the popular clamor for governmental control in place of free enterprise. It does not discuss the problems set by the serious shortcomings of an economic system based on the degree of economic freedom which was regarded as desirable and was allowed, say, around the turn of the century. And it does not attack fallacies in a very dramatic way, in comparison with the character of the thinking and argument on which they are actually based.

The author's treatment of the course of events leading to the Nazi dictatorship in Germany also strikes me as open to attack on the ground of over-simplification. He practically attributes everything to the Socialist movement and state paternalism toward labor and industry, including the cultivation of an attitude of contempt for business enterprise, in comparison with esteem for bureaucratic status on a salary. He explicitly relegates the militaristic tradition to a minor role. It seems to me that there are many factors in German history which would call for consideration in a balanced treatment. One thinks of the late survival of feudalism, retarding of national unification and industrialization, and the special circumstances surrounding these changes and the establishment of responsible government after the first World War. These last surely had much to do with the breakdown of parliamentarism, an undoubted fact and a vital factor in the establishment of the Hitler regime. I recall only a brief mention of anti-Semitism, which has a long history in Germany. These matters do not in my own mind invalidate the author's general conclusion but they weaken the argument as a presentation of his case.

In sum, the book is an able piece of work, but limited in scope and somewhat one-sided in treatment. I doubt whether it would have a very wide market in this country, or would change the position of many readers.

Reader's Report by Jacob Marschak[8]

December 20, 1943

The current discussion between advocates and adversaries of free enterprise has not been conducted so far on a very high level. Hayek's book may start in this country a more scholarly kind of debate.

The book will appeal to friends of free enterprise and give them new material: Hayek's interpretation of the modern English scene (labor and industrial monopolist driving jointly toward a collective economy) will be new to all American readers except those who have read or listened to William Benton's impressions; while Hayek's German background enables him to give new support to the contention that socialism is the father of Nazism.

Those who are not convinced in advance of Hayek's thesis will probably learn from his argument even more than those who are. Hayek (Chapter IV) has a wholesome contempt for the quasi-scientific method of "trends," "waves of tomorrow." Those who love planning because they love the inevitable will, perhaps, after reading Hayek revise either their faith or their tastes. Perhaps they will start to think in terms of ends and means instead of in prophecies.

It is true that Hayek himself gives little food for such concrete thinking. As he says himself at the end of the book (pages 177, 179)[9] the book is almost exclusively critical not constructive. Its technique is black-and-white. It is impatient of compromises (page 31). It is written with the passion and the burning clarity of a great doctrinaire. Hayek has the sincerity of one who has had the vision of a danger which the others have not seen. He warns his fellowmen with loving impatience.

Accordingly, the best chapters of the book are negative or formal. There is an excellent and truly inspiring chapter on the "Rule of Law" (Chapter VI); but Hayek has little to say as to how the Rule of Law (i.e., the avoidance of administrative decisions *ad hoc*) might be applied to create instruments for mitigating unemployment by monetary means, or for combating monopolists. On such points he gives only vague hints (page 90, 147). Since in this country the terms "plan" and "socialism" have often been used to include monetary and fiscal policies, social security, and even progressive income tax the American reader will possibly expect from Hayek a more concrete demarcation between what the book calls "planning in the good sense" and the (undesirable) planning proper. In fact, the non-economic chapters (that on "The End of Truth," for example) are more impressive than the economic ones.

[8][Jacob Marschak, reader's report, December 20, 1943, may be found in the University of Chicago Press collection, box 230, folder 1, University of Chicago Library. —Ed.]

[9][The page numbers in Marschak's report are taken from Hayek's original manuscript, hence do not correspond to the page numbers in the present text. —Ed.]

Those who read Walter Lippmann, Stuart Chase,[10] or the Fortune's discussions on the postwar world will also read Hayek. He is often less concrete than Lippmann or Chase; but his thinking is somewhat sharper, just because it is more abstract. Hayek's style is readable and occasionally inspiring.

This book cannot be by-passed.

J. Marschak

[10][American accountant, freelance writer and author Stuart Chase (1888–1985) was a popular writer in the interwar period. He was the author of such books as *The Tragedy of Waste* (New York: Macmillan, 1925) and provided the foreword to Thorstein Veblen, *The Theory of the Leisure Class* (New York: Modern Library, 1934). For more on Walter Lippmann, see chapter 2, note 8. —Ed.]

Foreword to the 1944 American Edition by John Chamberlain

The shibboleths of our times are expressed in a variety of terms: "full employment," "planning," "social security," "freedom from want." The facts of our times suggest that none of these things can be had when they are made conscious objects of government policy. They are the fool's-gold words. In Italy they debauched a people and led to death under the burning African suns. In Russia there was the first Five-Year Plan; there was also the liquidation of the three million kulaks. In Germany there was full employment between 1935 and 1939; but six hundred thousand Jews are now deprived of their property, scattered to the ends of the earth, or lying in mass graves in the Polish forests. And in America the pump never quite filled up after the successive primings; war alone saved the politicians of "full employment."

To date, only a handful of writers has dared to trace a connection between our shibboleths and the terror that haunts the modern world. Among these writers is F. A. Hayek, an Austrian economist now living in England. Having watched the congealing of the German, the Italian, and the Danubian social and economic systems, Hayek is horrified to see the English succumbing by degrees to the controlled-economy ideas of the German Walter Rathenau, the Italian syndicalists—yes, and Adolf Hitler, who had the courage to draw conclusions from the less forthright statism of his predecessors.[11] This book of Hayek's—*The Road to Serfdom*—is a warning, a cry in a time of hesitation. It says to the British and by implication to Americans: Stop, look and listen.

The Road to Serfdom is sober, logical, severe. It does not make for ingratiating reading. But the logic is incontestable: "full employment," "social security," and "freedom from want" cannot be had unless they come as by-products of a system that releases the free energies of individuals. When "society" and the "good of the whole" and "the greatest good of the greatest number" are made the overmastering touchstones of state action, no individual can plan his own existence. For the state "planners" must arrogate to themselves the right to move in on any sector of the economic system if the good of "society" or the "general welfare" is paramount. If the rights of the individual get in the way, the rights of the individual must go.

The threat of state "dynamism" results in a vast, usually unconscious fear among all producing interests that still retain a conditional freedom of action. And the fear affects the springs of action. Men must try to outguess the government as yesterday they tried to outguess the market. But there is this difference; the market factors obeyed at least relatively objective laws, while governments are subject to a good deal of whim. One can stake one's future on a judgment that reckons with inventories, market saturation points, the interest rate, the trend curves of buyers' desires. But how can an individual outguess a government whose aim is to suspend the objective laws of the market whenever and wherever it wishes to do so in the name of "planning"? Shrewdly, Peter

[11][For more on Walther Rathenau, see chapter 12, note 18. —Ed.]

Drucker once remarked that the "planners" are all improvisers.[12] They create not certainty but uncertainty—for individuals. And, as Hayek demonstrates, the end result of this uncertainty is civil war, or the dictatorship that averts civil war.

The alternative to "planning" is the "rule of law." Hayek is no devotee of laissez faire; he believes in a design for an enterprise system. Design is compatible with minimum-wage standards, health standards, a minimum amount of compulsory social insurance. It is even compatible with certain types of government investment. But the point is that the individual must know, in advance, just how the rules are going to work. He cannot plan his own business, his own future, even his own family affairs, if the "dynamism" of a central planning authority hangs over his head.

In some respects Hayek is more "English" than the modern English. He belongs, with modifications, to the great Manchester line, not to the school of the Webbs.[13] It may be that he is also more "American" than the modern Americans. If so, one can only wish for the widest possible United States audience for *The Road to Serfdom*.

John Chamberlain
New York, NY
July 1944

[12] [For more on Drucker, see chapter 2, note 9. Drucker's *The End of Economic Man*, op. cit., is discussed in chapter 14, note 2. —Ed.]

[13] [For more on Sidney and Beatrice Webb, see chapter 5, note 3. —Ed.]

Letter from John Scoon to C. Hartley Grattan[14]

Hayek: THE ROAD TO SERFDOM

May 2, 1945
Mr. C. Hartley Grattan
6 White Hall Road
Tuckahoe, New York

Dear Mr. Grattan:

I have been in the office about five minutes a day since I returned to Chicago, or you certainly would have heard from me before this. The reviews were sent to you over a week ago, however, and for your purposes they tell the main story.

THE ROAD TO SERFDOM came to us in December 1943, was read by two scholarly readers outside of the Press, and was approved by our Publications Committee (made up of faculty members from various departments of the University) at the end of that month. It was in page proofs when we first saw it, and about to be published by Routledge in England. The idea of the Press's publishing it in this country was suggested by a member of the Department of Economics at the University who had previously known Hayek and his work;[15] almost simultaneously another friend of the author's,[16] once at the University but then in Washington with the government, suggested the book to us and got us the page proofs.

The first report, a copy of which I am enclosing marked "A," was from a man who is very reliable, pretty middle-of-the-road in his political stand, and respected by both sides. He says in his report that he was on Hayek's side in this matter even before reading the book, so he recommended that we get another report from the opposition. This we did, and the report labeled "B" came from one of the most definitely "progressive" economists in the country, whose name you would recognize immediately if it were not our long-standing policy never to reveal readers' names. In other words, we simply could not have given the book a more objective trial: we didn't know a thing about it at that time, so we got reports from two opposing points of view and then laid them before a committee composed of thirteen men of differing shades of opinion. They approved publication of the book by the Press.

That was all before Mr. Brandt and I came to the Press at the beginning of January, 1944. We found this project in the vault with many others, part of the probable program

---

[14][Scoon's letter may be found in the University of Chicago Press collection, box 230, folder 3, University of Chicago Library. —Ed.]

[15][Frank Knight —Ed.]

[16][Aaron Director —Ed.]

for the year just beginning then. As the Press started to make up its new list, THE ROAD TO SERFDOM looked far from world-shaking. Then we read the page proofs ourselves, and decided to ask the author to be specific about the book's application to the United States, explicitly mentioning this country where he included it in his thought instead of slanting the book directly at an audience limited to England—"making no promises as to publication which might influence his judgment on this point," my memo read. It went on to say: "If he agrees, let's take it on. It will stir up trouble, but the author has a point and evidently has had excellent experience." (I should explain here that the committee's "approval" of a manuscript is not mandatory, so the question of publication had not yet been completely decided.)

This process was agreed upon by all parties, and we, a colleague of the author's,[17] and Mr. Hayek himself all set to work suggesting possible revisions. Specific changes were eventually agreed upon, Mr. Hayek of course having the final say about what was added, what was deleted, and the specific wording in each spot. Meanwhile we at the Press were worrying about a possible new title, the sort of sales the book would have (it was taken on purely as a scholarly work, and we knew it would either fall pretty flat or catch on very widely), and how best to introduce this work by a foreign author without much of a name in this country. After much conferring we decided to leave the title (a paraphrase of Bertrand Russell's ROADS TO FREEDOM),[18] to ask John Chamberlain to write an introduction to the book, and to have a first printing of 2,000 copies. This figure was definitely influenced by the competition the book faced in the previously published OMNIPOTENT GOVERNMENT, by Ludwig Von Mises, Hayek's one-time teacher in Vienna.[19]

About the time the contract for American rights was signed—the beginning of April—we began to hear about the book in England, which had been published there on March 10. The first printing in England was only 2,000, but it was sold out in about a month. It began to be quoted in Parliament and in newspapers, and a few newspapers over here began mentioning it now and then—but of course we were still uncertain as to how it would appeal to the United States. As a matter of fact, right up until publication date we couldn't get a bookstore even in New York excited about the book, although Joe Margolies, of Brentano's, did allow it some sales possibilities.

Into June the author was correcting our proofs, and publication, which we had hoped

---

[17][Fritz Machlup —Ed.]

[18][Scoon is wrong about the origin of the title. As Hayek once explained in an interview, "The idea came from Tocqueville, who speaks about the road to servitude; I would like to have chosen that title, but it doesn't sound good. So I changed 'servitude' into 'serfdom,' for merely phonetic reasons." F. A. Hayek, "Nobel Prize Winning Economist," ed. Armen Alchian. Transcript of an interview conducted in 1978 under the auspices of the Oral History Program, University Library, UCLA, copyright Regents of the University of California, p. 76. —Ed.]

[19][Scoon refers to Ludwig von Mises, *Omnipotent Government: The Rise of the Total State and Total War* (New Haven: Yale University Press, 1944). —Ed.]

for in July, was delayed until September 18, by which time the English edition was in its third printing. We sent out more advance copies and review copies than usual, and from the response we knew that the book would have a good chance of catching on: the first review that we saw was Orville Prescott's in the NEW YORK TIMES of September 20, which was neutral and called it "this sad and angry little book," but by the time we had seen Henry Hazlitt's front page review in the Sunday TIMES BOOK REVIEW we had ordered a second printing of 5,000 copies. In a few days we had requests for German, Spanish, Dutch and other translation rights, and on September 27 we ordered a third printing of 5,000 copies, upping it to 10,000 the next day. Requests for magazine rights came from several sources, but the READER'S DIGEST was first and made the best offer.

By the first week of October many stores were out of stock and we had a tremendous and intricate job of printing, binding, shipping and allotting to customers in both this country and Canada—by this time we had made an arrangement with Routledge to take care of Canadian orders too. From the start there was great enthusiasm for the book but the sales went by ups and downs and our advertising agency had a real headache getting space at the right times. A few book programs on the radio boosted the book, toward the end of October, but we knew that its sales would fall off after Christmas so we began casting about for something to do with it this year. Mr. Brandt got the idea of bringing Mr. Hayek over here; he called the departments of economics at several universities about the possibility, and all were very enthusiastic. As soon as definite arrangements had been made and it became known that Mr. Hayek was coming to this country, organizations and individuals of all sorts overwhelmed us with efforts to get hold of him and we had to turn the trip over to the National Concert and Artists Corporation.

The rest of the story you know. The book, now in its seventh printing, has sold nearly 50,000, but orders are coming in so fast that we don't know the exact total. Actually it has had one of the most eccentric sales careers a book ever had, and it has been very difficult to know what to do next with it: the DIGEST condensation caused a great spurt, but the spurt did not hold—very likely because of the Book-of-the-Month Club's distribution of the condensation, which has now reached a figure above 600,000.

Bitterness about the book has increased as time has gone by, rising to new heights as the book has made more of an impression. (People still tend to go off half-cocked about it; why don't they *read* it and find out what Hayek actually says!) You also know how the author feels about this: one of his regrets is that in a way his conclusions are down on paper, but not the process by which he arrived at them, and we are all wondering whether some day we should not bring out a fully annotated edition of the book. (This edition is being used as collateral reading in political science and similar courses at a number of universities.) Meanwhile Hayek has many other projects on hand, none of which we should talk about now.

I hope that this will suffice for your needs—I have gathered the material out of the files and may have lost something in perspective. If there is anything more that you would like to know, we will try to supply it.

Yours sincerely,

John Scoon
Editor

JS:MB

Introduction to the 1994 Edition by Milton Friedman

This book has become a true classic: essential reading for everyone who is seriously interested in politics in the broadest and least partisan sense, a book whose central message is timeless, applicable to a wide variety of concrete situations. In some ways it is even more relevant to the United States today than it was when it created a sensation on its original publication in 1944.

Nearly a quarter of a century ago (1971), I wrote an introduction to a new German edition of *The Road to Serfdom* that illustrates how timeless Hayek's message is. That introduction is equally relevant to this fiftieth anniversary edition of Hayek's classic. Rather than plagiarize myself, I herewith quote it in full before adding a few additional comments.

"Over the years, I have made it a practice to inquire of believers in individualism how they came to depart from the collectivist orthodoxy of our times. For years, the most frequent answer was a reference to the book for which I have the honor of writing this introduction. Professor Hayek's remarkable and vigorous tract was a revelation particularly to the young men and women who had been in the armed forces during the war. Their recent experience had enhanced their appreciation of the value and meaning of individual freedom. In addition, they had observed a collectivist organization in action. For them, Hayek's predictions about the consequences of collectivism were not simply hypothetical possibilities but visible realities that they had themselves experienced in the military.

"On rereading the book before writing this introduction, I was again impressed with what a magnificent book it is—subtle and closely reasoned yet lucid and clear, philosophical and abstract yet also concrete and realistic, analytical and rational yet animated by high ideals and a vivid sense of mission. Little wonder that it had so great an influence. I was impressed also that its message is no less needed today than it was when it first appeared—on this more later. But its message may not be as immediate or as persuasive to today's youth as to the young men and women who read it when it first appeared. The problems of the war and postwar adjustment that Hayek used to illustrate his timeless central thesis, and the collectivist jargon of the time that he used to document his assertions about the intellectual climate, were familiar to the immediate postwar generation and established an immediate rapport between author and reader. The same collectivist fallacies are abroad and on the rise today, but the immediate issues are different and so is much of the jargon. Today we hear little of 'central planning,' of 'production for use,' of the need for 'conscious direction' of society's resources. Instead the talk is of the urban crisis—solvable it is said only by vastly expanded government programs; of the environmental crisis—produced it is said by rapacious businessmen who must be forced to discharge their social responsibility instead of 'simply' operating their enterprises to make the most profit and requiring also, it is said, vastly expanded government programs; of the consumer crisis—false values stimulated by the selfsame rapacious businessmen seeking profits instead of exercising social responsibility and of course also requiring expanded government programs to protect the consumer, not least from himself; of the welfare or poverty crisis—here the jargon is still 'poverty in the midst of plenty,' though what is now described as poverty would have been regarded as plenty when that slogan was first widely used.

"Now as then, the promotion of collectivism is combined with the profession of individualist values. Indeed, experience with big government has strengthened this discordant strand. There is wide protest against the 'establishment'; an incredible conformity in the protest against conformity; a widespread demand for freedom to 'do one's own thing,' for individual lifestyles, for participatory democracy. Listening to this strand, one might also believe that the collectivist tide has turned, that individualism is again on the rise. As Hayek so persuasively demonstrates, these values require an individualistic society. They can be achieved only in a *liberal* order (I use the term *liberal*, as Hayek does—in the original nineteenth-century sense of limited government and free markets, not in the corrupted sense it has acquired in the United States, in which it means almost the opposite), in which government activity is limited primarily to establishing the framework within which individuals are free to pursue their own objectives. The free market is the only mechanism that has ever been discovered for achieving participatory democracy.

"Unfortunately, the relation between the ends and the means remains widely misunderstood. Many of those who profess the most individualistic objectives support collectivist means without recognizing the contradiction. It is tempting to believe that social evils arise from the activities of evil men and that if only good men (like ourselves, naturally) wielded power, all would be well. That view requires only emotion and self-praise—easy to come by and satisfying as well. To understand why it is that 'good' men in positions of power will produce evil, while the ordinary man without power but able to engage in voluntary cooperation with his neighbors will produce good, requires analysis and thought, subordinating the emotions to the rational faculty. Surely that is one answer to the perennial mystery of why collectivism, with its demonstrated record of producing tyranny and misery, is so widely regarded as superior to individualism, with its demonstrated record of producing freedom and plenty. The argument for collectivism is simple if false; it is an immediate emotional argument. The argument for individualism is subtle and sophisticated; it is an indirect rational argument. And the emotional faculties are more highly developed in most men than the rational, paradoxically or especially even in those who regard themselves as intellectuals.

"How stands the battle between collectivism and individualism in the West more than a quarter of a century [now half a century] after the publication of Hayek's great tract? The answer is very different in the world of affairs and in the world of ideas.

"In the world of affairs, those of us who were persuaded by Hayek's analysis saw few signs in 1945 of anything but a steady growth of the state at the expense of the individual, a steady replacement of private initiative and planning by state initiative and planning. Yet in practice that movement did not go much farther—not in Britain or in France or in the United States. And in Germany there was a sharp reaction away from the totalitarian controls of the Nazi period and a major move toward a liberal economic policy.

"What produced this unexpected check to collectivism? I believe that two forces were primarily responsible. First, and this was particularly important in Britain, the conflict between central planning and individual liberty that is Hayek's theme became patent, particularly when the exigencies of central planning led to the so-called 'control of engagements' order under which the government had the power to assign people to occupations. The tradition of liberty, the liberal values, were still sufficiently strong in Britain so that, when the conflict occurred, central planning was sacrificed rather than individual liberty. The second force checking collectivism was simply its inefficiency. Government proved unable to manage enterprises, to organize resources to achieve stated objectives at reasonable cost. It became mired in bureaucratic confusion and inefficiency. Widespread disillusionment set in about the effectiveness of centralized government in administering programs.

"Unfortunately, the check to collectivism did not check the growth of government; rather, it diverted its growth to a different channel. The emphasis shifted from governmentally administered production activities to indirect regulation of supposedly private enterprises and even more to governmental transfer programs, involving extracting taxes from some in order to make grants to others—all in the name of equality and the eradication of poverty, but in practice producing an erratic and contradictory mélange of subsidies to special interest groups. As a result, the fraction of the national income being spent by governments has continued to mount.

"In the world of ideas, the outcome has been even less satisfactory to a believer in individualism. In one respect, this is most surprising. Experience in the past quarter century has strongly confirmed the validity of Hayek's central insight—that coordination of men's activities through central direction and through voluntary cooperation are roads going in very different directions: the first to serfdom, the second to freedom. That experience has also strongly reinforced a secondary theme—central direction is also a road to poverty for the ordinary man; voluntary cooperation, a road to plenty.

"East and West Germany almost provide a controlled scientific experiment. Here are people of the same blood, the same civilization, the same level of technical skill and knowledge, torn asunder by the accidents of warfare, yet adopting radically different methods of social organization-central direction and the market. The results are crystal clear. East Germany, not West Germany, had to build a wall to keep its citizens from leaving. On its side of the wall, tyranny and misery; on the other side, freedom and affluence.

"In the Middle East, Israel and Egypt offer the same contrast as West and East Germany. In the Far East, Malaya, Singapore, Thailand, Formosa, Hong Kong, and Japan—all relying primarily on free markets—are thriving and their people full of hope; a far call from India, Indonesia, and Communist China—all relying heavily on central planning. Again it is Communist China and not Hong Kong that has to guard its borders against people trying to get out.

"Yet despite this remarkable and dramatic confirmation of Hayek's thesis, the intellectual climate of the West, after a brief interlude in which there were some signs of the resurgence of earlier liberal values, has again started moving in a direction strongly antagonistic to free enterprise, competition, private property and limited government. For a time, Hayek's description of the ruling intellectual attitudes seemed to be growing somewhat obsolete. Today, it rings truer than it did a decade ago. It is hard to know what explains this development. We badly need a new book by Hayek that will give as clear and penetrating an insight into the intellectual developments of the past quarter century as *The Road to Serfdom* does of earlier developments. Why is it that intellectual classes everywhere almost automatically range themselves on the side of collectivism—even while chanting individualist slogans—and denigrate and revile capitalism? Why is it that the mass media are almost everywhere dominated by this view?

"Whatever the explanation, the fact of growing intellectual support of collectivism—and I believe it is a fact—makes Hayek's book as timely today as it was when it first appeared. Let us hope that a new edition in Germany which of all countries should be most receptive to its message—will have as much influence as the initial edition had in the United States and the United Kingdom. The battle for freedom must be won over and over again. The socialists in all parties to whom Hayek dedicated his book must once again be persuaded or defeated if they and we are to remain free men."

The penultimate paragraph of my introduction to the German edition is the only one that does not ring fully true today. The fall of the Berlin Wall, the collapse of communism behind the Iron Curtain, and the changing character of China have reduced the defenders of a Marxian-type collectivism to a small, hardy band concentrated in Western universities. Today, there is wide agreement that socialism is a failure, capitalism a success. Yet this apparent conversion of the intellectual community to what might be called a Hayekian view is deceptive. While the talk is about free markets and private property—and it is more respectable than it was a few decades ago to defend near-complete laissez-faire—the bulk of the intellectual community almost automatically favors any expansion of government power so long as it is advertised as a way to protect individuals from big bad corporations, relieve poverty, protect the environment, or promote "equality." The present discussion of a national program of health care provides a striking example. The intellectuals may have learned the words but they do not yet have the tune.

I said at the outset that "in some ways" the message of this book "is even more relevant to the United States today than it was when it created a sensation . . . half a century ago." Intellectual opinion then was far more hostile to its theme than it appears to be now, but practice conformed to it far more than it does today. Government in the post-World War II period was smaller and less intrusive than it is today. Johnson's Great Society programs, including Medicare and Medicaid, and Bush's Clean Air and Americans with Disabilities acts were all still ahead, let alone the numerous other extensions of government that Reagan was only able to slow down, not reverse, in his eight years in office. Total government spending—federal, state, and local—in the United States has gone from 25 percent of national income in 1950 to nearly 45 percent in 1993.

Much the same has been true in Britain, in one sense more dramatically. The Labour Party, formerly openly socialist, now defends free private markets; and the Conservative Party, once content to administer Labour's socialist policies, has tried to reverse, and to some extent under Margaret Thatcher succeeded in reversing, the extent of government ownership and operation. But Thatcher was unable to call on anything like the reservoir of popular support for liberal values that led to the withdrawal of the "control of engagements" order shortly after World War II. And while there has been a considerable amount of "privatization" there as here, government today spends a larger fraction of the national income and is more intrusive than it was in 1950.

On both sides of the Atlantic, it is only a little overstated to say that we preach individualism and competitive capitalism, and practice socialism.

Note on Publishing History[20]

Hayek began working on *The Road to Serfdom* in September 1940, and the book was first published in England on March 10, 1944. Hayek authorized his friend Dr. Fritz Machlup, an Austrian refugee who pursued a distinguished academic career in the United States and was employed, in 1944, at the Office of Alien Property Custodian in Washington, DC, to sign up the book with an American publisher. Before it was submitted to the University of Chicago Press the book was turned down in the United States by three publishers—whether because they believed it would not sell or, in at least one case, because they considered it "unfit for publication by a reputable house."[21] Undeterred, Machlup showed the page proofs of the British edition to Aaron Director, a former member of the University of Chicago Economics Department who was to return to the university after the war as an economist in the Law School. Subsequently, Frank H. Knight, a distinguished economist at the university, received a set of proofs and presented them to the University of Chicago Press with Director's suggestion that the Press might want to publish the book.

The Press signed a contract with Hayek for American rights in April 1944, after persuading him to make some changes—"to be specific about the application to the United States . . . instead of slanting the book directly at an audience limited to England," as John Scoon, then editor at the Press, later recalled.

"About the time the contract for American rights was signed—the beginning of April—we began to hear about the book in England, which had been published there

---

[20]Much of this section is based on research carried out by Alex Philipson, promotions manager at the University of Chicago Press.

[21]See Hayek's foreword to the 1956 American paperback edition, p. 41.

on March 10. The first printing in England was only 2,000 but it was sold out in about a month. It began to be quoted in Parliament and in newspapers, and a few newspapers over here began mentioning it now and then—but of course we were still uncertain as to how it would appeal to the United States. As a matter of fact, right up until publication date we couldn't get a bookstore even in New York excited about the book."

The Chicago edition was published on September 18, 1944, in a first printing of 2,000 copies, with an introduction by John Chamberlain, then as now a well-known writer and reviewer of books on economic subjects. "The first review that we saw," Scoon went on to say, "was Orville Prescott's in the *New York Times* of September 20, which was neutral and called it 'this sad and angry little book,' but by the time we had seen Henry Hazlitt's front page review in the *Sunday Times Book Review* we had ordered a second printing of 5,000 copies. In a few days we had requests for German, Spanish, Dutch and other translating rights, and on September 27 we ordered a third printing of 5,000 copies, upping it to 10,000 the next day. . . .

"By the first week of October many stores were out of stock and we had a tremendous and intricate job of printing, binding, shipping and allotting to customers in both this country and Canada. . . . From the start there was great enthusiasm for the book but the sales went by ups and downs. . . .

"Bitterness about the book has increased as time has gone by, rising to new heights as the book has made more of an impression. (People still tend to go off half-cocked about it; why don't they read it and find out what Hayek actually says!)" Scoon's comment is still true today.

The *Reader's Digest* published a condensation in April 1945, and more than 600,000 copies of the condensed version were subsequently distributed by the Book of the Month Club.[22] In anticipation of the *Digest*'s condensation and also of a lecture tour that Hayek was scheduled to make in the Spring of 1945, the Press tried to arrange for a large seventh printing. However, a paper shortage limited the press run to 10,000 and forced the Press to reduce the size of the book to a pocket-size version. It is a copy from that printing, incidentally, that is in my personal library.

In the fifty years since its publication, the Press has sold over a quarter of a million copies, 81,000 in hardback and 175,000 in paperback. Chicago's first paperback edition was published in 1956. Hayek's son, Laurence, reports that nearly twenty authorized foreign translations have been published. In addition, underground, unauthorized translations circulated in Russian, Polish, Czech, and possibly other languages, when Eastern Europe was behind the Iron Curtain. There is little doubt that Hayek's writings, and especially this book, were an important intellectual source of the disintegration of faith in communism behind the Iron Curtain, as on our side of it.

Since the fall of the Berlin Wall it has been possible to publish the book openly in the

[22][See my introduction to this volume, p. 19, for further discussion of the 600,000 figure. — Ed.]

countries and satellites of the former Soviet Union. I know from a variety of sources that there has been an upsurge of interest in Hayek, in general, and *The Road to Serfdom* in particular in those countries.

Since Hayek's death in 1992 there has been increasing recognition of the influence that he exerted in both communist and noncommunist regimes. His publishers can confidently look forward to continuing sales of this remarkable book for as long as freedom of the press prevails—which, despite some erosion since he wrote, is nonetheless more secure than it would otherwise be precisely because of this book.

Stanford, California
April 14, 1994

ACKNOWLEDGMENTS

I would like to thank the staff of the Interlibrary Loan department at Jackson Library, UNC-Greensboro, for obtaining scores of books and articles for me to use, and reference librarian Mark Schumacher for his assistance in tracking down a number of Hayek's more obscure references. A number of individuals also helped me in this latter task, among them Jack Bladel, Valerie Cauchemez, Andrew Farrant, Wendula Gräfin v. Klinckowstroem, Rob Leonard, Harro Maas, Chris Tame, Yuri Tulupenko, Viktor Vanberg, and John Webb. Donald Moggridge corrected some errors in my introduction. Karl Schleunes, Dave Limburg, and Tim Williams assisted me with the translation of certain German phrases. Jude Blanchett at the Foundation for Economic Education provided me with the interesting 1945 article by Croswell Bowen on the "selling" of *The Road to Serfdom*. Finally, I thank John Blundell, Stephen Kresge, and Stuart Warner for many conversations about Hayek, and for their good advice about the volume.

I owe a special debt to Susan Howson for bringing to my attention the memo by Hayek found in the William Beveridge papers, for providing me with the LSE schedule of classes for the 1930s, and for alerting me to the correspondence between Hayek and Machlup in the Machlup collection, which is much more extensive than that in the Hayek collection.

I presented versions of my introduction at the Duke University Workshop in Political Economy, at a conference on neoliberalism at New York University, at the UK History of Thought Conference, and at meetings of the History of Economics Society and the History of Economic Thought Society of Australia, and greatly benefited from the comments of participants. Two anonymous readers for the University of Chicago Press caught a number of errors and made suggestions for strengthening the manuscript.

A number of people at the University of Chicago Press assisted me in the preparation of this volume. Catherine Beebe helped me find materials in the University archives, and my editor Alex Schwartz helped in innumerable ways to get the project to completion.

The last time I saw Hayek's son Laurence was at a conference at Kings College, Cambridge, in June 2004 to commemorate the sixtieth anniversary of the publication of *The Road to Serfdom*. At the end of the conference we took a tour to the top of Kings Chapel to see where Hayek and John Clapham had once done air raid duty during the war. Laurence had been a student at Kings and clearly relished reliving his own earlier clandestine visits to the chapel roof. Only three weeks later, on July 15, 2004, Laurence Hayek died at home of a heart attack. This volume is dedicated to his memory.

Bruce Caldwell

INDEX

Social Democrats (Germany), 50, 182n4,
182n5, 189
socialism: changing definition of, 54–55;
citizens' acquiescence to, 142–43; class
factions within, 144–46; competition
within, 7; competitive, 88–89n4; conservatism and, 45–46; Conservative
Socialism and, 192; democracy with
as utopia, 79; different experiences of
in U.K. and U.S., 22; ends and means
of, 83–84, 168–69; feasibility of, 7;
freedom and power in, 76–78, 78n4;
German opposition to, 4; German
tradition of, 74–75, 74n14; as heir to
liberal tradition, 78; as High Road to
Servitude, 78; in historical perspective,
67–68; hot, 44; individualist, 82; indoctrination and, 143; inevitability of,
199; and inevitability of totalitarianism,
28–31; market, 7, 24–28; monopolies
and, 206n51; nationalism and, 161–
64, 182–83, 192; Nazi objections to,
245–46; organizational, 184n9; power
politics and, 185–86; as precursor to
fascism, 28n101, 60, 63, 144–46,
145n10; pressure groups and, 143–44;
private income from property and,
135; Prussian tradition and, 62–63,
62n5; as purely theoretical, 162; Religious Socialism and, 192; role of in
German history, 23; Rule of Law and,
117; as slavery, 67, 67n4; as species of
collectivism, 84; unanimity regarding,
59–60, 59n3; welfare state versus,
30–31, 44, 54–55; "who, whom?"
and, 138–39
"Socialist Calculation: The Competitive
'Solution'" (Hayek), 88–89n4
Social Security (U.S.), 43n12
sociology of knowledge, 247, 247n5
Sombart, Werner, 74, 74n13, 93, 183–84
Sorel, Georges, 174, 174n4, 181
Soule, George, 22
Soviet Communism (Webb and Webb), 8
Soviet Union. *See* Russia
Spann, Othmar, 189–90n27

Sparta, ancient, 153
Spengler, Oswald, 173n3, 189–90, 189–
90n27, 190n32, 191
Spirit and Structure of German Fascism, The
(Brady), 201n31
Sraffa, Piero, 3
SS (Germany), 157–58n2
Stalin, Josef, 55n4, 69n8
Stalinism, as superfascism, 79
standard of living, rising, 70–71
Stein, Heinrich, 190n31
Stigler, George, 20, 28
Storm of Steel (Jünger), 189–90n27
Strachey, Lytton, 194–95n6
Streicher, Julius, 157, 157–58n2
Sweden, 54
Swiss, values of, 219
Switzerland, 234

Tacitus, Publius, 68, 68n6
Tatreis, 192n41
Tead, Ordway, 16, 16n52
technology: compulsory standardization
and, 96–97; habits of thought and,
72–73; inevitability of planning and,
91–92, 94–95, 96–98; monopolies
and, 92–93, 96–97
Temporary National Economic Commit-
tee (U.S.), 92–93, 92n3
Tennessee Valley Authority (U.S.), 228,
228n7
Tennyson, Alfred (Lord Tennyson), 233,
233n12
"Ten Points for World Peace" (Wells),
121n10
Thatcher, Margaret, 263
Thierack, Otto Georg, 178n12
Thomas, Ivor, 50, 50n24
Three Years of World Revolution (Lensch),
187–89, 188n2
Thucydides, 68, 68n6
Time and Tide (periodical), 231n9
Times (London), 231, 231n9
Tocqueville, Alexis de: on individual free-
dom, 77, 77n3; on new servitude, 48,
48n22; on socialism as slavery, 67; on

cation and, 142; individual dignity and, 130; postwar reconstruction and, 221–22; state as moral institution and, 115–16. *See also* morality

virtues, individualist and collective, 167–68, 219

Voigt, Frederick Augustus, 79, 79n7

Volksgemeinschaft, 183, 183n8

Voltaire, François Marie Arouet de, 118–19

von Papen, Franz, 108, 108n7

von Treitschke, Heinrich von, 194, 194n4

Waddington, Conrad Hal, 202–4, 202n35, 202n37

Wallace, DeWitt, 19

War against the West, The (Kolnai), 189–90n27

war and war metaphors: civil liberties and, 31–32, 32n108; German economy and, 185; German militaristic tradition and, 250; glorification of, 189–90n27, 200; postwar planning and, 204n49, 213–14; prevention of, 235–36; as sacred in Germany, 184; totalitarianism and, 168; veterans and, 204n48

wealth: equitable distribution of, 131–32; freedom and, 78; potential plenty and, 131n5; private property and, 136

Webb, Beatrice: British travelers' reaction to thought of, 219, 219–20n7; on cult of science, 8; Hayek and, 254; imperialism of, 163–64; on incapacity of legislature, 104n3; on math and science under totalitarianism, 177; on stifling of criticism, 175

Webb, Sidney: British travelers' reaction to thought of, 219, 219–20n7; on cult of science, 8; Hayek and, 254; imperialism of, 163–64; on incapacity of legislature, 104n3; on math and science under totalitarianism, 177; on stifling of criticism, 175

welfare state, 13, 14n45, 30–31, 44, 54–55

Wells, H. G., 121–22, 121n10, 184, 219, 219–20n7

Weltanschauung, 142–43, 146, 247

West Germany, East Germany and, 261

"What is the Public Interest?" *(The Economist)*, 51n25

"Why I Am Not a Conservative" (Hayek), 45n14

wickedness, dangers of selective attribution of, 61, 226

Wilhelm II (Germany), 194–95n6

Wilkie, Wendell, 1

Wilson, Woodrow, 197, 197–98n15

Wootton, Barbara, 12, 21, 28, 40n5

World War I: English flight from socialism and, 187; Germany's revolutionary mission and, 188, 190; National Socialism and, 182–83, 185; as war between liberalism and socialism, 191–92, 198–99

World War II: Hayek's war effort and, 9–15; lessons of, 224; postwar international law and, 235; postwar reconstruction and, 12–13, 214–15, 215n4, 221–22

youth, effect of planning on, 48–49

LaVergne, TN USA
14 June 2010
186008LV00001B/111/P